ENGLISH COSTUME FOR SPORTS AND OUTDOOR RECREATION

The Boy with the Bat

Thomas Hudson (1701-1779)

ENGLISH COSTUME
FOR SPORTS
AND
OUTDOOR RECREATION

FROM THE SIXTEENTH TO THE NINETEENTH
CENTURIES

PHILLIS CUNNINGTON
& ALAN MANSFIELD

COLOUR FRONTISPIECE
64 PLATES AND 254 DRAWINGS

BARNES & NOBLE, Inc.
NEW YORK
PUBLISHERS & BOOKSELLERS SINCE 1873

FIRST PUBLISHED 1969
BY A. AND C. BLACK LIMITED

FIRST PUBLISHED IN THE UNITED STATES, 1970
BY BARNES & NOBLE, INC.

SBN 389 01162 2

Printed in Great Britain by
W. & J. Mackay & Co Ltd, Chatham

CONTENTS

6 *Contents*

THE PLATES

ACKNOWLEDGEMENTS

We wish to thank the following for valuable help and advice: Mr W. R. Batty, Hon. Sec. of the York Cricket and Rugby Union Football Club, Berry Bros. & Rudd Ltd, Blackheath Football Club, Blackheath Royal Golf Club, Burberry's Ltd, The Business Archives Council, Mr Ronald W. Clark (*re* Mountaineering), Miss E. R. Clarke (*re* Physical Education), The Dunlop Company Ltd, Mr F. G. Emmison, Essex Record Office, Mr F. W. Fenton, York (*re* Cycling), The Football Association, Mrs Madeleine Ginsberg, Miss Zillah Halls, Mr R. L. James (*re* Archery at Harrow School), Kent County Cricket Club, Mr James Laver, Lillywhite Frowd Ltd, Lillywhites Ltd, London Electrotype Agency, The L.P.E. Ltd, Marylebone Cricket Club, Messrs. Meyer & Mortimer, Mr R. Patterson, Curator of the Castle Museum, York, Miss Diana Rait-Kerr, Royal and Ancient Golf Club of St Andrews, Mr and Mrs John Smith (*re* Riding), Miss O. Spafford, O.B.E. (*re* Physical Education), Mr A. A. Whife of *The Tailor and Cutter*, York Cricket and Rugby Union Football Club; and the staff of the following Museums, Art Galleries and Institutions: *Birmingham,* City Museum and Art Gallery, *Colchester,* Castle and Holly Trees Museum and Public Library, *Coventry,* Herbert Art Gallery and Museum, *Exeter,* Royal Albert Memorial Museum, *London,* British Museum, Courtauld Institute of Art (Witt and Conway Libraries) The Geffrye Museum, Gunnersbury Park Museum, London Museum, Tate Gallery, Victoria & Albert Museum, *Manchester,* Gallery of English Costume, *Norwich,* Strangers Hall Museum, *Worthing,* Museum and Art Gallery, *York,* Castle Museum.

We are very grateful to Mrs Ralph Luckham and Mrs Alan Mansfield for their constant help throughout, and I personally, P.E.C., owe a special debt of gratitude to Miss Catherine Lucas, M.Sc., not only for her untiring help in research but also for reading my text before publication and making valuable suggestions for its improvement.

PREFACE

For variety of divertisements, sports and recreations no nation doth excel the English.

Edward Chamberlayne *Angliae Notitia or The Present State of England*. 1st Ed. 1669.

The period covered by this book extends from Tudor to the end of Edwardian times. Our starting point has been chosen because it was in the sixteenth century that definite growth in the popularity of sport seems to have begun. A gradual evolution of special clothing designed for sport has been traced from this time onwards and a marked acceleration and diversification in the nineteenth century has been noted and followed. Not long after 1900 an expansion took place so great that its description would require a separate volume; hence the decision to terminate the present book with the reign of Edward VII.

Women were not only late in developing a taste for sport but slower than men in defying convention and escaping the dictates of fashion so as to achieve an adaptive costume. As late as 1904, Mary Hezlet, the golf champion, though she advised ladies to wear "short skirts", meant by "short" only six inches off the ground. However her discussion of the efforts made by women at various times to free their limbs for strenuous exercise, makes it clear that the opening of the century was a turning point:

> In games especially, dress is an important factor; the girl of the present day must be suitably attired for the various sports, or she cannot do herself justice in them, or derive the benefits which are to be obtained in their pursuit. The time is past when it was thought necessary for a girl . . . who indulged in athletics to make a perfect fright of herself, and to try to imitate men as much as possible; and it has been discovered that . . . this does not make sport easier but only attracts much undesirable attention. The "new woman" and the "athletic woman" are no longer subjects for comic papers . . . and the majority of girls endeavour to combine comfort and grace . . . when indulging in their sports.
> Mary Hezlet, *Golf*, 1904.

It has been impossible for the present book to cover every kind of sport, and indoor games have therefore been omitted. Some outdoor recreations not strictly in the category of "sports" have, however, been included and the book ends on a restful note with picnics.

CHAPTER I

CRICKET

BY ALAN MANSFIELD

Hail CRICKET, glorious, manly, British game, First of all sports, be first alike in fame.

James Love, 1770.

I. TO THE END OF THE EIGHTEENTH CENTURY

That cricket is, and has been for the past two and a half centuries at least, the Englishman's national game is not to be denied. Even today, when a multitude of other pastimes surround us to entice us from allegiance to King Willow, it stubbornly refuses to give place to other claimants, old or new, and despite the trials and tribulations suffered by "big" cricket, in town parks and on village greens, in school playgrounds and on waste sites, its devotees of all ages and classes dedicate the summer months to what G. D. Martineau has described as our national art, "no less artistic for taking the form of a game, and no less national for remaining unappreciated by all but a minority of the nation". (*Bat, Ball, Wicket and All*).[1]

The origins of the game are, like many a British institution, obscured by the mists of time; some writers attribute its origin to a Saxon game played with a crook shaped bat or stick (criece); and Edward II as a youth in 1300 is well known to have played "ad Creag' et alios ludos". It was the seventeenth century, however, which saw the game gaining a place in the chronicles and literature of the day, and it was in the south-eastern counties that it first achieved a status higher than that of the pastime of an idle hour for school-boys and yokels. In the early eighteenth century the game was patronized by the Prince of Wales. Frederick Louis, and many of the nobility quickly followed his example. Although the death of the Prince, from the effects of being struck by a cricket ball, in 1751, was a severe blow to the national development of cricket, by the end of the eighteenth century there was a revival, pioneered by the famous team based on Hambledon, a village in Hampshire.

[1] With acknowledgement to the Author and Publishers, Sporting Handbooks Ltd.

Originally, no doubt, as in other active pursuits, the cricket players made no more sartorial concessions to the game than that of discarding their outer garments for ease of wielding the bat and ball and moving about the field. Although there are sixteenth and seventeenth-century records of the game no illustrations appear to be extant, if, indeed, any artist thought fit to portray the contemporary equivalent of Kipling's "flannelled fools". However, it is perhaps reasonable to assume that the countryman clad in a "shyrt of canvas hard and tough" with a "strawer hat upon his head" and a "payre of startuppes" on his feet[1] would have as happily played at cricket in such a garb, as he would have gone about his daily work. The "startuppes" on his feet were a type of short boots, loose fitting, and with wooden pegs in the soles. Between the shirt and the boots would have come either hose, or breeches and stockings. Perhaps, in the face of demon bowling a second pair of stockings would have served as primitive pads. Such additional overstockings, reaching to the knee, were worn by some countrymen when at work.[2]

It is with the new found popularity of cricket among the upper classes in the eighteenth century that the first definite descriptions and illustrations of the game and its players appear, increasing in numbers and detail as the century progresses. (Frontispiece.)

A painting attributed to the early 1740s in the Tate Gallery shows the players, generally, clad in breeches and shirts, though two are also wearing waistcoats, and one a light blue short-tailed jacket. The shirts are white, the breeches brown or black. White stockings and black shoes, and a black jockey-style cap, possibly of velvet, complete the teams' costume. The umpires and scorers wear the long fullskirted coat and three-cornered cocked hat of the day. An engraving of 1743 shows all the players wearing white or light coloured breeches.

In a painting ascribed to Francis Hayman, R. A., in 1743, of Cricket on the Artillery Ground, Finsbury, of the nine players shown all wear white shirts without neckcloths, some open at the neck, and no hats. The batsman, however, wears a brewer's cap. (Plate 1.)

Another painting of Hayman's, also of about 1743, shows similarly clad players, many of them again wearing jockey caps. These caps were fashionable wear among young "sparks", who sported them on all occasions:

---

1 *Debate between Pride and Lowliness* Francis Thynn (?). *c.* 1568.
2 See engraving in *Boke of Husbandrye*, J. Fitzherbert. *c.* 1525.

Set of Sparks who choose rather to appear as Jockeys and it is seldom or never they are to be seen without boots, whips . . . and black caps instead of hats. . . .

Universal Spectator, 1739.

They were originally intended, as the name implies, for wear on horse-back, and the cricketers no doubt adopted them for their superiority of staying on the head, in contrast to the usual cocked hat. They were often trimmed with a buckled band:

A small round jockey cap, with a green and gold hatband, buckled in front with a high polished steel buckle.

The Ipswich Journal, 1788.

The Eighth Earl of Winchilsea is stated to have dressed his team in hats with a gold or silver binding and ribbons of an unstated colour. These hats were presumably the three-cornered cocked hats, on which it was customary to have some form of braid to bind the brim.

Sky blue or azure blue appear to have been adopted as uniform colours for the coats of some cricket clubs, many of which sprang up in the latter half of the century. Hambledon wore sky blue coats with gilt buttons, nankeen waistcoats and breeches and drab beaver hats, lined with green. Frederick Reynolds, the playwright, upon being elected to the M.C.C. a few years after its formation in 1787 "immediately assumed the sky blue dress, the uniform of the club. . . ." It is interesting to note that from the seventeenth century azure blue had been the livery of Eton. These blue coats, being discarded on the field, served principally to identify their owner's allegiance when not actually playing: in many ways they are akin to the hunt evening coats and the famous "bright blue dress coat, with gilt buttons, displaying a bust, and the letters P.C." of a later day. (Charles Dickens, *The Pickwick Papers*).

From mid-century onwards it was fashionable to have portraits of young boys, either alone or in a family group, painted as dressed for cricket: they generally wear breeches, stockings and shoes, and a waistcoat over a white shirt (Fig. 1). The shirt collar may be worn buttoned up, with a black neck ribbon, or from about 1770, left open and turned down over the coat or waistcoat.

During the 1780s a portentous development in boys' garments occurred. Trousers, previously a rare and unfashionable garment, were introduced for wear by boys, and within a few decades superseded breeches and stockings for males of all ages. The painting by W. R. Bigg, R.A., variously known as "Generous Schoolboys" or "The Soldiers Widow" or "Schoolboys' Collection", exhibited at the Royal Academy in 1798, shows a group of boys ready for cricket: some wear breeches and stockings, others tight ankle length trousers, or pantaloons (Fig. 2).

1. Boy cricketer. 1768.   2. Boy cricketers. One wears ankle-length
                                           trousers. 1798.

The end of the century also witnessed the introduction to the cricket field of another hitherto unfashionable garment—the jacket. This was a short, fitting, coat resembling a sleeved waistcoat. The jacket was worn both by soldiers and sailors; the painting by David Allan of 1784–5 of the Cathcart Family shows three young men in a group posed by an open-fronted tent; in the background is a cricket match in progress: one of the young men wears a military jacket and leans upon a bat; a second sits upon the ground on a military coat, with a bat by his side, and wears a sleeved waistcoat. The third young man wears a sleeveless civilian waistcoat. (Plate 2.)

In 1783 a parson in Wales writing of a local cricket team says that:

Players to wear swanskin[1] jackets with sleeves edged with coloured riband

[1] A downy surfaced flannel material.

PLATE I

Cricketers in shirts, breeches, stockings and shoes. The batsman wears a brewer's cap. 1743.

Oil painting attributed to Francis Hayman, R.A. Collection of the late Sir Jeremiah Coleman, Bt.

PLATE 2

The Cathcart Family. Waistcoats, one with sleeves: military
jacket. 1784–5.

*Oil painting by David Allen. By kind permission of Earl Cathcart. Photo-
graph by courtesy of the Royal Academy.*

. . . which will not stand each person above 2s. 6d. or 3s. 6d. at the utmost.
Letter to J. G. Phillips from Rev. James of Pontyglas, Carmarthenshire, 1783:

and in 1798 a tailor charges:

> Repairing 2 cricketing jackets 8s.
> To a shooting jacket £1. 10s. 0d.
> Altering a Regimental jacket 2s.

Kent Records, 1798.

The three-cornered cocked hat which had reigned through most of the eighteenth century began to give way to the round, tall crowned hat in the 1770–80s. An engraving by Cook published in the *Sporting Magazine*, June, 1793, shows players, scorers and umpires in this type of headgear.

Throughout this period the Umpires wore the usual day dress of the time and held a bat, in the manner of a walking stick. Was this a badge of office, a first aid in case of disaster overtaking the striker's bat, or a weapon to enforce disputed decisions?

Despite the evidence of paintings and prints, which agree upon the coloured breeches of the players during most of the century, there is allusion to the now traditional white of the cricketer's garb from the pens of at least two versifiers of the game: James Love, one of whose verses heads this chapter, refers to teams:

> In decent white most gracefully array'd;

and George Huddesford wrote in 1791:

> But come, thou genial son of Spring,
> Whitsuntide, and with thee bring
> Cricket, nimble boy and light,
> In slippers red and drawers white,
> Who o'er the nicely measured land
> Ranges around his comely band,
> Alert to intercept each blow,
> Each motion of the wary foe.

The engraving by Cook mentioned above has the players clad in white jackets and white breeches and stockings, and the general appearance is very uniform and workmanlike; except, perhaps, for the tall hats and wigs.

2. THE NINETEENTH AND EARLY TWENTIETH CENTURIES

During the early decades of the nineteenth century the main change in the cricketer's dress was the substitution of trousers almost universally for breeches and stockings—although a few of the older hands retained the style of their youth. E. H. Budd is said to have been the last to wear the old style, doing so up to the end of his playing days, which continued into the 1850s.

Miss Diana Rait-Kerr has pointed out[1] that trousers took longer to become acceptable on the cricket field than they did in every day life. She cites a drawing of Robert Cruickshank of 1827 as the last picture in which teams are shown wearing breeches, and notes that this drawing depicts the first match employing the experimental round-arm bowling and suggests a connexion; trousers being better adapted for the coy wearing of some type of hidden pad. Against this is the opinion of the Rev. John Mitford, who in 1833, protested against the wearing of white trousers, not only on the grounds that they were unbecoming, but also inconvenient as they might get in the way of the ball.

Robert Cruickshank calls to mind his brother George, who was an illustrator of Dickens, and it was of the year 1827 that Dickens wrote when describing the garb of the Dingley Dellers and All Muggletonians:

> Straw hats, flannel jackets, and white trousers—a costume in which they looked very much like amateur stone masons.

Mary Russel Mitford writing in 1823 also spoke disparagingly of the figures cut by cricketers arrayed for the fray—this time it is the M.C.C. team, gentlemen and players together, she describes as

> dressed in tight white jackets (the Apollo Belvedere could not bear the hideous disguise of a cricket-jacket), with neck cloths primly tied round their throats, . . . japanned shoes, silk stockings and gloves. . . .
>
> 1823, letter to B. R. Hayden.

Here then are breeches, although implied by Mary only by reference to the stockings—breeches of all things were *not* mentioned, less still written about, by well brought up young women in the 1820s. Miss Mitford contrasts the fine clothes of the London team with the "unbuttoned collars . . . loose waistcoats, and . . . large shirt sleeves" of the local village team who are to

---

[1] *Playfair's Cricket Monthly*—January 1966.

be their opponents. Here her maidenly modesty does not allow her to mention the nether garments at all—we can only suppose that *something* was worn below the waistcoats and shirts: perhaps "trousers", like the Muggletonians and Dingley Dellers. Alas, we shall never know.

By the 1830s trousers were well established, mostly white (which was a fashionable colour, in nankin or jean, for summer wear: Peel's new "Bobbies" were issued with white duck trousers in 1829), although judging by contem-

3. Batsman in checked trousers. 1834.

porary engravings coloured and even check trousers were also worn (Fig. 3). Tight and narrow at the beginning of the century they became wider and easier with the years, no doubt much to the improvement of the game and the comfort of the wearers. Braces were the commonest means of support, although a sash or belt could be used. A picture of "Squire" Osbaldeston, probably drawn between 1808 and 1818 shows him wearing short white jacket, shirt and neckcloth, with his nether garments (this is not modesty— the picture is only three-quarter length) secured by a sash which passes around the waist, under the flap of the small falls and is tied in a bow on the right hand side. He also wears a round tall hat with the brim turned down (Fig. 4).

Jackets are still to be seen on cricketers of the 1830s, but they appear less frequently. They are not always white at this period—green, and blue and white, are mentioned as distinguishing livery for clubs:[1] a stage between the azure coats of the eighteenth century and the blazers of a later day.

4. Cricketing jacket. Sash round waist. *c.* 1812.

F. Gale writing in the 1880s of the cricket of his youth in 1830 describes a local team wearing white duck trousers and flannel jackets, with either tall black hats or straw hats. One player wore black leather slippers with one spike in the heel, which he claimed as his own invention.[2] To prevent soiling their trousers

> A few old fogies, veterans who played, had a silk pocket-handkerchief tied to the left knee so that they could drop down on it . . . for . . . old fashioned fieldsmen would drop on one knee, so that if the ball went through their hands by a false bound their body was in the way.
>
> F. Gale in The Badminton Library: Cricket. 1888.

From the 1790s onwards the tall hat crowned the cricketer as characteristically as it perched on peer and postman, parson and policeman, and held its

[1] Martineau p. 91.
[2] Robert Robinson of Farnham who flourished 1792–1819 is credited with the wearing of spikes.

sway over batsman, bowler and fielder (not forgetting umpires) for some sixty years—despite challenges from straw hats and soft caps. It seems incredible to a generation that eschews hats almost completely that such a headgear should ever have found its way on to the cricket field—however, some players must have attempted to put it to practical use, for a Law of 1820 ruled that "if any person stops the ball with his hat the ball is to be considered dead".

The 1840s and 50s were great days and glorious is the Roll of Honour of those decades: Pilch, Mynn, Lillywhite, Sir Frederick Bathurst, Wenman, and "Felix", to name but a few; and an increasing amount of publicity accrued to the game, and portraits of players and pictures of matches became more and more numerous (Plate 3), whilst the Staffordshire potteries turned out thousands of mantelpiece ornaments based on illustrations of favourite players. Details of dress thus became more plentiful.

5. Trousers with small falls and braces. 1843.

In the early 1840s the jacket is still to be seen—short and tight fitting, with either shawl or stepped collar, waist length, single-breasted with four or five buttons, one button cuffs. Increasingly however, the players are represented in shirt sleeves—thereby exposing their braces, which had not as yet become an object too shameful for public display.

On 22nd July, 1843, the *Illustrated London News* published a drawing of the great bowler William Lillywhite (Fig. 5). He wears trousers held up by braces of enormous proportions, loose sleeved shirt, with a dark neckcloth around a

6. A celebrated Yorkshire cricketer. White flannel jacket and trousers
and bottom boots with cloth tops. *c.* 1840.

high collar, and a black top-hat. The front fastenings of his trousers are small falls, though fly-fronts were becoming more popular; as early as *c.* 1840 Richard Letby (Fig. 6) was wearing fly-fronted trousers, and in the lithograph of the XI of England of 1847 (Plate 3) the majority of the trousers are thus equipped.

In this XI of 1847 we also find two players wearing large soft-crowned, peaked caps, and one a wide-brimmed round hat, possibly straw, the rest have the usual tall top-hat. Of the two wearing caps, one is "Felix", in real life Nocholas Wanostrocht, a school master and left-handed bat, who in 1845 had published that classic of cricket literature, *Felix on the Bat*. In this book Felix describes just such a cap:

> made of chequered woollen: it is light and cool to the head, absorbs perspiration, and (which is not an insignificant fact) is not likely to blow off and hit the wicket.

In 1847 Eton and Harrow took to straw hats, but Winchester stuck to tradition and the topper until 1851, when caps of white flannel with dark blue ribbon were introduced.[1]

Felix also recommends "an under flannel vest, or thin Jersey", which he "holds to be exceedingly useful in preventing the too fast evaporation of the heat of the body. For the same reason a cotton shirt is better than a linen one."

Is this the outcome of discarding the jacket? Perhaps: on the other hand he would appear to recommend a jersey as a substitute for the shirt itself; after complaining of the loose sleeves of a shirt, whereby a ball may be deflected on to the wicket, or the umpire's view impaired, he says:

> The best plan is to have a Jersey not too tight in fit, with a shirt collar made to button on the top.

There is a picture of Felix with Alfred Mynn dated 1846 which shows them wearing what appear to be such jerseys (Fig. 7). They look like modern long-sleeved vests, but with collars worn with neckcloths—the neck openings are buttoned with a three-button flap slightly left of front centre. In one case the flap is piped with red, in the other with blue. They both wear fly-fronted trousers supported by belts passing through loops on the waistband: these belts echo the colour of the neck piping.

Felix recommended that trousers should be of flannel, although it was some years before this became the general rule. He also favoured the belt as against braces:

> which must be exploded[2] whilst in the active service of hitting.

It was in 1845 that Edwin Ade, of 415 Oxford Street, patented a cricket belt, and this firm in later years became famous for its belts, many fitted with

[1] MS. Notes: Miss Diana Rait-Kerr, M.C.C.

[2] The noise was likely to have been confused by careless umpires with that of popping creases.

elaborate lock-plates or buckles. The Patent Office Records for this year speak of vulcanized rubber for belts, and it was a rubber belt Felix favoured.

7. Jersey-like shirts, cricketing belts, trousers with fly fronts. 1846.

Although he does not mention jackets, Felix evidently wore one at times:

> Felix . . . fell to the ground . . . Mynn . . . walked up to him, took hold of him by the collar of the flannel jacket. . . . (? 1846).
>
> Haygarth, quoted in *Lords and the M.C.C.*
> Harris & Ashley-Cooper, 1920

As well as neckcloths, which should be of cotton, "because silk is a non-conductor of heat and does not absorb perspiration" and socks or stockings (not cotton or silk), Felix speaks of shoes, and recommends three spikes.

> the two under the bend of the foot should be nearer to top of the sole than is now the custom . . . the one in advance should be between and close under the division of the first and second toes.

This is an advance on the primitive heel-spike mentioned in 1830, and it is of interest that Felix talks of shoes and makes no mention of boots. We read of the Rugby team wearing, in about 1840, untanned yellow cricket shoes.

Tom Brown's School Days, 1857.

but at much the same time Richard Letby was being painted wearing square toed, cloth topped, buttoned boots (Fig. 6). However the boot was not popular on the cricket field during these years.

The dress of umpires did not change during the first half of the nineteenth century—except as the normal fashions of the male of the day changed: thus trousers replaced breeches, the tail- or frock-coat the full-skirted coat or frock of the eighteenth century, and the tall hat took over from the three-cornered cocked hat. The practice of carrying a bat was gradually abandoned, although a picture of a match at Maldon, Essex, in about the year 1848 (Essex Record Office) shows an umpire with one carried under his arm.

During the 1850s the standard dress for players is white trousers and shirt, with a collar and large bow tie, black or coloured. Belts have replaced braces, and the top hat has almost disappeared by 1853. The United XI of All England, drawn in 1852 (Fig. 8), shows only one top-hat, but while three

8. The Eleven of All England. Hemispherical hats. 1852.

players wear Felix's soft woollen cap, the majority are proudly wearing the new "Hemispherical Hat", which

> is becoming very general for morning wear.
>
> *Gentleman's Herald of Fashion*, 1853.

The "Hemispherical" hat was bowl-shaped, with a flat brim—a sort of proto-bowler, and must have been almost as inconvenient as the top hat.

Flannel was by now perhaps the most common material for trousers: one club ruled in 1856 that:

> The XI appointed to play in a match to appear in white flannel trousers, and that the recognized colour of the Club be a cap.
>
> Lillywhite: Collected in Miss D. Rait-Kerr's MS. notes.

9. "How *did* you hurt your legs? And how can you go about in that distressingly swelled condition?" See text. 1854.

Leech in *Punch* of 1854 shows a "stout party" clad in shirt, trousers, belt and neckcloth, losing a somewhat battered tall hat as he runs. He wears three-spiked shoes.[1] Tenniel in the same year of *Punch* shows a young man wearing

---

[1] "Spiked soles, 6/–"—1850 advert. of Lillywhite Bros.

what appears to be a tight fitting jacket, buttoned over the chest on the right-hand side and a large bow tie. He sports a striped muffin-shaped cap with a peak (Fig. 9). There is quite a wide variety of hats and caps exhibited during the 1850s and one wonders what form the hat took that was presented to H. Stephenson at Sheffield in 1858 for taking three wickets with consecutive balls—a bowler, perhaps?

Towards the end of the 1850s a fashion for coloured or fancy shirts began to appear. The use of patterned shirts for sporting wear goes back at least to the 1830s, when "aquatic" shirts, later known as "Regatta" and "Rowing" shirts were introduced for wear on the river:

> Bob Jones is a rowing man . . . He wears a blue checked shirt. . . .
> Kenny Meadows, *Heads of the People*, 1841.

but had not hitherto appeared as part of the fashionable cricketer's attire. The All England XI of Wm. Clarke adopted a red-striped or spotted-shirt in the later 1850s, and during the 1860s and 70s the fancy shirt flourished and even lingered on into the 1880s.

Spots, checks, stripes, quarters, devices of bats and balls, county emblems —all these appeared on the backs of the fashionable players. The team George Parr took to the Antipodes in 1863–4 were depicted clad in checked, striped and dotted shirts and with a variety of headgear from bowler hats to a straw "sailor" (Fig. 10). The first English team to tour Australia, under H. H. Stephenson in 1861–2, were clad in sober white shirts, but

> were supplied with helmet shaped hats around which were different coloured ribbons, and each man wore a different coloured sash . . . in order that the public might be able to identify each individual player.
> *Scores and Biographies*, 1862.

In the photographs of this team they appear in conventional cricket belts, which during this decade were as colourful and varied in design as the shirts. Some were webbing, striped vertically or horizontally, some printed with designs of bats, stumps, balls, etc. Indiarubber and elastic were much favoured, and so were canvas belts worked in Berlin woolwork by the loving hands of sisters and wives. It was a favourite pastime of young ladies to so embroider braces and belts and the women's magazines gave suitable patterns away to their readers:

A pattern for a cricket belt in Berlin woolwork.

Young Ladies Journal, 1868.

These belts were often fastened by elaborate clasps, moulded or chased in designs of bats, etc. or showing portraits of favourite players.

10. Test players. Bowler hats and spotted shirts. 1863–4.

The Museum at Lords shows many fine examples of belts of this period, including one bearing the truly democratic and sporting legend

The Prince and peasant by cricket are united.

As well as belts the M.C.C. possess among their treasures examples of printed flannel shirting, one bearing in blue the Sussex martlets within a shield. A shirt of similar date bearing figures of cricketers printed on it is in the Strangers Hall Museum, Norwich.

The Excelsior Cricket Club, Islington, were painted in a moment of triumph by Henry Garland in 1864, and the visitor to Lord's may share that triumph today—the hero of the match is chaired on the shoulders of two of his team mates, he is clad in sober white but his supporters wear, one a blue, the other a scarlet shirt. Others of the team wear red or violet shirts. All wear white trousers and brown and white shoes or low boots. These players are all youths, and it is youths too who are portrayed in Routledges *Every Boy's Annual for 1866* very similarly clad.

But it was not only youths' and schoolboys' teams of the 1860s who adopted bright self-colours, and the Harlequin's uniform of crimson and buff shirts and blue trousers may be taken as typical of the exuberant nature of many club clothes.

In 1861 the Cambridge University XI appeared at Lord's in light blue, and a year later Oxford took the field in their own varient of that colour, while the Royal Engineers not to be left behind in the race were coming along in 1864 on legs clad in stockings of the Corps colours—red and blue stripes— above which were the newly introduced knickerbockers, a reversion to the fashion of a century earlier.

11. Pill box hat and striped jersey. 1870s.

During the 1870s the stripes moved upwards and encircled the players' chests, decorating jerseys with round necks and no collars which were worn over the trousers; these are almost indistinguishable from the football jersey (Fig. 11). Also during this decade pill-box caps were added to the varieties of headgear in fashion; and occasionally the white flannel trousers were decorated by a coloured piping down the side seam.

One member of Parr's XI in 1863 is shown wearing a jacket (Fig. 12) but a jacket quite different from those previously fashionable: Tom Lockyer has a loose single-breasted jacket, buttoned by the top button only, which is cut on the lines of the newly introduced "lounge jacket"—of which two favourite varieties were the Paletot jacket and Tweedside jacket.

12. Soft cap: jacket: wicket-keeper's gloves and pads. 1863–4.

In 1878 the first representative Australian XI visited these islands, and they were photographed in loosely cut, single breasted jackets vertically striped and pill-box hats in the same colours. In the same year the *West End Gazette* published a fashion plate of a cricketer in a similar jacket, but of plain flannel (Fig. 13).

Throughout the 1870s and 80s the coloured or patterned shirt persisted, although the plain white one was steadily regaining its popularity: and shirts of all kinds were now to be seen occasionally worn without ties, and even, by the younger generation, with open necks, as had been the fashion a century earlier. The sleeves also were now increasingly seen to be rolled up to the elbow—a fashion which appears to have begun not before the 1860s.

In 1880 the *Boy's Own Paper* published a coloured lithograph showing twenty-one leading cricketers of the day. White, pink, spotted shirts: striped jerseys; a striped jacket in M.C.C. colours: belts; scarves; plain, striped and checked peak caps; all are represented. The trousers are white, cut full, all with fly-fronts. Brown and white laced shoes or boots are worn.

13. Cricket cap: flannel jacket: brown and white leather shoes. 1878.

By 1888 W. G. Grace writing in the Badminton Library volume *Cricket* states that

> White is now usually worn, and it certainly looks better and cooler than any other colour.

He recommends white flannel or cloth for trousers, with a strap and buckle at the back to help support them as

> braces are not worn when playing cricket.

Loops for a belt or scarf are also mentioned, and Grace recommends a scarf rather than a belt, as

> You will not run the risk of being given out caught at the wickets through the handle of the bat coming in contact with the buckle of the belt and the noise being mistaken by the umpire for a snick off the bat. I once saw a man given out for this very thing.
>
> *Cricket:* The Badminton Library, Longmans, Green & Co., 1888.

Grace recommends also a cap, not a hat, and a "jersey or sweater" for playing in cold weather in preference to a jacket. The jacket, he says, can be used when fielding but certainly not when bowling or batting. As for footwear

> I prefer lace-up boots, and think most cricketers who play a good deal do the same. Have them made of brown or white leather. . . . I should advise all cricketers who play often to have two pairs of boots, one with short spikes or nails which will hold and prevent slipping on a hard dry ground, and the other with longer spikes for a soft wet spongy ground.
>
> Ibid.

A "Spy" Cartoon of 1889 (Fig. 14) shows a modern looking wicket-keeper (Hylton Philipson, Oxford Union) clad in white shirt and trousers with a dark blue cap, and dark blue scarf around the waist; a square folded with the point hanging down behind. He wears brown leather boots, as did W. G. himself. A similarly clad player appears in *Punch* (6th August) in 1890, but here brown and white boots are indicated. In 1897 (7th August) a *Punch* cartoon shows Salisbury and Chamberlain dressed as cricketers—their garb is similar to the foregoing, but no scarves are apparent around the waists, and they wear white boots.

In 1892 the cricketing jacket or blazer was described as having:

> The back with no seam, front not cut away below the bottom button. Patch pockets. A small watch pocket is sometimes placed inside the upper patch pocket. . . . Step collar. Sleeves sometimes lined with . . . thin material. White, coloured, or striped flannels used.
>
> *Minsters Gazette of Fashion,* June 1892.

Such blazers are seen in the plate of the Bishop's Stortford Club XI in 1893 (Plate 4). It will be noted here that the now popular straw hat predominated. Boots are either white or brown. The shirt collars are worn without a tie, open at the neck.

During the 1890s when playing cricket, as in other active pursuits, the trouser bottoms were sometimes worn turned up.

PLATE 3

(*a*) Kent *v*. Sussex. Top-hats, trousers and braces. 1849.
Contemporary print. Photograph by courtesy of Lillywhite Frowd.

(*b*) The Eleven of England. 1847.
Coloured lithograph from a drawing by "Felix".

PLATE 4

(*a*) A Club Team. Blazers and boaters. 1893.

Photograph of Bishops Stortford XI. Essex Record Office.

(*b*) Batting gloves. 1910.

Author's Collection.

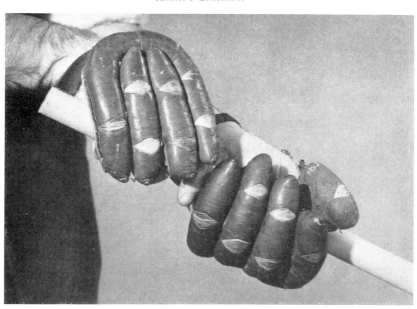

14. "Oxford cricket". Scarf round waist. 1889.

The long white coat of the umpire in this photograph was introduced in the 1860s, replacing the dark frock-coat hitherto worn.

By the early years of this century the cricketer's costume had settled down in essentials to what it is today.

As Miss Rait-Kerr says:

> the photograph of the first M.C.C. touring team taken in Australia in 1903 might almost be a present-day side.

White canvas boots had been introduced as a cheap substitute for white leather—of which white buckskin was the favourite. My Father, who played much school and Club cricket in Yorkshire in the days before the First War recollects that it was every boy's ambition to possess a pair of white buckskin cricket boots.

During the years immediately preceding the Great War a necktie was frequently worn around the waist to support the trousers, which by now were made with a permanent turn up.

CRICKET PADS AND GLOVES

There is no armour against Fate

James Shirley. 1717.

Some form of protection for the legs seems to have been desired by some cricketers from the eighteenth century, although it was not until the nineteenth century was well advanced that pads, and gloves also, were widely used.

The eighteenth century protection, when used, did not extend beyond:

White silk stockings with another pair rolled over his instep.

Lord Charles Russell, quoted in *Lord's and the M.C.C.*
Harris & Ashley-Cooper, Herbert Jenkins 1920.

Such were worn by the Rev. Lord Frederick Beauclare, D.D., who was against the use of pads as unfair to the bowler.

I have seen it suggested that the artificial padded calves worn by those not well endowed by nature might on occasion be slipped round to the front of the leg—though I have come across no contemporary evidence of this.

Robert Robinson of Farnham is said to have worn pieces of board fastened on his legs. The date is not known, but Robinson flourished from 1792 to 1819 (*Bat, Ball, Wicket and All*, G. D. Martineau, 1950). Such boards were probably adapted from the "beaters" or thigh pads of wood worn by some ploughmen.

Dench, a Brighton player, in 1825, used sacks stuffed with straw, and leather leggings are also spoken of (Martineau op. cit.). These devices may also be traced to agricultural or industrial use: even in medieval times we read of smiths that "their shanks are sheathed against sparks of fire" (B.M. MS. Arundel 292) probably with leather.

Both the M.C.C. and Kent C.C. have specimens of early pads in their collections. An M.C.C. specimen (Fig. 15b) is no more than a knee pad and is fastened by tapes. Such knee pads were advertised in 1843. Here again the influence of the thatcher's, flint-knappers,' and stone-breaker's knee pads can be seen.

The Kent specimen, at Canterbury, is larger, 21½ inches overall, including an extension for the knee, and shaped to the foot (Fig. 15a). It is fastened by flaps which button together down the back of the leg.

H. Daubeney is credited by James Pycroft (*The Cricket Field*, edited by S. F. Ashley-Cooper, 1922) with the invention of true pads in 1836; but *Scores and Biographies* gives the honour to James Nixon in 1841.

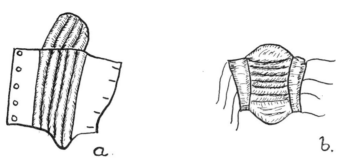

15. Early pads: (*a*) at Canterbury, (*b*) at Lords.

By 1845 Felix was recommending the use of concealed padding within the trousers:

> The padding which I recommend as most becoming in its appearance, and most effective in its intentions, is to have longitudinal sockets, made (inside the legs of the trousers) of linen, half an inch apart, extending from two inches above the knee-pan down to the lower part of the trousers. Long slips of Indian rubber, half an inch thick, can always be inserted therein, and taken out as they go or come from the wash. And here let me strongly urge that your practice be conducted as much like match-playing as possible. Heedless hitting off careless bowling is worse than no practice at all; it is like shutting your eyes at Billiards, and hitting hard for the chances of the table. Lest I should not be rightly understood about the directions for the trousers, those of the right-handed hitter would require the sockets to be placed so as to defend the outside of the knee-pan of the left leg, and calf and outward ankle-bone, the inside of the knee-pan of the right leg, the shin-bone and the inner ankle. The trousers of the left-handed hitter would of course require the opposite to this.
>
> Felix, op cit.

In 1849 Bell's *Life in London* deplored the use of pads by wicket keepers and longstops, showing that by then their use had spread from the batsman.

In 1851 Lillywhite & Sons were advertising "newly invented leg guards", stuffed with horse hair, which they exhibited at the Great Exhibition of that year.

The use of pads was not universally recognized in the 1850s as Tenniel's drawing in *Punch* in 1854 shows (Fig. 9). However, concealed padding on the Felix principle no doubt accounts for the apparent absence of pads in the photos and drawings of the time.

These early pads were tied around the leg with tapes or strings, but in 1862 Lillywhite was advising buckles and straps.

Writing in 1888 W. G. Grace says of pads:

> I cannot call to mind anyone who plays without them. It is much safer to wear them, and when they are properly made and fit well they but slightly affect the freedom of the legs. The sense of confidence that comes from wearing them more than makes up for the slight loss of freedom.
>
> W. G. Grace, op cit.

He goes on to say that "the present arrangement of buckle and strap . . . meets with general approval", but "some makers of the present day have them fastened by loops and a long strap lacing up the back of the leg".

In the early years of this century "skeleton" pads had a vogue. They were in shape like the normal pad, but instead of being solid consisted of connected longitudinal strips of cane or whalebone lightly padded and covered with buckskin (Fig. 16). They were presumably designed to be lighter and cooler than the normal pad. The vogue did not last and the original style was triumphant, remaining with but slight modifications until today. Brown leather pads also enjoyed a certain popularity at the beginning of the century.

Padded finger-stalls were said to have been worn in the 1830s, but it is the inventive Felix who is generally credited with the introduction of batting gloves in 1835 or 1837, although the Earl of Bessbrough writing in *The Cricket Field* in 1893 says William Caldecourt in 1834–8 was wearing leather gloves padded with wool. Felix's gloves were of white kid with small blocks of indiarubber glued on at different points. Caldecourt was advertising "india-rubber padded gloves" in 1842. These were all for batsmen: the wicket-keepers were wearing in the 1850s gloves or gauntlets of, apparently, an ordinary kind: dog leather was recommended for young beginners. In the 1860s the palms were stuffed and the gloves, which were ventilated back and front, had 4-inch gauntlets (Fig. 12).

PLATE 5

Lady cricketers. Match played by the Countess of Derby and other ladies
in 1779.

Marylebone Cricket Club Collection.

PLATE 6

Kent match. Lady cricketers in 1838.

Marylebone Cricket Club (Jeremiah Coleman Collection).

In 1865 a Henry Emmanual sprang upon a wondering world his "improved extensible and collapsing guard or pad" and also gloves of vulcanized caoutchouc "or other substance capable of being inflated and contracted". These technological triumphs were constructed on the principle of the bicycle tyre and could be blown up as required. These remarkable pieces of equipment seem to have been based on the indiarubber tube crinoline cage of a decade earlier, and probably failed through the same cause—unexpected and embarrassing punctures.

16. Skeleton pads. Early 20th century.

W. G. Grace in 1888 said:

> Gloves are generally made of leather, with strips of thick fluted india-rubber sewn on the back to protect the fingers and hand. . . . It is not many years since they were made with leather on the inside, which covered the palm of the hand, preventing, as everyone knows, a firm grip of the bat; however, that is a thing of the past, and now a good number of players not only wear gloves without anything covering the palm of the hand, but go so far as to cut out pieces of the inside covering to the fingers. . . .

Gloves are generally fastened at the wrist by a band of elastic sewn on the top and buttoned. You can . . . have the thumb separated from the body of the glove and sewn on to a piece of elastic, the other end of which is fastened to the back of the glove, and long enough to pass once round the wrist; this contrivance will keep the glove well in its place.

W. G. Grace, op cit.

This latter device was developed in the early 1900s into a skeleton glove, rather like a bunch of bananas, one of which is on a long lead. The pair I have bears the date 1910 written by my father when he bought them. The left-hand glove—for my father was a left-handed bat—has four joined finger-stalls, padded on the outside, with the thumb-stall separate and on a piece of elastic about 15 inches long. The right-hand glove is a mere padded protection to cover the back of the four fingers only—no thumb piece is needed—which is secured by an elastic loop for the wrist and leather loops at the end of each finger. The gloves are of brown kid with white kid insets at the finger-joints (Plate 4). Brown gauntlet gloves were worn by wicket-keepers at this time.

Bibliography

Badminton Library. *Cricket*. Longmans, Green and Co., 1888
Harris, Lord and Astley-Cooper, F. S. *Lord's and the M.C.C.* Herbert Jenkins, 1920.
Martineau, G. D. *Bat, Ball, Wicket and All*. Sporting Handbooks Ltd, 1950.

WOMEN CRICKETERS

BY PHILLIS CUNNINGTON

A very early mention of the word "crickett" was made by John Derricke in 1593 when he tells us that he attended the "free School of Guldeforde, he and his fellowes did runne and play there at crickett and other plaies". It was not until two centuries later that women began to "run and play at cricket", and this happened in 1745.

> The greatest cricket match that was ever played in the south part of England was on Friday the 26th of last month, on Gosden Common, near Guildford, between eleven maids of Bramley and eleven maids of Hambledon dressed all in white. The Bramley maids had blue ribbons and the Hambledon maids red ribbons on their heads. The Bramley girls got 119 notches and the Hambledon girls 122.
>
> There was of both sexes the greatest number that ever was seen on such an occasion. The girls bowled, batted, ran and caught as well as any men could do in that game.
>
> *The Derby Mercury* 16th August, 1745.

Although we are told that these girls were all dressed in white, we are not told what they wore, probably for the simple reason that they followed the fashion of their day. Strange to say, garments suitable for exercise of any sort were not adopted by women until late in the nineteenth century. Cricket matches between women continued spasmodically to the end of the eighteenth century and in order that spectators might be able to recognize each side, distinctive colours were often worn. In a match played in 1747:

> The women of the Hills of Sussex will be in orange, and those of the Dales in blue.

In John Collet's famous picture of "Miss Wicket and Miss Trigger", 1770, Miss Wicket does appear to have made an effort to secure runs more easily as she wears a short (for that date) sporting skirt, called then a petticoat. She also wears a short jacket and waistcoat; but her bergère hat with dangling ribbons and her shoes with Italian heels must have outweighed all the advantages of the short skirt (Fig. 17).

In 1777 a remarkable cricket match was played in private by the Countess of Derby and some other ladies of quality and fashion (Plate 5).

17. Lady cricketer. 1770.

Here again, fashion strikes the note for their costumes. All are dressed alike in morning wear, consisting of jacket and petticoat, a style very fashionable in the 1770s.

> The most fashionable morning dress and home undress for all day is a dishabille which consists of a short jacket and petticoat. The coat [petticoat] is generally puckered round the bottom about a quarter of a yard deep. . . . The jacket is short, not above a quarter of a yard on the hip . . .
>
> *Gentleman's and London Magazine,* February, 1777.

The fitting bodice with low neck was typical. The ladies in this match have long sleeves with ruffles (frills) at the wrist, and again they all wear bergère hats which seem to have been correct for their cricket matches in the eighteenth century.

The "Cricket Match Extraordinary" made famous by T. Rowlandson's caricature, took place in 1811 (Fig. 18). The players, who represented Hampshire *v.* Surrey, were all women and of all ages.

18. "Cricket Match Extraordinary". 1811.

In Rowlandson's drawing all the women wear plain dresses bunched up round the waist so as to shorten the skirts above the knees, with nothing much underneath. Some wear ribbons in their hair, but no special head-gear. Their frocks are of all colours.

It should be noted that other descriptions of the players' costume do not correspond with Rowlandson's picture. Pierce Egan in his *Book of Sports*, written in 1832, reports as follows:

A grand cricket match has been played this month (October) between eleven *women* of Surrey and eleven *women* of Hampshire, for 500 guineas . . .

The combatants were dressed in loose trousers with short fringed petticoats descending to the knees, and light flannel waistcoats, with sashes round the waist—The performers were of all ages and sizes, from 14 years to up-wards of 50, and were distinguished by coloured ribbons—Royal purple for the Hampshire, orange and blue for Surrey.

The weather being favourable on the 2d [*sic*] day, much skill was dis-played, but the palm was borne off by a Hampshire lass who made 41. [Hampshire won]

In the 1830s fashions of the period were still worn by women cricketers, the only concession to utility being a shortened skirt. In the lithograph "Keeping the Wicket" (Fig. 19) the young woman wears a low-necked tightly-laced dress with gigot sleeves and short laced boots. The only un-fashionable item is her male top-hat.

19. "Keeping the wicket against All England". *c.* 1830.

At the Kent match of the ladies of Maidstone versus the ladies of Rochester in 1838, the dresses are again of the period and inconveniently long. All the players wear feather-trimmed bonnets or hats (Plate 6).

By 1875, however, a group of schoolgirls seem to have been given some freedom of movement for the game.

> Steps came down the corridor; no mincing feminine ones this time, but a man's bold decided tread. I lay down my stitching to listen. The door opens, a head is popped in—"Cricket?" says a loud clear voice, the door is shut again, and down go work and thimbles, a babel of delighted cries goes forth and upstairs pulling off ribbons, gowns, crinolines [i.e. crinolettes], all our feminine belongings, and pulling on knickerbockers and blouses. Yes knickerbockers! Let no one blush or look shocked for they are long and ample, and tied modestly in at the ankle: and as to the blouse, which descends below the knee, and is trimly belted in at the waist, it is as decent and uncompromising as that worn by Dr Mary Walker; our costume being in short, nothing more or less than that which is designated by the somewhat opprobrious title of "Bloomer". The knickerbockers bring comfort, the tunic confers respectability. It is a lovely thought that I can kick up my heels to my heart's content, and yet preserve decorum.
>
> As to what manner of female I look, I care nothing; my sensations are all I think about, and they are blissful.
>
> Helen B. Mathers, *Comin thro' the Rye*, 1875.

Schoolgirls, however, were allowed more freedom than adults. Since bloomers were a failure with adults, divided skirts were strongly recommended, similar to those advised for tennis and walking by Miss Ballin in 1885 (See p. 91).

> Cricket [she says] is a very good game for girls and the same remarks as to dress apply to this as to lawn tennis. It is necessary, however, that girls who play cricket should have a protective pad to be worn over their bosoms, in order to prevent any harm which might possibly arise from a chance blow from a cricket ball. A loose well-wadded pad can be placed between the dress-body and the underclothes: it may be kept in place by two bands on either side, one passing above and one beneath each arm, and fastening at the back. This will, I think, be preferable to having the bodice of the dress, the underbodice, or the stays, wadded, as if the pad is loose it can be removed when the game is not being played. It should not however be removed immediately after playing, as this might cause the player to take cold in the chest.
>
> Miss Ada Ballin, *The Science of Dress*, 1885.

In 1890 the English Cricket and Athletics Association made the following announcement:

> The Original English Lady Cricketers . . . equipped with regulation outfit
> by Messrs. Lillywhite, Frowd & Co., and elegantly and appropriately
> attired . . .

were ready for the game. The *Illustrated London News* of 24th May depicted
them at play. All the women wear dresses with the small gigot sleeve fashionable at this date, but the skirts are shortened to just below the knees. The
peaked caps for women were now coming into fashion for sport. The wicket-
keeper and batsman both wear pads (Plate 7). The elegant trimming on the
skirts and round the sailor collars must have been specially designed for this
occasion, since the increasing popularity of outdoor activities for women
evoked the following comment from a contemporary:

> . . . the enthusiasm with which the perfectly plain skirt is welcomed shews
> clearly which way English taste lies. 1890.

A slightly similar style is shown in a picture from the *Illustrated London
News* of 1897, but the skirt is above the knees, showing knickerbockers
below (Fig. 20). These were now known as 'rationals'. The peaked cap is still
in evidence. This, however, was going out of fashion in the nineties. In a
photograph of Lady Cricketers at Royal Holloway College, *c.* 1895, they all
wear boater hats with striped ribbon bands. Most of them have a stand
collar and tie to their blouses and surprisingly long skirts.

Some kind of head-gear seems to have been the rule, generally, for lady
cricketers. In a country game in 1890, in which the girls were being coached,
they wore boaters.

> In the immediate foreground, an effective bit of colour was supplied by the
> party of cricketers. . . . They were chiefly of the fair sex, but there were
> two or three young men in flannels among them, engaged in the congenial
> occupation of coaching and improving.
> "Are you going down to see the cricket Betty?" . . . The triumphant
> bowler made her way towards Betty . . . "Well," she said, "do you think
> we are improved?" . . . She was a pretty dark haired girl . . . She was
> dressed, like most of the other girls, in a gay shirt with a stiff front, and a
> knowing little tie, and wore a plain sailor hat with a red ribbon. Trying as
> the costume was in itself, on her it had an oddly piquant effect that was not
> unbecoming, as Betty felt, though she disapproved the style.
> *Cassell's Family Magazine,* 1890.

Surely this is not surprising!

PLATE 7

"The original English Ladies Cricket Match."

Illustrated London News, *24 May 1890.*

PLATE 8

Cricket team of Bedford Physical Training College, 1919. Typical gym tunics. Batsman wears pads. Some wear snoods to control the hair.

By the turn of the century head-gear ceased to be worn during play.

Skirts remained long even as late as 1905, but from about this time the "gym tunic" began to be adopted by most players. In Plate 8 we have a photograph of a cricket team in 1919 where women are at last allowed free-

20. Lady cricketer in "rationals" just showing below a short skirt. 1897.

dom of movement. Madame Bergman Osterberg, the Swedish teacher, had introduced the gym tunic for physical training in 1885, and from then on-wards it had been increasingly used by schools and the P.T. Colleges for gym and games. Tunics were knee length, sleeveless and worn with a washable blouse. They had three box pleats down the front and back and were tied round the waist with a sash-like belt of braid. They were usually made of navy blue serge, but clubs had their own colours which might be brown or dark green.

Appropriate underwear was now necessary and close fitting knickers matching the tunic were introduced. The name "bloomers" came to be applied to this new undergarment. Corsets were replaced by loose unboned supports with suspenders, such as 'liberty bodices'.

Comfort had at last conquered fashion and produced a fashion of its own.

Note: A brief history of women's cricket is given in Nancy Joy's *Maiden Over*. Sporting Handbooks Ltd, London, 1950.

CHAPTER 3

FOOTBALL

BY ALAN MANSFIELD

The country swains at football here are seen,
Which each gapes after for to get a blow,
The while some other one, away runs with it clean,
It meets another at the goale between.

Henry Peacham, 1612.

A seventeenth-century visitor to England has left us his impression of the game of football as it was in his day, an impression which ascribes some merit to it as an exercise but is by no means enthusiastic about either the subtlety of the play or the skill of the players.

In winter foot-ball is a useful and charming exercise. It is a leather ball about as big as one's head, filled with wind. This is kick'd about from one to t'other in the streets, by him that can get it, and that is all the art of it.

J. Misson, *Memoirs and Observations of M. Misson in his Travels over England*, 1697.
(English trans. 1719)

Even in Misson's time football was of a venerable antiquity as a semi-ritual game played on Shrove Tuesday in both town and country. A hand-ball game, hurling, has certain affinities with ancient football and was popular in the West of England. In Lincolnshire an ancient game, the Hood Game, is traditionally played using, not a ball, but pieces of tightly rolled canvas. These, and other games of a similar nature throughout the British Isles, have all, perhaps, contributed to the two types of football, Association and Rugby, played today.

Unlike cricket, football did not crystallize from its ancient forms, when whole villages or parishes took part on each side, until the nineteenth century, and it was the public schools rather than the public that turned it into a popular game once again after a period of eclipse during the eighteenth century.

The players of those early varieties of proto-football did not make much concession in the way of costume as the misericord at All Souls, Oxford, shows (Plate 9). This is of the first half of the fifteenth century and so outside our time, but by the sixteenth century no more advance had been made than the doffing of an upper garment. In 1519 the curate of St Mary's Church, Hawridge, Berks, is said to have been deprived of his living for "ludit ad pilam pedalem in camisia sua", on a Sunday. ("Playing at football in his shirt.") (Letter in *Morning Post*, 20th August, 1930, quoted in M. Marples *A History of Football*, 1954).

21. Men playing football in doublets, breeches and shoes. *c.* 1611.

Shirts are also evident in 1611, but doublets in some cases were not discarded (Fig. 21). Of a hurling match in 1654, played in Hyde Park, it was said that one side wore red caps, the other side white. (*The Moderate Intelligencer*, 4th May 1654, quoted in M. Marples, op cit.)

For a game somewhat akin to hurling, played in East Anglia, the participants seem to have partially disrobed, for the goals were said to be piles of the coats of the players—a method of construction still in use by small boys playing *ad hoc* football. This game was camp-ball or camp, and a variety of it known as "kicking-camp" could be played with or without shoes being worn. It is uncertain whether the ball or the opposing team was the target of the kicking in the eighteenth century; by the nineteenth it was more civilized and according to C. J. B. Marriott (*The Rugby Game and how to play it*, 1922) early in that century teams wore uniforms of different coloured flannel jackets.

The traditional Lincolnshire Hood Game was played in a red jacket or shirt, and a hat wreathed with red flowers.

A print of about 1760, "Football in the Streets of Barnet", shows eight men playing. They wear breeches, stockings and shoes; four are in hats, and the only difference from normal outdoor attire is that they have discarded their coats and are in waistcoats, and shirt sleeves extending to the wrists.

An illustration "Playing at Football" to a children's book, *c.* 1760 (from Andrew Tuer *Forgotten Children's Books*, ed. 1898) shows two boys in shirts, breeches, and shoes. The shirt sleeves again descend to the wrists (Plate 9).

A painting of 1839 shows village boys at football wearing trousers, jackets or waistcoats, trousers or breeches: some are wearing hats or caps. Still no attempt had been made in the village to adopt a specialized garb, although Harrow School were said to have worn uniform white trousers and black gaiters for the game as early as 1836, and Winchester in about 1840 had similar white trousers with the added refinement of striped shirts or jerseys, one team red and white, the other blue and white.

At Rugby, though,

> They are hanging their jackets, and all who mean real work, their hats, waistcoats, neck-handkerchiefs and braces on the railings,
>
> T. Hughes, *Tom Brown's School Days*, 1856, but set in *c.* 1840.

just like the village boys.

An engraving of football at Rugby School in 1845 shows trousers, shoes, a miscellany of shirts or jerseys and jockey-style caps, some with parti-coloured panels or sectors. Eleven years later, at the same school forage-type caps are depicted. In both pictures some of the players appear to be stripped to the waist, and shoes are the footwear.

Shoes appear to have been the standard wear for the feet, although a writer in 1892 (A. G. Guillemard, President of the Rugby Union, quoted by M. Marples op. cit.) writing of the 1860s speaks of "navvies", special boots for "hacking", described by another old player as having a toe resembling the ram of an iron-clad. Guillemard recalls how one player at Rugby was reproved for unnecessary violence and threatened to have his "navvies" removed and slippers substituted. Of shoes Sir. J. D. Astley writing of his Eton schooldays in the 1840s, says of a schoolfellow:

> He was a brilliant football player, but a terribly untidy fellow, and his shoes were always down at heel, so much so indeed that I have often seen his shoe fly after turning the ball, or when he made a kick.
>
> Sir J. D. Astley, Bart., *Fifty Years of my Life*, 1894.

Astely himself, in 1850, played in a regimental game dressed in a suit of scarlet flannel.

So far we have talked of "football' in the nineteenth century as one game, of which a variety of forms were played, mostly by schools; however, by mid-century it was felt that the time had come to define the game and thus clear up the confusion caused when players of different varieties met together, as occurred in the universities, in which the popularity of the game had been revived by the influx of undergraduates who had played it at school, and in the clubs now beginning to be formed.

Codes of Rules based on the Rugby variety had been drawn up in 1846 and 1848, and in 1863 a meeting of schools and clubs in London founded the Football Association.

Law No: 14 of the new Association stated:

> No player shall be allowed to wear projecting nails, iron plates, or gutta percha on the soles or heels of his boots.

—probably proposed by someone with painful memories of "navvies".

For nearly thirty years this law was in force and it was not until 1891 that leather studs and bars on the heels and soles were allowed. In 1900 referees were authorized to examine players' boots before a match.

In 1867 it was said:

> Your hard workers at football gird up their loins with a broad leather belt, and donning their oldest and dirtiest trousers, and oldest and dirtiest tight jersey, with no covering on their heads, and a faithful and trusty pair of boots on their feet . . . Be that as it may, there is the light division to be thought of, and the pretty Football players . . . Well, for such as these, useful and excellent fellows in their way, the prettiest costume is a coloured velvet cap with a tassell, a tight striped jersey, white flannel trousers, boots à discretion, only no projecting plates or gutta percha.
>
> *Handbook of Football*, Routledge, 1867.

Every Boy's Annual for 1866 from the same publisher (Routledge) contains a coloured plate "Football" showing such coloured caps, but the other garments worn by the players are a medley of shirts, jackets, and trousers of varied hues (Plate 10).

Neither did the Rugby code allow nails. William Allison quoting a letter of his written at preparatory school in Rugby:

> Oakfield,
> Oct. 23rd, 1864.
>
> . . . I got a piece about ¾ of an inch long taken right out of my leg.
> The fellow who did it must have had nails in his boots, which are not allowed.
>
> W. Allison, *My Kingdom for a Horse*, 1919.

Allison also alludes to the flannel trousers as mentioned by Routledge:

> Rugby School.
> 22nd Dec. 1867.
>
> . . . I shall probably get my flannels, which is being allowed to wear flannel trousers instead of ducks [coarse white linen]—a great comfort in more ways than one.
>
> Ibid.

Later in the same letter he says "I had to cut the laces of my boots all the way down." By this date boots had evidently replaced the earlier shoes as normal wear.

Flannels, like caps, were only given after House Matches, and Allison in fact had to wait two years for his. Presumably the granting of "flannels" died out as the dress for the game was rationalized: probably the "cap" survived because it became the accepted wear of the schoolboy, in a less ornate form than the ceremonial games cap, and the insignia of his Alma Mater.

Why trousers—even flannel ones—were elevated to such an honourable status I cannot conjecture: the cap has, perhaps, a more obvious dignity. Were not crowns and coronets and caps of maintenance marks of greatness and esteem? And was not the Victor Ludorum crowned with a wreath? And did not, in 1858, H. H. Stevenson receive a hat as a reward for taking three wickets with three consecutive balls?

Head-gear of some type appears as an essential article of the footballer's dress in the 1860s, and apparently survived on some heads until the 1880s, though by the nineties it seems to have died out, only to survive in the modern Rugby scrum-cap.

Knickerbockers, a loose type of breeches originally part of the Volunteers' uniform, became popular from about 1860 for country wear by civilians. They spread to the football field, and a photograph of a Harrow School team in 1867 shows them wearing matching vertically striped knickerbockers and shirts, and striped caps to match, some worn with the peaks to the rear. The team also wears high ankle boots and light coloured stockings. (Photograph reproduced in *A Hundred Years of Soccer in Pictures*, F. A. Heinemann, 1963).

22. Pillbox cap, knickerbockers. 1878.

Pillboxes, skull-caps, and knitted "brewers" caps (sometimes called "fishermens" or "pirate" caps), as well as the peaked cricket style cap are all to be seen in drawings and photographs of the 1870s; bare heads are also evident (Figs. 22 and 23).

Rugby School still played in trousers in 1871, but knickerbockers generally triumphed, although as late as 1888 a goalkeeper was photographed in goal and long trousers. Both codes adopted the knickerbockers, and they persisted into the early 1890s in some cases (Fig. 24).

The codification of the Rugby and Association games and the subsequent

PLATE 9

(*a*) Medieval football. 1st half 15th century.

Misericord, All Souls College, Oxford. Photograph by courtesy of S. Whiteley, Hatch End, Pinner.

(*b*) Children playing football. *c.* 1775.

18th-century book illustration from Andrew Tuer, Forgotten Children's Books. *1898–9.*

PLATE 10

Schoolboys playing football. Trousers: jackets: shirts: caps and bowler hats. 1866.

23. England *v* Scotland. Scotland in dark jerseys with lion badge.
England light jerseys with leopards badge. Elastic sided boots on one
player. 1872.

greater control and organization of matches led naturally to teams and clubs
adopting a standard design and colour of jersey and cap, and in some cases,
stockings.

In 1867 it was advised,

> if it can previously be so arranged, to have one side with striped jerseys of one
> colour, say red; and the other with another, say blue. This prevents confusion
> and wild attempts to . . . wrest the ball from your neighbour. I have often
> seen this done, and heard the invariable apology—"I beg your pardon, I
> thought you were on the opposite side."
>
> Routledge, op. cit.

Early jerseys seem to have been self-coloured, or with horizontal stripes
(Fig. 22): vertical stripes and halved or quartered part-colours became popular
in the 1880s (Fig. 25).

> Jerseys and stockings in a great variety of patterns, solid colours, stripes . . .
> horizontal and vertical . . . in all combinations of colours.
>
> Advertisement, *Tailor and Cutter*, 1894.

24. Blackburn Rovers *v* Notts. County. Knickerbockers and long
shorts. 1891.

Badges appear in the mid-sixties on the breast of the jersey and in 1871 the
first English International Rugby team bore a large embroidered rose over
their hearts. In 1879 the English Association team carried a shield of three
leopards and the Scottish team the lion of that country (Fig. 23).

Later, horizontal stripes were monopolized by Rugby players, and vertical
ones became the insignia of the Association player—is there here a subconscious
symbolism of the position so often assumed by players of the former game?

Up to the 1870s jerseys had a plain round neck, sometimes quite low.
Towards the end of the decade a short centre-front opening and two buttons
appeared. By the 1880s turn-down collars were popular and a more shirt-like
appearance was evident. (This type of jersey was in fact seen on Rugby teams
as early as 1871, worn with a bow tie in some cases.)

During the 1880s knickerbockers gave place to shorts. At first these were
long and close fitting (Figs. 25, 26), but became shorter in the 1890s, and by
the early 1900s were, if long by modern standards, much wider in the leg
(Fig. 27). The Football Association, perhaps worried by too great a display
of male calves, originally ruled that shorts should extend below the knee.

Plain stockings, or stockings striped throughout their length (Fig. 22) were mostly worn until the mid-1890s, when coloured stripes to the turnover tops only began to appear (Fig. 27). Thick woollen jerseys and ordinary cloth caps as goalkeeper's wear seem to have been introduced in the early years of the present century.

25. Jersey coloured in halves: long shorts: boots with bars. 1886.

Despite the increasing science and skill shown over the years, and the decreasing savagery of the players, the shins remained a very vulnerable area of the players' body. Early attempts to guard against injury seem to have been frowned upon:

> . . . Moreover, anything in the nature of a guard for the shins was anathema maranatha. I remember seeing a boy very severely beaten for being found to have stuffed copy-books inside his stockings when he played football.
>
> W. Allison, op. cit.

Nevertheless, shin-guards eventually triumphed over Spartanism, and in 1880 they were first mentioned in the laws of the game. They are said to have been invented, or introduced, by S. Widdowson of Nottingham.

26. Rugby: long shorts; high boots. 1887.

Certainly, in 1882, Richard Daft, of that town advertised:

S. W. Widdowson's Registered Shin guards.
Football: A Weekly Record of the Game. Vol. I, 1882–3.

In the early days they were formidable things, like mini-cricket pads, worn outside the stockings and secured by straps. In 1887 they extended from just below the knee to the ankle. Throughout the 1880s and most of the 90s they appear in photographs and drawings fastened outside the stockings— from the mid-90s they become less common and seem to have moved inside. Of the season 1900–1 I have seen only one pair shown outside the stockings. From thence onwards none are to be seen in photographs.

According to Gibson and Pickford:

Law 12 regulates boot studs and prohibits clips, buckles, etc. on shin guards.
Association Football, Vol. IV.
A. Gibson & W. Pickford, Caxton, 1905–6

27. Oxford *v* Cambridge. 1903.

Basically the dress of the immediately pre-Great War footballer was what it still is today—new materials are in use, shorts have got shorter, boots have got lighter, but photographs of players of the 1900s and the 1960s seem very much alike, and one is struck by the similarities rather than the differences. In the four hundred years of football that we have considered, it is the forty years from 1860 until 1900 that saw the development, rationalization, and standardization of the footballer's kit. And if our footballer, past or present, feels justly sore at Kipling's unkind description, he can resort to

Pond's Extract . . . absolutely unrivalled as an application for sprains and bruises.

NO ATHLETE SHOULD BE WITHOUT IT.

Advertisement: *Football: A Weekly Record of the Game,* Vol. I, 1882–3.

Bibliography

Football Association. *A Hundred Years of Soccer in Pictures.* Heinemann, 1963.
Marples, Morris. *A History of Football.* Secker and Warburg, 1954.

CHAPTER 4

HOCKEY AND CROQUET

BY PHILLIS CUNNINGTON

HOCKEY

There appears to be strong evidence that hockey of some sort is a very ancient game. On the wall of an Egyptian tomb, date 2000 B.C., there is a picture which depicts two men "bullying".

The game, with sticks of the hockey design, spread through Persia, Japan and Greece and it had been adopted in England by the fourteenth century. There it persisted, although Edward III tried to suppress the practice of "useless" games, including "hockey", since "the realm is likely in a short time to be destitute of archers."

28. Hockey-player; detail from a stained glass window, Gloucester Cathedral, c. 1350.

In the East window of Gloucester Cathedral there is a roundel of stained glass dating c. 1350 depicting a player with a stick which is thought to be a

29. Men in knee-length shorts as described in text. Some wear short
gaiters and caps with peaks, most are bare-headed. 1892.

hockey stick. Hockey did not become a popular game, however, until the
late nineteenth century. The Blackheath Hockey Club was in existence in
1861 and the players wore either a red or a blue hat to indicate for which
team they were playing.

In 1871 the Teddington Hockey Club was founded and the men then wore
yellow shirts and white flannel trousers.

The present form of the game came under national control when the Hockey Association was founded in 1886. The Costume then worn was a sweater
or a heavy woollen shirt, sometimes coloured or striped; knickerbockers,
long woollen stockings and leather football boots.

Shorts, at first about knee-length, replaced knickerbockers and have become shorter ever since.

By the twentieth century cotton shirts, variously coloured, became the rule and light-weight ankle shoes with studded rubber soles replaced boots, but long stockings remained.

30. Ladies' hockey match. All wearing long skirts and boater hats.
1893.

Women undergraduates took to hockey at Lady Margaret Hall, Oxford in 1887 and from the 1890s enthusiasm for the game spread. We are told by a writer on sport in 1910 that:

> The wide increase in the popularity of hockey and its rapid development as a woman's game in the last twenty years is unique in the history of games.
>
> *Encyclopaedia of Sport.*

The first international ladies' match between England and Ireland was played in 1897. They all wore ankle-length skirts, red for England, green for Ireland. All wore shirt blouses with collars and ties. The Irish team wore peaked caps, but, except for the captain, the English team was bare-headed. Heavy skirts of considerable length continued to be worn for hockey by ladies' clubs and the Universities (Plate 11), right up to 1914.

PLATE II

(*a*) Bedford College Hockey Team, 1896. All wearing long skirts, blouses and college ties.

Photograph kindly supplied by the Librarian, Bedford College for Women.

(*b*) British International team, 1912. All in long skirts, still correct at this date.

Photograph kindly lent by Miss E. R. Clarke.

PLATE 12

Hockey players wearing gymn tunics and boots; some have protective ankle pads. 1914.

By 1893 schools and students of physical training were already wearing, for hockey, the short gym tunic and appropriate underwear described on p. 45, but it was an up-hill struggle for others to achieve tunics or even short skirts. Miss Clarke, who captained the All England team in 1912 (Plate 11(b)), tells us that failing a tunic she compromised by wearing a knee-length skirt and was then asked by the All England Council to have her red England skirt made longer as it was "so important on these occasions to avoid all criticism"! However by 1915 gym tunics had won the day and were worn by all the first teams in England.

Short canvas boots with rubber studs were general. Ankle pads and padded gloves were adopted by some (Plate 12).

In 1900 a garment known as a djibbah was introduced at Roedean School. It was a knee-length dress with a round neck and short sleeves, fitted the figure fairly closely and flared out from the hips without pleats. The djibbah had no general popularity; indeed the typical gym tunic had no serious rival for hockey players until it was ousted at last by shorts.

CROQUET

The hey-day of the game of croquet was in the 1860s.

Whether it was derived from a game introduced from France in the seventeenth century and called paille-maille and later pall-mall, is doubtful. Pall-mall was played with a ball, a mallet and two hoops on a hard surface. There is no doubt, however, that true croquet was brought from Ireland to England in the 1850s and Lord Lonsdale, the sporting peer, was one of the first to lay out a court on the lawns of his home in the Lake District. During the 1860s and 1870s it was probably the most popular outdoor game for ladies in England.

Costumes worn for croquet were merely those in the mode of the day. Men tended to wear country suits for casual games, but frock coats and top hats for special matches. In the crinoline period of the 1860s women's skirts were slightly shorter than previously and for croquet were generally hitched up over this cumbersome hooped petticoat so that ankles became evident.

> Not long ago, some twelve years back (*c.* 1860) . . . Pretty ladies were soon seen thumping those bright balls about with tiny mallets; and this game quickly became popular. . . . Consider curiously the simultaneous appearance in the world of "tight croquet" and short petticoats with fascinating

borders. Does it not almost seem as if the process of croqueting and the fact that young ladies have pretty ankles, were discovered at one and the same moment of time. . . . The fact, also, that it is the only game that brings gentlemen and ladies together in the open air cannot be rated too highly. Whether for flirtation or downright hard play, croquet has unquestionably achieved this result and every other pastime has failed.

Arthur Lillie, The Book of Croquet, c. 1873

31. Ladies in crinolines, with skirts hitched up so that petticoats and even drawers are exposed. 1862.

Although the cage petticoats, generally known as crinolines, must have interfered with the ease of wielding the mallet, they had their uses.

There are two modes of playing the game. The first is the severe and self-glorifying style advocated by the writers. . . . There is also the social and "jolly" style where a young lady is known to carry her ball in the ample folds of her dress after it has been ungallantly driven off, to a position which she prefers, and when called to account she sits on the grass and requires her attendant squire to help her up before any further progress can be made; producing more hearty merriment than the finest strokes of play.

Croquet, a New Game of Skill, 1867.

Suitable clothes for ladies to play croquet in were suggested by a gentleman in 1864.

> Some . . . may consider that we are scarcely justified in suggesting the proper croquet costume for young ladies. . . . As one of the prominent reasons of the pleasure that men take in the game is the sight with which they are indulged of a neatly turned pair of ankles and pretty little boots, we hint that young ladies, when playing croquet, should don their prettiest boots, provided that they are adorned with good strong soles. . . . We request that they banish from the game those hideous boot-coverings known as goloshes, or (vulgarly) crushers.

32. Style of 1864. Men players wearing lounge jackets, knickerbockers and hats.

The dress should be looped up, or not only will it spoil many a good stroke, but with its sweeping train will probably disturb the position of some of the balls . . .

If a young lady's hands are very tender and apt to blister, we advise her to wear a pair of old kid gloves. She must be careful, however, that they fit well or, as they prevent the hands taking a firm hold . . . they are sure to deaden the force of the stroke.

Then follows advice to gentlemen:

The best costume for gentlemen (that which the late Mr. Thackeray [died 1863] characterized as "the prettiest dress for boys that has been invented these 100 years") is knickerbockers. Most men will look almost graceful when dressed in white flannel knickerbockers, with jacket, waistcoat, shirt and cap to match. Cricketing shoes, *minus* the spikes which would chip the balls, and perhaps stick into them, are to be recommended in consequence of the softness of the leather.

A game of croquet, played by people dressed as we have suggested, presents a more charming appearance than possibly most people imagine.

Edmund Routledge, *Handbook of Croquet*, 1864.

33. Men in beach wear. Girls in bathing dresses. 1870.

PLATE 13

Ladies playing croquet in the height of fashion, as also is the gentleman in frock-coat and top-hat. 1874.

Print in James Laver Collection.

PLATE 14

Lady croquet champion in smart summer outfit.

The Bystander. *1906.*

A letter from a girl staying in the country, describes a "Mr Tightman" aged 56 who tried to pass himself off as a young gallant. He wore "very modern clothes" and well brushed hair and whiskers. On escaping from being "croqued" [*sic*],

> jumping in the air . . . he split three buttons of his frock coat which was fastened in order to shew off his fine figure . . . he limps after the ball when he is croqued as actively as the tight patent-leather boots he sports will allow him. Ibid.

Evidently Mr Tightman showed how *not* to dress for croquet. The urbane individual in Plate 13 at least wears his coat open.

34. Man in early style morning coat, trousers and bowler hat. Woman in the style of 1870 with draped over-skirt and bustle.

The popularity of croquet was such that it was even played on the beach in bathing suits. (Fig. 33.)

In the 1870s fashionable costumes were worn by ladies, with ground-length skirts and all the drapery of this period. Hats were always worn (Plate 13).

> At 4 o'clock Miss Meredith Brown and her beautiful sister Etty came over to tea with us and a game of croquet. Etty . . . was dressed in light grey with a close fitting crimson body which set off her exquisite figure. . . . But the

greatest triumph was her hat, broad and picturesque, carelessly turned with flowers and set jauntily on one side of her pretty dark head, while round her shapely slender throat, she wore a rich gold chain necklace with broad gold links. (1875.)

Francis Kilvert, *Diary 1870–1879.*

35. Detail from "Spring Meeting of the All England Croquet Club, Wimbledon". Man in lounge suit and wearing a deer stalker hat with flaps turned down. 1872.

Men were not always smart (Fig. 35). As the craze for croquet subsided smart clothes were no longer considered essential, even for women, and in the 1890s and after, a blouse and skirt was usual; but even then the skirt was long (Plate 14). Men usually dressed in an ordinary day suit but to prevent them from becoming too slack, this warning was pinned to the board of a croquet club:

Gentlemen are requested not to play in their shirt sleeves when ladies are present.

Bibliography

Anon. *Croquet, a new Game of Skill.* 1867.
Battersby, H. F. *Hockey,* London, Ward, Lock & Bowden. 1895.
Lillie, Arthur. *The Book of Croquet.* London, Jaques & Son, 1872.
Pollard, Marjorie. *Your Book of Hockey.* London, Faber & Faber, 1959.
Routledge, Edmund. *Routledge's Handbook on Croquet.* London, 1864.

CHAPTER 5

GOLF

BY ALAN MANSFIELD

Oh often may she wear it,
Her bonny golfing bonnet!
And as she deftly ties her dainty head its shade within,
Though down she looks demurely,
Full well she knows securely
She holds my heart a captive in the bow beneath her chin.

Jenny Betts Hartswick.

The game of golf has, like many games, an involved ancestry. It first appears in recognizable form in the fifteenth century. In 1457 James the II of Scotland prohibited the playing of the game, and the prohibition was enforced by James IV in 1491, when he decreed against

fut bawis, gouff, or uther sic unproffitable sportis.

In England, our own Henry VIII was not opposed to it.
In 1513 Catherine wrote to Wolsey

I thank God to be busy with the golf, for they take it for pastime; my heart is very good to it and I am horribly busy making standards, banners, and bagets.

Unfortunately we have no record of what these early golfers wore to play the game: contemporary pictures from the Low Countries where the game or a similar game was also popular show the players wearing doublet, slops[1], stockings and shoes. Hats were also worn by the players. The golfers on Blackheath where the game is said to have been introduced in 1608 presumably wore similar garb.

A late sixteenth century reference to expenditure in Scotland refers to:

Ane hatt lint with velvet.

Haddington Burgh Book, 1576.

[1] Wide knee breeches.

This item is included with one for golf balls, and the hat may have been for wear when golfing, but there is no definite proof, neither is there any clue as to whether the hat differed in any way from the normal head-wear of the time.

It has been said that there is no evidence that the Scots ever played in the kilt, although a reference to St Andrew's of unknown date speaks of the gentlemen golfers dressed in the "old Scottish dress". (Rev. Walter Wood, *The East Neuk of Fife*. n.d.)

From the middle of the eighteenth century "companies" of golfers formed themselves into clubs, and like the cricketers and hunters of that time they adopted a club uniform.

These uniforms generally consisted of a red frock, breeches and white stockings, worn with shoes, the usual men's dress of the day; uniformity being the colour of the frock, that is, a loose fitting coat with a small collar, an informal garment in the early eighteenth century.

By the end of the century clubs were distinguishing themselves by the colour of the frock collar (known as the 'cape') and by devices or badges on the buttons, or on the frock itself:

> Red coat with dark blue velvet cape, with plain white buttons, with an embroidered club and ball on each side of the cape, with two large buttons on the sleeves.
> Royal and Ancient Golf Club of St. Andrews 1784,
> quoted in H. H. Hilton & G. G. Smith. *The Royal &*
> *Ancient Game of Golf*, 1912.

According to Kay's *Edinburgh Portraits*, published in 1842, the Leith Club in about 1815 wore a

> Scarlet single breasted coat with green collar and plain gilt buttons, badge on left breast, with the device of the thistle embroidered with gold on green cloth, the trousers white.
> Quoted by W. Dalrymple, MS. notes.

In the early days in Scotland golf was played on the common links by all classes of society, peer and plumber, surgeon and shopkeeper:

> Then the greatest and wisest of the land were to be seen on the links of Leith, mingling freely with the humblest mechanics in pursuit of their common and beloved amusement. All distinctions of rank were levelled by the joyous spirit of the game.
> Unacknowledged source, quoted in *Golf*,
> Badminton Library, 1902. ed.

The formation of the clubs, however, brought a certain exclusiveness to the game; in general the clubs recruited their members from the upper and middle classes. In St Andrews at the middle of the eighteenth century, there were said to be two clubs, one for the nobility, gentry and professions (they of the red coats), and one for the tradesmen, who wore a green uniform. Later, in about 1784, Earl Balcarres and ten of his friends played at St Andrews in a uniform frock, buff in colour, with red collar and white buttons.

36. Golfer at Blackheath: round hat, short frock. See text. 1790.

The Blackheath Royal Golf Club, the earliest evidence of which is in the eighteenth century, although the game was played there as early as 1608, appear to have worn a short red military style frock, with long narrow revers faced with green, blue stand-fall collar and blue cuffs, both braided (or laced) with gold, and gold epaulettes, buff breeches, white waistcoat and stockings (Fig. 36).

In some, if not all, clubs, a penalty was exacted if the club uniform was not worn by members when they played in matches.

The Glasgow club, flourishing between 1786 and 1833 fined their members a bottle of rum if they did not wear the regulation frock or jacket, a grey one, when playing for the club (*Golf Illustrated*, 25th September, 1903).

The jacket, reaching just below the hips, was sometimes worn in place of the frock; it was a popular garment for sportsmen in the latter half of the eighteenth century (Fig. 37). It also was often red, faced with a different colour.

37. Golfer in red jacket, faced blue, blue waist-coat and breeches. "Bicorne" hat. Badge on left breast. Uniform of Hon. Co. of Edinburgh Golfers. *c.* 1780–90.

In the closing years of the eighteenth century the top-hat, sometimes white, began to be worn, and continued as an alternative to bonnets and caps in the nineteenth (Fig. 38).

In the early years of the nineteenth century trousers generally began to replace breeches, no less on golfing legs than on others. In 1820 the St Andrew's Club adopted plain blue for the coat or jacket, with club buttons: at a later, unrecorded, date they reverted to red.

In the 1820s and 1830s dark jackets and tail coats were to be seen, worn with white or light coloured trousers. Tam o' Shanters and top hats, white or black, crowned the players' heads, and sometimes spats embellished the other end.

Contemporary evidence shows that the red or other coloured uniform coat or jacket was by no means universal in the nineteenth century—no doubt the fines of earlier days had lapsed. The professional players of the 1840s and 1850s appear to have settled down to tweed or cloth jacket and trousers, and a soft peaked cap (Fig. 39).

In England golf seems to have had little following from the mid-1600s until a revival occurred in the 1860s, although it lingered on among a few enthusiasts, as at Blackheath, and a club was formed in Manchester in 1815.

38. Golfer in red coat with blue collar and top hat. Badge on left breast. *c.* 1818–20.

The famous club at Westward Ho in North Devon was founded in 1864, and the course at Wimbledon was laid out in the same year. During the next twenty years or so the game increased enormously in popularity, despite certain references by devotees of other games to "Scotch croquet", or, as in the case of the legendary Regimental Serjeant Major, "'ockey at the 'alt".

The game was played before 1864 on Wimbledon Common by the London Scottish Volunteers, and from them it may have spread to other Volunteer regiments who frequented the Common for rifle shooting. A feature of the uniform of these Volunteers was a loose form of breeches known as knickerbockers; a garment which rapidly caught on as civilian dress for country and sports wear. Knickerbockers soon vied with trousers and by 1892 there was a run on very loose knickers, buttoning at the knee for cycling and golf, a Scotch game that is gaining favour.

Tailor and Cutter, 1892.

(See Fig. 40).

The red coat was not so popular in England as in Scotland, and in both countries it tended to die out during the 1890s, by which decade the game was well established in favour south of the Border.

39. Professional golfers: jackets, trousers and cloth caps. *c.* 1850–60.

40. Knickerbockers and spats on the links. 1891.

However, in 1894 it was still being said:

These jackets are made in all sorts of materials, but the Golf jacket proper is scarlet serge, some clubs being recognised by the collar, which is of different coloured cloth, faced.

Tailor and Cutter, 1894.

In some instances in England where golf was played on public commons, such as Wimbledon, it was compulsory under local by-laws for the players to wear red coats: that such a rule was not financially prohibitive is shown by an advertisement:

> Golfing coats and vests, made of a specially good scarlet flannel . . . as low as14s.
>
> Advertisement, 1894.

Some of the reluctance of English players to wear the red coat, unless compelled to, may have been due to the opinion held by many that it was the mark of the "maestro", and that with it one might also unforgiveably put on "side".

But the glory of the red coat was in part replaced by the exuberance of the check patterns of coats, waistcoats and trousers or knickerbockers, and the gaiety of the knitted stockings worn with the latter leg-wear.

> But in the matter of Norfolk jackets and knickerbockers, spats and parti-coloured stockings, checks and stripes, the golfer is a bird of bright and varied plumage.
>
> Horace Hutchinson, *Golf,* Badminton Library. 1902. edit.

There is some evidence that in the nineteenth century the coat or jacket was sometimes discarded for the freedom of waistcoat and shirtsleeves.

Gloves were generally worn in the eighteenth century and frequently in the nineteenth.

In the 1890s the soft, peaked, cloth cap, generally made of tweed became the favourite type of head dress for golfers, almost entirely ousting the deer-stalker, straw, and other forms of hat. Originally made to fit close to the head, it increased in size as the century drew to a close:

> Caps with small peaks and which fit the head close and low down behind are the prevailing shape.
>
> *Tailor and Cutter,* 1894.

> The Golf cap is enormously popular. The crown continues to increase in size and is now made very full and overlaps the peak. It is in striking colours.
>
> *Tailor and Cutter,* 1898.

The earlier close fitting caps, made in eight segments, survived on into the early years of the twentieth century, but gradually died out by the time of the Great War.

At the beginning of this present century the common wear for golf was a Norfolk suit with knickerbockers, patterned stockings, sometimes spats, and heavy shoes or boots, with the caps as described above, or sometimes a tweed or soft felt hat (Fig. 41). Trousers occasionally replaced knickerbockers, and were generally worn with turned-up legs—which could be a hazard, as in 1910 when a driven ball was lost, subsequently to be found in the turn-up of a spectator's trousers.

41. Golfer: knickerbocker suit; "golf" cap: stockings and shoes. *c.* 1909.

42. Golfer in very loose knickerbockers, check waistcoat and large "golf" or "motor" cap. 1914.

From about 1910 onwards rather loud check waistcoats were fashionable; and by 1914 the knickerbockers had become very loose and baggy, approximating to the plus-fours of the mid-1920s (Fig. 42). The Norfolk jacket was often replaced by one cut on lounge lines.

In some clubs the red coat in the form of "tails" lingered on as evening dress for captains and ex-captains.

When women took up golf we do not know. There is a tradition that Mary Queen of Scots played. The first recorded instance appears to be in the Minutes of Musselburgh Golf Club for 1810 when it was resolved to present by subscription "a handsome new creel and shawl to the best Female golfer" playing in the annual New Year's Day match. Two of "the best Barcelona silk handkerchiefs" were also included in the prize. Perhaps surprisingly this offer was apparently only made to the "Fish ladies" of the town, and this together with the creel might indicate that those hard working and muscular women were the sole female devotees at the time.

43. A lady golfer at Westward Ho: fashionable gown with flounced, apron-fronted skirt: tall, elaborately decorated hat. 1873.

Half a century or so later, in England, we find ladies genteely putting at Westward Ho (Fig. 43) clad in all the inappropriate finery of 1873.

In 1885 the lady's garb in the du Maurier drawing (Fig. 44) is more practical and she tops it with a tweed deer-stalker like her husband's. To quote a contemporary author on dress for "any active outdoor exercise":

> In construction it must be as simple as possible, leaving the limbs unimpeded in action, and having no useless extraneous ornaments. The hat should cover the head, and if for rough work should be one which obviously will not

become draggled and spoiled by wet. Ostrich feathers or plush trimmings
are wholly unfitted for this kind of dress.

L. Higgin, *Art as Applied to Dress,* 1885.

The first Ladies Championship was held at Lytham St Anne's in 1893, and
at about this date it was said:

. . . as for golf, all the variety that comfort requires is to have the skirt a
trifle shorter, and the sleeves and bodice a thought looser than usual to ensure
freedom of stroke.

Mrs Douglas, *The Gentlewoman's Book of Dress.* n.d. (but after 1889).

44. She in tight bodice and draped overskirt;
deer stalker hat: he in Norfolk suit; son in
knickerbockers, sailor hat and jacket. 1885.

The question of "freedom of stroke" also exercised the male mind:

We venture to suggest seventy or eighty yards as the average limit of a drive
advisedly; not because we doubt a lady's power to make a longer drive, but
because that cannot well be done without raising the club above the shoulder
. . . the posture and gestures required for a full swing are not particularly
graceful when the player is clad in female dress.

Lord Moncrieff, *Golf,* Badminton Library, 1902 edit.

This possible lack of grace when making a full-length drive was one of the
reasons why many clubs in the 1890s made special ladies' links with short holes

well within the players' capabilities without offending susceptibilities by raising their arms above their shoulders.

That their sportsmanship was superior to their gamesmanship in this respect is, however, evidenced by pictures of lady golfers of the time. Such a one is the young lady of 1894 clad in skirt, shirt-blouse and golfing cap (Fig. 45).

45. Lady golfer in blouse and skirt and golf cap. 1894.

Golf gained immense popularity among women as well as men during the 1890s, and being a game playable in summer and winter allowed of a variety of female dress ranging from blouses and skirts and straw hats to heavy tweed costumes, with thigh length jackets (Plate 15).

Golf capes were introduced about 1893: they were hip length, kept in place by straps crossing in front, and were often tartan-lined.

Hats were of straw, boater-shaped, often decorated with ribbons or artificial flowers, or of felt, or might take the form of a cap.

At the beginning of the present century ladies' jackets became shorter, and were often in the Norfolk style (Plate 15). In spring flannel was used for jackets or coats:

Double breasted reefer of striped flannel: Panama hat.

The Ladies Tailor, April 1902.

Skirts were shorter than previously.

> In wet weather the long skirt hampers every movement . . . and is very tiring to drag about. A short skirt—really short, not simply a couple of inches off the ground—looks infinitely nicer and more workman-like, and makes an inestimable difference in comfort.
>
> Mary Hezlet, *Ladies Golf*, 1907.

"Really short" is, of course, a comparative term, and in Edwardian days meant about six to eight inches off the ground, and even at that length they took a great deal of wear and tear at the hem, so leather was often employed to reinforce the skirt bottom.

> It is a good plan to have a broad strip of leather round the hem, as this lasts well, and when covered with mud can be washed with very little trouble.
>
> Ibid.

The use of leather in this way was not confined to golf, but was often found in country skirts and dresses and for shooting, walking and the like.

Shorter skirts meant smarter footwear, and boots, or shoes, should be

> properly looked after and kept on trees while not in use . . . brown [boots] are usually made of softer leather and perhaps look smarter.
>
> Ibid.

Shoes should be worn with leather or cloth gaiters, and flat heels were recommended for shoes and boots.

Nails or studs were sometimes worn in the soles and heels.

Knitted jerseys and cardigans were also acceptable wear for golf, as for other outdoor activities.

> The fashionable golf jerseys are sold at Evans in all colours for only 6*s* 11*d*. They are very nice for the seaside, for golf, for boating or tennis. I think they look best in red. . . .
>
> *The Housewife*, 1895.

Scarlet jerseys were very fashionable in 1906, an echo of the man's golf jacket, which by this time was only very rarely seen on the links. Blouses or shirts were high-necked, of cotton or flannel, generally, with either a turn-down attached collar or a high stiff linen collar. Ties were worn with both varieties. Sleeves were sometimes rolled up.

Hats were of a wide variety, but generally more practical in design than during the previous decades—the Tam o' Shanter and the motor cap seemed especially in favour. The motor cap was a peaked soft cloth cap on the lines of the golf cap, but flatter and larger in the head; they were often made of the same cloth as the skirt or costume. Despite the popularity of the Tam o' Shanter (Fig. 46), not every fashion writer had commended it:

> Not every one who goes to Scotland should wear a Tam o' Shanter. It is only by skilful management that this trying woollen monstrosity is ever rendered becoming . . . It has a disconcerting way of lurching over just at the wrong time.
>
> Mrs Douglas, op. cit.

46. Lady in short check skirt, blouse, collar and tie and Tam o' shanter. 1903.

By 1909 some women players copied the American fashion of no hat.
Gloves, that hallmark of the Perfect Lady,

> should always be worn for golf, as they do not interfere at all with the grip on the club, and are a great protection to the hands, saving them from the disfiguring marks of chaps and blisters. Soft, washing chamois leather are the best kind, and men's old white kid ones turned inside out are also excellent.
>
> Mary Hezlet, op. cit.

By the end of our period the woman golfer had attained a practical style of dress for her upper half, shirt or blouse, or jersey, and a knitted cardigan for added warmth on cold days. For the lower woman, however, the traditional long skirt still encumbered her legs despite the hesitant shortening it had undergone during the previous twelve or so years.

For both sexes what to wear on the links posed questions, both moral and material; "When anyone is outrageously dressed," said Mary Hezlet, "it casts a slur on the whole society of lady golfers": and H. G. Hutchinson reminded his male readers that "there are certain points of etiquette, such as those connected with dress, which differ locally, and you should ever endeavour to conform yourself to the etiquette of the links on which you are playing." To pick a safe path between etiquette, custom, and in the case of ladies, womanliness, on the one hand, and ease and efficiency of play on the other was not always easy, and when it came to clothes perhaps the safest advice was that of the old professional (with the garment suitably amended in the case of the ladies):

> Ye should never play a match in a pair of new breeks, for ye'll aye be thinking about them, when ye should be looking at yer ba'.

Bibliography

Badminton Library. *Golf.* Longmans Green & Co., ed. 1902.
Hezlet, Mary. *Ladies Golf.* Hutchinson & Co., 1907.

MISS MOIR

MRS MACFIE

PLATE 15

(a) Ladies at St Andrews: coat and skirt, frilled blouse, broad belt; and skirt with long coat of differing colour, shirt, stiff collar and tie. "Boater" hats. 1893.

The Gentlewoman, *August 1893.*

(b) Lady golfer in tweed Norfolk jacket and short skirt, high stiff collar, buttoned gaiters, Trilby style hat with veil. 1904.

The Lady's Realm. *1904.*

CHAPTER 6

TENNIS

BY PHILLIS CUNNINGTON

Tennis is a game of no use in itself, but of great use in respect it maketh a
quick eye and a body ready to put itself into postures. *c.* 1600.

Attributed to Francis Bacon.

A short account of tennis is necessary before describing costume.

Tennis originated in France where it was popular all through the thir-
teenth, fourteenth and fifteenth centuries. It is uncertain when it first came to
England but it is mentioned in Gower's *Balade c.* 1400. The great days of
tennis in England, however, started with the Tudors and this game, apart from
a decline in the eighteenth century, has been popular ever since.

Tennis played on a covered-in court (as distinguished from lawn tennis)
was usual in the early days. At Hampton Court, such a tennis court can still
be seen. It was built in 1530 and much patronized by Henry VIII. Open-air
tennis, called field tennis or long tennis, was, however, often played many
years before lawn tennis which became such a popular game in the nineteenth
century. A description of field tennis in 1591 is quoted by J. Nichols in *The
Progresses and Public Processions of Queen Elizabeth*:

> The same day after dinner . . . ten of my lord Hartford's servants, all
> Somersetshire men, in a square green court before her Majesty's windows
> did lay up lines, squaring out the form of a tennis court and making a cross
> line in the middle. In this square, they (being stript of their doublets) played
> five to five, with the hand ball, at bord and cord (as they term it) to the great
> liking of Her Highness.

In France, in the fifteenth century, tennis balls were stuffed with wool and
covered with sheepskin. In England in the sixteenth century the balls were
usually of leather stuffed with human hair.

> The old ornament of his cheek hath already stuffed tennis balls.
> Shakespeare, *Much Ado About Nothing,* Act III Sc. 2 (1599–1600).

Tennis was generally played by hand until the sixteenth century when the racket was usual. The racket was, however, in use much earlier, as it was mentioned by Chaucer *c.* 1382 in his *Troilus and Cryseyde* "playen racket, to and fro". And again in Shakespeare's Henry V, Act I Sc. 2, we read:

> K. Henry: What treasure, uncle?
> Exeter: Tennis balls, my liege.
> K. Henry: We are glad the dauphin is so pleasant with us; His present, and your pains, we thank you for: When we have matched our rackets with these balls, We will, in France, by God's grace play a set Shall strike his father's crown into the hazard. (1600).

In Comenius's *Visible World*, three figures are depicted playing tennis in a covered court (Fig. 47).

In a tennis court they play with a Ball which one throweth and another taketh

47. Tennis players in 1664.

and sendeth back with a Racket and this is the sport of Noblemen to stir their body. 1664.

Early tennis was certainly the "sport of Noblemen" and royalty. As early as 1536 a restrictive Act was passed forbidding servants and labourers to play "idle games" such as tennis. Even three centuries later we read:

> From the Palace Yard (Westminster) we moved on . . . till we came to the tennis court, but could not for my life imagine what place that could be, hung round with such a deal of network . . . He informed me 'twas a conveniency built for the noble game of tennis, a very delightful exercise, much used by *persons of quality* . . .' it is very healthful to him that plays it, and it is very profitable to him that keeps it.
>
> Ned Ward, The London Spy, 1698–1703.

Ordinary clothes were worn.

King Henry VIII was a keen tennis player and some of his tennis clothes have been recorded.

> Item Delyuerd by the King's comaundement to Hilton iii yerds of blacke veluete for a Tenes Cote for the King's grace.
>
> Item delyuerd to Hilton iii yerds qrts of blew velwete. Delyuerd by the King's comaundement for a Tenes Cote for the King.
>
> Inventory of Henry VIII's Wardrobe, 1517

The cote at this date, worn over the doublet, was a short jacket or jerkin. Some had sleeves that were full above and long to the wrist, others short sleeves or none at all.

This would not be a garment worn during play, but intended for wear after the game was over. This is shown by the Venetian Ambassador's account, in 1519, of Henry VIII playing tennis.

> The King . . . extremely fond of tennis at which game it was the prettiest thing in the world to see him play, his fair skin glowing through a shirt of the finest texture.

The King's shoes are also recorded in the Royal Accounts of 1517.

> It'm for sooling of syxe paire of shooys with feltys, to pleye in at tenneys, of oure greate wardrobe.

Shirts were correct wear for tennis players in the sixteenth and seventeenth centuries, though ordinary clothing was also worn, as shown in some contemporary illustrations; but shirts were preferred:

> He courts ladies . . . and sometimes venters so farre upon the vertue of his pomander [a receptacle containing scent] that he dares tell 'hem, how many shirts he has sweat at tennis that weeke".
>
> > Ben Jonson, *Cynthia's Revels*, Act. II Sc. 1 (1601).

> I ha' cause to weep: I lend gentlemen holland shirts, and they sweat 'em out at Tennis and no restitution, no restitution.
>
> > T. Dekker, *Northward Hoe*, Act. IV Sc. 3 (1607).

Shirts made of holland, a fine linen first imported from Holland, were the fashion.

Prince Henry to Poins:

> What a disgrace is it to me to remember thy name, or to know thy face tomorrow or to take note how many pair of silk stockings thou hast: *viz.* these and those that were thy peach-coloured ones! Or to bear the inventory of thy shirts; as one for superfluity, and one other for use, but that the tennis-court keeper knows better than I; for it is a low ebb of linen with thee, when thou keepest not racket there, as thou has not done a great while; because the rest of thy low-countries have made a shift to eat up thy holland; and God knows whether those that bawl out the ruins of your linen shall inherit his kingdom.
>
> > Shakespeare, *II Henry IV*, Act II Sc. ii (1600).

With "shirt tops" ordinary leg wear was worn:

> Renouncing clean
> The faith they have in tennis and tall stockings, Short blister'd breeches. . . .
>
> > Shakespeare, *Henry VIII*, Act I Sc. iii (1613).

Blistered meant slashed and was a form of decoration to the breech or upper portion of trunk hose, as then worn. The long stockings were the lower portion.

Tennis shoes at this date were similar to those of the sixteenth century:

> The fellow waits on him, now, in tennis-court socks or slippers sol'd with wool.
>
> > Ben Jonson, *Epicoene or The Silent Woman*, Act I Sc. i (1609).

Charles I was a keen tennis player and a record of his expenses in 1643 states:

> 4 yds of taby, 2 ells & $\frac{1}{4}$ of teffety to be a tennis suit, and 2 pairs of garters and roses, with silk buttons and other necessaries for making up the said suit.

Taby was a coarse kind of thick taffeta, glossy and watered. Roses were decorative rosettes for shoes.

By now the shirt outfit for tennis seems to have declined as is seen in the illustration of James Duke of York as a child in *c.* 1641 (Fig. 48). He wears a doublet, long breeches known as Spanish hose, and stockings with turn-over tops edged with lace, all in the fashion of the day. Charles II too was a keen tennis player and in his wardrobe accounts of 1679, the following items occur:

> Making a paire of tennis drawers XXXd 1 Ell of Taffata for Tennis drawers XIIs VId To John Pate for Shooes, Galoshes, tennis shoes, slippers & Boots LXXXXIIIl 7s.

48. Prince, afterwards James II, when about 8 years old. *c.* 1641.

The drawers were an undergarment; the galoshes were protective wear and at this date were wooden-soled over-boots, buckled on. They certainly would not have been worn at play, but might have been put on over the thin tennis shoes after the game was over, if part of his tennis outfit.

49. Short doublet and full breeches. Round-crowned cap. 1688.

In the woodcut in Comenius's *Visible World*, 1664 (Fig. 47), the players wear doublets, and are taking full advantage of the prevailing fashion for very wide breeches open at the knee, much like women's tennis shorts of the twentieth century.

An example of playing tennis in clothes of ordinary cut is shown in a drawing in R. Holme's *Academy of Armorie and Blazon* (See Fig. 49). It is interesting to note that the player is described as "cloathed all in white". This seems to be a foreshadowing of what, much later, became *de rigeur*.

In the eighteenth century the fervour for tennis declined and it ceased to be a game mainly patronized by the aristocracy. A picture by an unknown artist shews a tennis player, in about 1720, wearing a sleeved waistcoat— waistcoats were always sleeved at this date—open at the neck, and a night cap. This last was a common day wear, worn indoors for comfort over the shaved head when the wig was removed. Wigs at this date were worn by all. The night cap, worn for tennis is referred to even in 1803. Clearly a wig was too hot and a shaved head unsightly (see Plate 16).

> June 24th, 1803 . . . We stopped to see Ld. Villiers play at Tennis ball, it was a most comical sight to behold his Lordship (who is reckoned a handsome man) in a night cap without a neckcloth and destitute of waistcoat and coat, it was a very good match.
>
> *The Wynne Diaries,* ed. by Anne Freemantle, Vol. III.

Towards the end of the eighteenth century a tennis revival was anticipated.

> Field tennis threatens 'ere long to bowl out cricket.
>
> *Sporting Magazine* Vol. II. 29th September, 1793.

In 1775 "Thick tennis shoes and flannel socks" were recommended for Lord Herbert[1] who was a keen tennis player. Tennis played in the open air became popular in the early nineteenth century.

> *Long or open tennis.* This game is played in the open air . . . The players take off their coats and wear a loose flannel jacket that allows the free exercise of their limbs. Some wear also a foreaging cap; but it is better to play with the head bare. The neck should be free. A belt is worn round the middle. Soft pliant slippers that yield to the feet, are absolutely necessary; for it is impossible to play the game properly in boots or strong shoes.
>
> Donald Walker, *Games and Sports,* 1837.

The advice to play "with the head bare" was not strictly followed until the twentieth century.

In 1875 the Rev. Francis Kilvert, writing to his father, says:

> This morning Teddy set up the net and poles in the field opposite the dining room windows and we began to play "sphairistike" or "lawn tennis" a capital game, but rather hot for a summer's day. 28th July.

---

[1] Henry, Elizabeth and George (1734–80), *Letters and Diaries* . . . ed. Lord Herbert, 1939.

In 1873 Major Walter Wingfield, said to be the founder of lawn tennis, took out his patent for "a new and improved court for playing the ancient game of tennis". From then on women at last joined in the game which now swept croquet aside.

But although men were aiming at wearing clothes suitable for such physical exercise, women, as with other sports, let fashion prevail over comfort and sometimes even played in tight skirts with trains (Fig. 50).

50. Tie-back trained dresses and "new lawn-tennis shoes, black with India rubber soles". 1878.

The following year Messrs. Jay brought out an improvement on this costume and advertised a Jersey tennis costume which at least gave freedom of movement below the knees where the skirt was kilted. (See Fig. 51).

In the 1880s aprons with pockets for holding the tennis balls were fashionable (Fig. 52).

> A costume of pale blue flannel with deep kilted skirt and long basque bodice, an embroidered apron with pocket to hold the balls, and a long overcoat which is intended to be removed for playing.
>
> *The Field,* 1885.

A dawning consciousness of the unsuitability of ordinary clothes for women tennis players began to show itself in the 1880s. A writer in *The Field* had this to say:

> The present healthy custom of indulging in active outdoor amusements is sadly interfered with by the ordinary costume. . . .
>
> Lawn tennis has taught women how much they are capable of doing and it is a sign of the times that various games and sports which would have been tabooed a few years ago as "unladylike" are actually encouraged at various girls' schools.
>
> *The Field,* 1885.

51. Jersey tennis costume. 1879.

Lady Harberton, founder of the National Dress Society, later the Rational Dress Society, did her best to persuade women to adopt suitable clothes for sports wear. In 1887:

> Under the auspices of the National Dress Society, Viscountess Harberton delivered a lecture on ladies' dress at the Westminster Town Hall on Wednesday . . . with Mrs Oscar Wilde in the chair. . . . The reform she preached was a radical one . . . if compression (from corsets) oppression,

and dragging were not inseparable from petticoats, there would be no need of a National Dress Society. . . . Besides the loss of health entailed by a bad system of dress, there was a distinct loss of pleasure resulting from the in-activity of the muscles . . . for in the present style of dress, it was im-possible for a woman to walk properly.

The Pictorial World, 1887.

52. Tennis player wearing apron with pockets for the balls. 1880.

So bloomers were advised.

Even *The Queen* in 1880 depicted two women tennis players in "rationals" or what were usually known as "bloomers" after Mrs Amelia Jenks Bloomer who tried to introduce them from America in 1851. Bloomers, however, were considered not only unfeminine but ugly and they were rarely adopted for tennis, Oscar Wilde speaks of:

the ugliness, the want of proportion, in the Bloomer costume which in other respects is sensible.

Pall Mall Gazette, 1884.

Miss Ada Ballin in 1885 in her book *The Science of Dress,* had another sugges-tion to make for women tennis players:

Lawn tennis is perhaps the best game for girls. For this and other games which require the player to run easily, divided skirts are very comfortable[1]. . . Provided the sleeves are made . . . to allow free movements of the arms, no special dress is required for this game; but jerseys are very comfortable to play in and on the whole the prettiest tennis dresses are those made of white flannel with loose sailor bodices, or like . . . the expanding dress. [See illustration for walking (p. 342)]. The expanding dress is the best dress for lawn tennis of which I know. It is charming in white cashmere or flannel.

53. The Bloomer Costume for tennis. 1880.

The dread of appearing "unladylike", however, hampered dress reform at this time and ladies continued to wear ordinary clothes for tennis until the end of the nineteenth century.

A further explanation, no doubt was a desire to attract the attention of onlookers, especially those of the male sex, to the players, wearing pretty clothes, rather than to the game.

A great many descriptions of alluring tennis costumes designed for ladies in the last decades of the nineteenth century have been recorded in contemporary magazines and similar publications, from which the following accounts are selected:

[1] See pp. 340-342.

A cream merino bodice with long sleeves edged with embroidery; skirt with deep kilting, over it an old-gold silk blouse-tunic with short wide sleeves and square neck. The tunic looped up at one side with a ball pocket sewn to it. Large straw hat of the coal-scuttle type. 1879.

With this an apron with ball pocket would be unnecessary.

Tennis costumes of flannel, nun's veiling, sateen or gingham; colour crushed strawberry, yellow and cream stripes, cream and crimson checks. Banded bodice with long basques caught up into panniers. The skirt short and full, often embroidered in cross-stitch or pompoms. Scarf drapery, or long pointed tunic; some with side pocket convenient to carry the racket when partaking of refreshments or when holding a parasol. Worn with black stockings, gauntlet gloves, patent leather pumps with silk bows; and sailor hat with silk handkerchief twisted round the crown. (1883.)

Bustles were the height of fashion in the 1880s and our next quotation shews that they were also worn for tennis.

54. Playing tennis wearing fashionable dresses with bustles, also hats.
One lady on left has an apron with a ball pocket. 1885.

Tennis costumes are of striped flannel the skirt plain in front and in wide pleats behind, measuring 2¾ yards round the hem. Tunic is either long on one side and turned up to the waist on the other in the 'milkmaid style' or short and drawn back, ending in two long sash ends. Or the skirt is in the 'peasant style' round and full with two or three tucks rather wide, and a fall of lace. The bodice is round-waisted with band and fancy buckle. The skirt has an alpaca foundation with one steel and a *horse-hair bustle*. The collar and cuffs are frequently replaced by a loosely knotted handkerchief. (1884.)

Tennis Costume, worn by a champion player; a black merino skirt with kilted flounce and . . . drapery reaching three inches above the ankles; a grey jersey bodice with stiff collar band, the shoulder seam reaching almost to the elbow, and a blue flannel cricketing cap pierced with black-headed pins (1890).

Even the writer exclaims: "What a strangely incongruous figure".

55. Lounge jacket, knickerbockers and cap. 1880.

Skirts were beginning to be shortened in the middle nineties, but was this for convenience or display?

Tennis Costume, two inches off the ground, of serge lined with check silk (glimpses of which would be revealed as she trips hither and thither) cut in one with the corselet which has narrow shoulder straps and laces down the back, thus precluding all possibility of a glimpse of petticoat or staylace—secrets which are frequently seen revealed—check silk shirt; large turndown collar and turnback cuffs. (1894.)

Special tennis dresses were also being designed for children.

I have just seen a pretty lawn tennis frock for a child, made in blue woollen stuff, but printed all over in white with shuttlecocks, balls, and racquets.

Cassell's *Family Magazine,* 1890.

56. Man in jersey and trousers, round cap. 1886.

Men's costume for lawn tennis in the 1880s and 1890s varied slightly, but almost invariably the head was covered.

This aristocratic and fashionable game (lawn tennis) . . . opinion is equally divided between trousers and knickerbockers . . . usually a lounge to button up close; a vest[1] is but seldom worn and often while the game is being played the lounge is thrown aside.

The Gentleman's Magazine of Fashion, 1882.

Flannel cricketing shirt, trousers with sash round the waist. 1886.

Ibid.

[1] Waistcoat.

The double-breasted reefer jacket was still popular in the 1890s but was being replaced by a flannel blazer, white or striped with patch pockets. White flannel trousers were now usual and soft canvas shoes with rubber soles. In the 1880s shoes with steel points were tried, but their day was short lived.

57. Tennis player in long skirt and zouave jacket. 1893.

In 1893, 1st June, *The Tailor and Cutter* made the following statement about tennis:

> This is now such a popular game in garden and other parties as to render it imperative that one of our Plates during the season should be devoted to a suitable dress. . . . The lady's jacket is something between the zouave and the Eton. The scarf is a necessary accompaniment and occupies the space between the top of the skirt and the jacket. The jacket and skirt are trimmed with white cloth or braid. . . . Fine navy serge is the material from which the dress is usually made.

A zouave was a short jacket like a bolero.

Then follows the description of a male tennis costume:

> The fancy flannel jacket bound with blue ribbon, and white trousers, constitute the fashionable attire for gents at lawn tennis parties; the cap is made of the same material as the jacket. The pockets are generally patched . . . the badge on the breast pocket indicating the club to which the wearer belongs.
>
> The jacket is cut in the lounge shape, a little easier than the ordinary wear and not quite so long.

With the exception of clothes worn by girls at a training college for gymnastics, such as that founded in 1885 by Madame Osterberg, women continued to play tennis in unsuitable clothes until about 1920. At Madame's College, as early as 1890, the girls played tennis in gym tunics or skirts at least six inches above the ground and corsets were forbidden; whereas in 1905 a lady champion wore a dress of white lawn with a skirt that swept just clear of the grass on ordinary shots, but brushed the ground on stooping. However

58. Tennis costume. 1890. See text.   59. Tennis suit for 1908. See text.

1903 short skirts, that is skirts well above the ankles, were being adopted by many players. White was advised as appearing neater than any coloured skirt, and from now on became the rule.

As already stated, the change for suitable tennis clothes for women did not occur until about 1920 when Mlle. Suzanne Lenglen appeared on the scenes and set an entirely new fashion which was very widely copied.

By Edwardian days it was conventional for men players to wear white flannel trousers, with turn-ups.

Their complete outfit was advertised by the *Tailor and Cutter*, 1908, as follows (Fig. 59):

> flannel suit . . . made easy fitting at all parts and without lining. There are three patch pockets . . . with a ticket pocket in the front facing . . . three buttons . . . cuffs . . . with holes and buttons.
>
> Trousers are . . . easy fitting and of full length as they will frequently have to stand cleaning, which is sure to shrink them more or less.
>
> The vest is an optional part of this suit.

Bibliography

Lord Aberdare. *The Story of Tennis*. London, 1959.
Marshall, Julian. *The Annals of Tennis*. London, "The Field" Office, 1878.
Smyth, J. G. *Lawn Tennis*. London, Batsford, 1953.

CHAPTER 7

RIDING

BY ALAN MANSFIELD

"It aint the 'unting on the 'ills
    that 'urts the 'osses 'oofs
But the 'ammer, 'ammer, 'ammer on the
    'ard 'igh road."
Trad.

Although in most parts of the world today horses are ridden solely for sport and amusement, until comparatively recently the exercise was performed also as a purely utilitarian one—as a means of travel. It is therefore to be noted that

60. Early 15th century woman rider, riding astride. Gown with hose underneath. Large hat and goffered head veil. Spurs.

the development of riding clothes was not originally connected with the sporting aspects of the art: that a suitable attire for riding was a necessity and was by no means confined to the wardrobe of the "sporting" man or woman. In the Middle Ages such attire appears to be the usual day dress adapted as required to sit a horse, and its variety and lack of specialization can be seen from Chaucer's description of the Canterbury Pilgrims, from the Knight's "fustian-tunic" to the Wife of Bath's hose, which "were of the finest scarlet red", and her "heels spurred sharply" (Nevill Coghill's translation—Penguin Classics 1951). Her hose, like modern tights, were pants and stockings combined, and being made of stout cloth would be an admirable under-garment for riding astride[1]—as she did according to the Ellesmere MS (Fig. 60), and as implied by Chaucer's mentioning a *pair* of spurs.

61. (*a*) Woman rider. Gown with low square neck filled in with "partlet": puffed elbow sleeves. Reticulated caul on back of head. Second half of 16th century.

(*b*) Man rider. Slashed jerkin over doublet. Trunk hose: long boots turned down at top: Copotain hat with plume. Second half of 16th century.

By the sixteenth century astride riding by women had gone out and the female method of riding became side-saddle sitting on a docile palfrey; even those Dianas who went hunting or hacking on horseback saw no need to modify their normal costume (Fig. 61a). But we do begin to see a trend towards specialized garments in the second half of the century. There was an overskirt, known as a "safeguard" worn when riding as a protection against dirt and weather. Cloaks or long capes were used when travelling and a mask or half mask, covering the upper part of the face, could be worn to protect the complexion. Boots or buskins of fine leather would be worn and a hat or bonnet would be added to the cap or caul usually worn indoors. The caps were generally of linen when used under a hat, and the caul was reticulated,

[1] I am assuming that she wore male hose; the female type was merely a pair of stockings. It is suggested that if she wore the latter, she would also wear a triangular pild, in the manner of a baby's napkin.

rather like a hair net, of goldsmiths work, silk or hair.

For men (Fig. 61b), hose of breeches and stockings all in one were in use throughout the sixteenth century, although separate breeches and stockings came in during the 1570s, as well. The hose were attached to the doublet, the upper body garment, by ties on the hose and eyelet holes in the doublet. These ties were known as "points".

> Their points being broken,
> Down fell their hose.   I *Henry IV*, II iv, l. 242.

62. The Earl of Essex in a long cloak and tall-crowned hat. 1587.

Over the doublet might be worn a loose fitting jacket or coat, sometimes with a hood.

> I bequeth to Gylbert Pemberton my Ryding
> cote of whyte russett wythe the hode
> to the same.   Essex Record Office, 1519.

Instead of the jacket a jerkin (Fig. 61b), following the lines of the doublet, might be worn, the jerkin was often sleeveless. Long cloaks, and from 1510–60 the gaberdine, a long loose overcoat with wide sleeves, were popular for wear on horseback (Fig. 62).

Boots were generally unfashionable except for riding and travelling. They might be long reaching to the knee or higher, and turned over at the top, in the earlier part of the century; and to the thigh in the latter part, when they were turned down to below the knee. In both cases a coloured lining, or boot

PLATE 17

Habit of long coat and waistcoat and stiff skirt: "tricorne" hat
and wig. 1715.

*"The Countess of Mar" by Sir Godfrey Kneller, 1715. Earl of Mar and
Kellie. Photograph by A. C. Cooper, Ltd.*

PLATE 18

Original specimen of velvet habit. Short coat, large collar.
Trained skirt. 1777.

York Museum.

hose would be exposed. Boot hose were originally coarse over-stockings worn with boots to protect the under-hose: later they became elegant and ornamental, richly decorated. Fastenings of these long boots were laces, buckles, or buttons. Some long boots of very thin stretchable leather had no fastenings and were worn like stockings, with lace topped boot hose showing above.

63. Doublet and trunk hose. Long "French" cloak, tall-crowned hat, long boots and spurs. 1602.

Short boots, less than knee high, were also worn.

Large spurs were commonly worn with all these boots.

All the types of hats and bonnets fashionable during the century could be worn when riding, often over caps (known as "night caps") as was the case with women. The countryman might merely wear a cap with the addition of ear flaps:

> And a knit night cap of coarsest twine,
> With two long labels [flaps] buttoned to his chin;
> So rides he mounted on the market day.
> Hall's *Satire II* Book IV 1597–8.

At the beginning of the seventeenth century men's clothes differed little from those at the close of the sixteenth (Fig. 63).

Trunk hose, of upper stocks or breeches sewn on to tailored nether stocks or stockings persisted until about 1610: a variation had short nether stocks, called canions, ending about the knee and requiring separate stockings as well.

64. Doublet, Spanish hose, bucket-top boots and boot-hose, spurs with butterfly spur leathers: "French" cloak with "sailor collar", plumed hat. 1645.

In the late sixteenth century breeches of various types were introduced and these all gained in favour during the seventeenth century, and were added to as the century progressed. Venetians were a wide-topped breeches narrowing to button or tie below the knee; oval breeches, gathered at waist and knee; Spanish hose, with a high waistline and ending below the knee, were also known as "long breeches" (Fig. 64); breeches open at the knee, like shorts, were introduced from Holland. Separate stockings, reaching above the knee, were either tailored, or, increasingly, knitted.

Later in the century breeches with immensely wide legs, pleated into a waistband and reaching to the knees, were introduced. These resembled a divided skirt and were known as "pantaloons" at this time (1660–70), or "petticoat breeches". These were extravagantly trimmed with ribbon-loops. Although petticoat breeches were mainly a fashion for Court wear they were, strangely, also worn for riding.

The support of breeches during the seventeenth century was by hooks and eyes to the doublet in place of points, or by a waist band with strap and buckle at the back, or ties at the front.

Doublets from about 1630 developed either an easier, higher waisted cut than hitherto, or became short and skimpy. The jerkin was still fashionable as an over-jacket: a military buff jerkin of oxhide became popular from 1620 until some years after the Restoration.

The cassock, a short loose coat widening towards the hem and with a vent at the back; riding coats with hoods; and the gaberdine, were all common over garments on horseback in the first half of the century. Knee length cloaks were also worn for riding (Fig. 64).

65. Long, unwaisted, coat and waistcoat. 1670–80.

From 1665 onwards the coat and waistcoat began to replace the jerkin and doublet. The coat at first was long and loose from the shoulders, the waist-coat on similar lines (Fig. 65); from 1690 the fit became better with a defined waist and a flared skirt.

For the fashionable man suits were of silk or velvet, and these materials were impracticable for any serious work in the saddle, so cloth suits became accepted as riding clothes:

> I went home and put on my grey cloth suit and faced white coat, made of one
> of my wife's pettycoates, the first time I have had it on, and so in a riding
> garb back again.
>
> Pepys *Diary*, 13th June, 1660–1.

Mrs Pepys' petticoat was either a skirt, not an undergarment, or, perhaps a
white flannel under-petticoat used as facings to the coat.

The unfashionable and the poorer classes normally wore cloth suits and no
distinction for riding or travelling would be necessary.

From the 1650s on a loose coat or jacket, known as a "jump" was popular.
It reached to the thighs, with a centre vent at the back. This was worn as an
overcoat on horseback (Plate 26).

Boots were either thigh length and close fitting, with laces, or easier
fitting with the tops turned down and doubled up again below the knees;
or from 1628, short, with bucket tops, which increased in size after 1648. In
the early years of the century boots were, generally speaking, only worn for
riding:

> As hap was his boots were on and them I dusted, [i.e. made dusty] to make
> people think he had been riding.
>
> Dekker, *The Honest Whore*, 1604.

Spurs with large rowels, were attached by means of broad spur leathers,
sometimes butterfly shaped in the front (Fig. 64). Boot hose, or over-stockings,
protected the stockings and were made with decorative tops to turn down over
the boot.

> For 2 yards of lace for ye boothose tops £1. 3. 0.
>
> James Master's *Expense Book*, 1650–5.

Later in the century heavy jackboots became common, perhaps as a result
of the military influence during the Civil War and Commonwealth. These
were of stiff hard leather, some with square bucket tops above the knee. A
clumsy type of riding boot with a cut out portion at the back of the top for
ease in bending the knee also appeared; both these, and some of the jackboots, had spur rests, or leather blocks above the heels to support the spurs.
Boots, which for about fifty years from 1610 had been popular for walking,
became less fashionable and were chiefly worn when riding, a reversion to the
mode at the beginning of the century.

And so by boate home, and put on my boots, and so over to Southwarke
to the post-house, and there took horse.

Pepys *Diary*, 16th January, 1660–1.

It is noteworthy that Pepys, a conscientious chronicler of his clothes, only
mentions a change of footwear before riding, after a day spent around
Whitehall and Westminster.

In the early days of the seventeenth century a popular woman's garment
was the jacket or waistcoat, also called a doublet, which article of men's
attire it closely copied. It had an easy close fitting bodice, flaring from the
waist. This garment, from about 1625, was specifically worn for riding. Later
coats, also copied from the man's garment, became popular for riding wear.

> I find the Ladies of Honour dressed in their riding garbs, with coats and
> doublets with deep skirts, just, for all the world, like mine . . . so that, only
> for a long petticoat dragging under their men's coats, nobody could take
> them for women. . . .

Pepys *Diary*, 12th June, 1666.

(Sam goes on to remark that this was an odd sight, and one that didn't
please him: not unnaturally for one of Sam's tastes.)

More feminine attire was also worn, but perhaps for State occasions and
short journeys only. Elizabeth of Bohemia is said to have had two riding
gowns of metal brocaded satin, with tissue sleeves.

The Safeguard, in the form of an over-skirt, or of a large apron, protected
the skirt of suit or dress, and kept out the cold. Joyce Jeffries in 1638 had a
scarlet safeguard, and a coat and hood laced with red, blue and yellow.

A favourite hat for riding at this time was the "cavalier", which had a
moderate-sized crown and a broad brim, worn flat or cocked up at the side.
The trimming was a hatband, and perhaps a plume (Fig. 66).

> The Queene was now in her cavalier riding habite, hat and feather, and
> horseman's coat, going out to take the air.

Evelyn: *Diary*, 13th September, 1666.

Towards the end of the seventeenth century Celia Fiennes riding by the
seaside at Penzance was caught in a "great storme of haile and raine", but
"the wind soone dry'd my dust coate." . . . (My Great Journey to Newcastle and to Cornwall, 1698, Christopher Morris, *The Journeys of Celia
Fiennes*, 1949.) In the opening years of the eighteenth century a "dust gown"

was "an upper garment worn by women, commonly called a Safeguard" (Phillips, 1706). Celia who wrote in a lively style about commerce and manufacture was disappointingly silent about her clothes, and gives us no clue to the design of her dust coat. As she is writing of mid-September in the West Country it is to be assumed she was not wearing winter clothes, and her "dust coate" may have been a light over-garment to keep the dust of the roads and tracks from her clothes, as in the case of the early motorists, rather than the heavier "safeguard". This possibility is supported by her report of it quickly drying in the wind.

66. Basqued bodice with balloon sleeves. "Cavalier" hat with hatband
and plume. 1625–40.

The eighteenth century has left us a considerable body of contemporary evidence as to costume in all its varieties, and in this respect we are on much firmer ground than when dealing with earlier ages. Actual garments are by no means rare, and the pictures, letters, bills and diaries of the time give much valuable information. Again, the growth of the newspaper, periodical, and novel during this century adds immeasurably to our knowledge of how the men and women of the day dressed and behaved.

At the beginning of the century women's riding coats resembled those of men, as had been noted by Pepys forty years previously, and were worn with a waistcoat. Both coat and waistcoat were long, almost knee length, with back and side vents, the latter pleated and buttoned. There was either no collar, or a small round turned down one. When a collar was worn, it, and the turned back sleeve cuffs, might be faced with another colour from that of the garment. The petticoat or over skirt was full and long (Plate 17).

> Coat and waistcoat of blue camlet, trimmed and embroidered with silver: a cravat of the finest lace, . . . a little beaver hat edged with silver and made more sprightly by a feather . . . a petticoat of the same with the coat and waistcoat.
>
> Steele, *The Spectator*, 29th June, 1711.

> Ladies who dress themselves in a hat and feather, a riding coat and a periwig, or at least tie up their hair in a bag or riband, in imitation of the smart part of the opposite sex.
>
> Addison, *The Spectator*, 19th July, 1712.

Both Steele and Addison, like Pepys, disliked this "immodest custom" of "the mixture of two sexes in one person", but their public, as Pepys's private, criticism, had no effect—feminine equestrian habits continued to ape the masculine, finally breaching the walls of man's last sartorial stronghold and assuming the fundamental garment of the sterner sex.

By mid-century the riding coat had become shorter and less decorated (Fig. 67), and the skirt of the coat might be extra flared by being joined to the body by a seam at the front: some coat skirts were circular in cut. The London Museum has a specimen of a habit *c.* 1740–50 of fine woollen material, drab coloured and lined with yellow silk with a very flared skirt cut in more than a full circle. There is a small round turned down collar and this and the cuffs are faced with yellow silk matching the lining. There is an attached false waistcoat front sewn to the lining on each side. Two slanting vertical slit pockets each have three buttons: the coat has nine buttons and the waistcoat front ten, in both cases on the right side, as on a man's coat. The petticoat, or skirt, is plain, long, but full, and of the same material as the coat. It has a flared section at the front and then three widths of material. The whole is simply gathered at the waist on to a draw-tape, and lined with a coarse stiff gauze resembling book-muslin.

During the centuries the position taken up by women in the side-saddle had altered from one where they faced sideways to one where the shoulders were approximately at right-angles to the horse's spine. This, and the addition of a second crutch on the saddle to support the right leg higher (an invention attributed to Catherine de Medici in the sixteenth century) probably had some effect on the design and material of the skirt of the habit. Whether the more practical seat was a result of easier, less elaborately stiff clothes, or whether the adoption of softer materials followed the altered position in the saddle it is difficult to decide. A French book of equitation published in 1770 emphasized the forward facing position and in a sketch illustrating this shows a skirt short enough to show both feet. Such a skirt was worn in England *c.* 1750 (Fig. 67). Certainly the riding clothes of the mid- and late eighteenth-century woman are simpler and softer in line than those of preceding ages. Broadcloth (a fine wool cloth), superfine cloth (of Merino wool), camlet (a silk and wool or hair mixture), and grogram (a thick silk taffeta) are examples of the materials used.

67. Riding habit: short coat flared from waist, waistcoat, full skirt. Navy blue trimmed with gold (uniform of Charlton Hunt). Black wide-brimmed hat trimmed with white feathers. *c.* 1759–60.

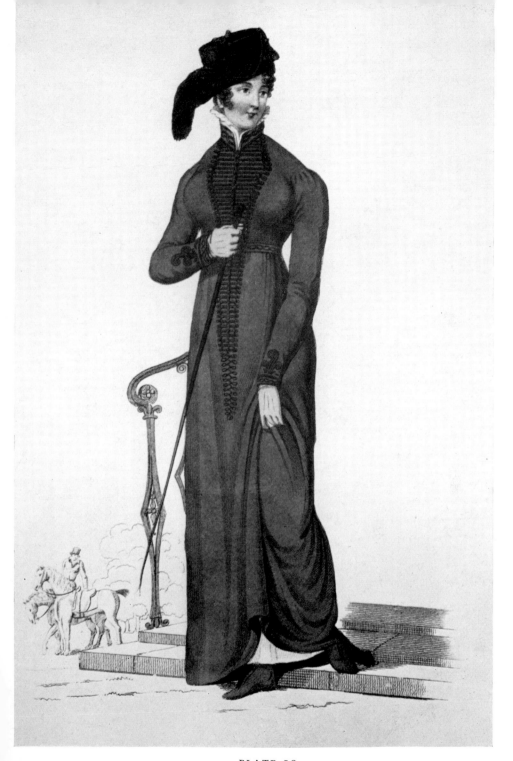

PLATE 19

Bright green one-piece habit (riding dress) laced with black.
Black beaver hat and plume, black half-boots laced with
green. York tan gloves. White under petticoat. 1812.

Fashion plate. La Belle Assemblee. 1812.

PLATE 20

Original specimen of habit. Blue cloth: short bodice trimmed
with braid. Voluminous skirt. (See text.) 1855.

London Museum.

Colours were varied:

A blue riding habit trimmed with silver.

Smollett, Roderick Random, 1748.

One silk grogram Riding Habit, trimmed with gold lace . . . one camblet ditto with gold loops, one green, one blue, one cloth velour.

Hereford Archives, 1740.

The skirt or petticoat became longer again in the last decades of the century, and the coat or jacket developed large lapels and a deep collar (Plate 18); sometimes it was double-breasted. The jacket skirts were increasingly curved from the front backwards, or disappeared in the front, leaving a short rounded coat-tail behind. In the 1790s the waist became higher, as it followed the fashion, and the coat-skirt became a frill like tail.

Women's coats and waistcoats buttoned left over right, male fashion, in the eighteenth century.

Some ladies in the 1780s and 1790s modelled their habits on military uniforms: perhaps in revenge for the adoption by the Royal Navy of dark blue and white for its officers' coats, said to have been inspired by the riding habit of the Duchess of Bedford some forty years earlier.

. . . the ladies begin to wear Morocco half boots and Hussar riding habits.

Ipswich Journal, 1786.

A quite new development occurred in about 1785 when the Great Coat or Riding Coat dress was introduced. It had a close fitting bodice with lapels and a deep double or triple cape-collar, after the style of a coachman's coat; and a long straight, full skirt, buttoned through: the bottom buttons often left undone to show the under petticoat. This fashion apparently crossed the Channel and returned from France as the "Redingote" at the end of the century. The redingote was a light overcoat fastening across the bosom.

A greatcoat proper, of similar design to the above, but in some cases only knee length, was worn when riding from *c.* 1780 onwards. Cloaks, hooded capes, and in the early years of the century, the safeguard, were also worn. A caped overcoat, or cloak buttoning down the front was known as a "Joseph". This was frequently worn on horseback and was often green in colour.

Dressed in a green joseph, richly laced in gold, and a whip in her hand. . . .

Oliver Goldsmith, The Vicar of Wakefield, 1764.

Hats of all kinds were fashionable for riding—the three-cornered cocked-hat (named the "tricorne" in the nineteenth century) was generally worn with a wig. Black velvet jockey caps were popular until the hair styles after the 1760s ruled them out. Cocked hats with a tall crown; beehive shaped hats; large brimmed hats; and small beavers with a deep round crown and narrow brim, were all to be seen on the equestriennes' heads during the century. In most cases they would be trimmed with feathers, often with ribbons as well (Fig. 68).

68. Riding habit: short cut-away coat, double-breasted: lapelled waistcoat: ruffled chemise front. Tall crowned hat with plumes and ribbon. *c.* 1780.

Plain, short gloves, with or without a small gauntlet were worn. They were sometimes known as "habit gloves".

> To a pr. of Habit gloves for Nancy pd. 0—1—6.
> *Parson Woodforde's Diary*, 1782.

Boots worn on horseback tended to be shorter than in previous times, and in the latter part of the century were sometimes laced up the front.

Men's dress for riding in the eighteenth century was confirmed as breeches, waistcoat and coat, a style which with variations of design and cut has persisted from the latter half of the seventeenth century until modern times. The coat at the beginning of the century had a flared skirt reaching slightly below the knees, with side and back vents. From about 1740 onwards the skirts at the front began to curve back and thus open up in the front. For riding, a continental fashion from the late seventeenth century was to turn and fasten back the skirt at the front, and this fashion is said (Kohler, p. 339) to have influenced the design of the English frock worn for riding.

The frock was similar to the coat, but was less rigid in cut and was distinguished by a flat turn-down collar known as a "cape". (Fig. 69.) The curve

69. Man in "riding frock" with small flat collar: (this garment did not become fashionable until about 1730). Heavy jackboots: round hat. Woman in gown and head kerchief, carrying face-mask for protection from the weather. *c.* 1704.

back of the front line followed that of the coat and became pronounced in the 1770s—by the 1790s the skirts were becoming nothing more than coat-tails, both in the coat and the frock. Although examples are found of the narrow skirts of the frock being caught back, the frock itself seems in England to have developed from the workman's garment of that name, a protective over-garment, of the early eighteenth century, and not to owe its origin to the Continent.

From mid-century the coat became shorter, ending above the knees and the flare and waist were little in evidence. For riding the frock was almost universal; it was generally shorter than the coat, and was always of plain, never embroidered, material. It was usually fastened with metal buttons, although at the end of the century mother-of-pearl became popular. The metal buttons were sometimes decorated.

Of a country squire:

> . . . even the button's of his clothes are impressed with figures of dogs, foxes, stags and horses.
>
> *The Connoisseur*, July, 1755.

> Mother-of-pearl buttons are likely to take the lead in the fashionable world: those of steel soon rust.
>
> *The Times*, 1794.

Another fashion in the last quarter of the century was for buttons of enamel, with hunting devices.

Buttons and buttonholes of the frock often reached below the waist, but never down to the hem.

Towards the end of the century double-breasted frocks were sometimes worn, especially for riding.

Waistcoats were at first long, but became shorter as the century advanced. At the end of the century double-breasted waistcoats were common, first appearing about 1760 (Fig. 70).

Cloaks were worn at the beginning of the century, particularly a knee-length buttoned variety with a cape collar known as a Roquelaine or roccelo, and numerous other variants of spelling. These were generally red in colour.

> Roquelo or hanging cloak of scarlet cloth.
>
> *The Postman*, 28th December, 1714.

> Scarlet Roccelo or Cloak trimmed with gold lace and large old fashioned buttons.
>
> *Daily Advertiser*, 23rd June, 1744.

By the 1730s, however, the cloak was largely replaced by the surtout or greatcoat or cape coat. Like the cloak it had a back vent for wear on horseback and a cape collar. A double breasted pattern was popular for riding.

> Gentleman with the cape-coat, whip and boots.
>
> *Gentleman's Magazine*, 1739.

A double breasted light-coloured great coat, with a blue-grey frock and scarlet waist-coat.

Ipswich Journal, 1749.

A fine Bath-coating surtout with Newmarket Cape (fit for any gentleman to wear). Holes and Edges bound. £1. 7. 0.

Advertisement, *Ipswich Journal*, 1766.

70. Man in a frock, probably double-breasted: double-breasted waistcoat, breeches buttoning at knee. French top boots, "Tricorne" hat. *c.* 1770.

From 1790 a popular top-coat was the Spencer, a tail-less waist length double-breasted jacket which was worn over the frock or coat.

The economical garment called a Spencer.

Sporting Magazine, 1796.

Knee-breeches were at first ill-fitting with a short body part, the breeches hanging round the hips without other support. The legs ended just below the knee with a knee-band and short slit on the outside closed by three or four buttons. Later the waistline became higher, the breeches were cut and fitted better and closer. The legs became shorter in the 1750s, but lengthened again in the 1760s onwards. With the higher waistline the hips no longer served as a support and braces or gallows began to be worn.

The kneeband was secured by a buckle, small in the first part of the century, becoming larger as the years passed, and finally towards the close of the century giving place to ties or strings.

Up to about 1750 the legs were covered by stockings pulled up over the knees of the breeches; later the breeches were buckled below the knees, over the stockings.

Leather breeches were often worn; buckskin particularly for riding:

> To be sold. Buck and doe skins and Buckskin breeches and others ready made . . . and every other article in the glove and breeches-making way.
>
> Advertisement, *Ipswich Journal*, 1761.

In the 1790s pantaloons, not to be confused with the garments of the same name a century previously, were beginning to be worn. The pantaloons in this reincarnation were close fitting tights shaped to the legs, and ankle length. They were buttoned on the outside of the leg up to the calf.

Riding boots in the earlier years of the eighteenth century were much of a pattern with the late seventeenth century—heavy bucket topped jack boots (Fig. 69), or light jackboots with a cut away U-shaped dip at the back and buttoning down the side. The jockey-boot or half jackboot ended below the knee and had a turn over top of softer and lighter coloured leather (Fig. 70). These became increasingly popular and the heavy jackboot fell into general disuse; the light jackboot continued to be worn by the unfashionable. With jackboots the protective boot stockings were still worn.

The jockey-boot developed two styles, the French and the English. In the English style the turned over top sloped down to a point in front; the French top was cut straight round. During the 1780s the term "top-boots' replaced the name of "jockey-boots".

In some instances leather straps, known as boot garters, were attached at the back of the boots and fastened round the leg above the knee to keep the boots in position when riding.

Hussar boots or buskins, and Hessians, two types of short boots decorated with tassels, came in during the closing decades of the century. Hessians were worn with pantaloons.

As an alternative to boots spatterdashes of cloth or leather, or gaiters of leather could be worn with shoes.

Spurs, some with large star-shaped rowels, were usually worn.

The universal hat of the eighteenth century man was the three-cornered cocked-hat, worn on a wig. The width of brim and style of cock gave rise to many varieties, each with a distinctive name.

In the 1770s the round hat of various shapes began to appear and became popular for riding and other sporting pursuits (Fig. 95), and in the 1780s the cocked-hat with its brim turned up high at the front and back only (the so-called "bicorne"—a modern name) was frequently worn on horseback.

Throughout the century the jockey-cap of velvet or cloth was worn occasionally for riding.

Riding whips or switches were carried.

To sum up the eighteenth century horseman, here are two mid-century contemporary descriptions.

> I was dressed in my blue riding frock with plate buttons, with a leather belt round my waste, my jemmy turn-down boots, my brown scratch wig and my hat with the narrow silver lace cocked in the true sporting fashion.
>
> *The Connoisseur*, November, 1754.

"Jemmy boots" were specially smart top boots.

> A well dressed man . . . had on a dark blue-grey suit of cloathes black breeches a tye-wig, a gold laced hat, a pair of boot stockings, with steel spurs and a cane swish in his hand but without a greatcoat.
>
> *Ipswich Journal*, 1766.

It is sad to say that the well-dressed man had hired a horse and then disappeared with it into thin air: hence his description appearing in the local paper. However, we must be thankful that even from this piece of villainy some good has issued, that we in this generation are richer by the bereaved livery-stable keeper's vivid pen picture of a well-dressed horse thief.

In clothes and in sport, as in all else, the nineteenth century saw vaster and more rapid changes than had any preceding era. It started with the ladies wearing the high-waisted and straight-skirted styles popular at the end of the eighteenth century. All in one dresses were popular in the first decades (Plate 19).

> Of bright green ornamented down the front and embroidered at the cuffs à la militaire, with black; small riding hat of black beaver with gold cordon and tassells; long green ostrich feather in front. Black half boots fringed with green. York tan gloves.
>
> *Ipswich Journal*, June, 1812.

A habit of the late 1820s in the Worthing Museum is of dark blue woollen cloth, with a full skirt and a waist-length jacket bodice with vestigial tails, and with a large collar—the sleeves are plain and tight fitting.

The late eighteenth and early nineteenth century fashion for light-weight, clinging, female garments, had drastically reduced the number of under petticoats worn, and in their absence the wearing of drawers, or trousers, became the fashion;

> drawers of light pink now the ton among our darling belles.
>
> *The Chester Chronicle,* 1804.

By the 1820s these somewhat masculine garments were being worn by the more advanced equestrienne; of silk, or cotton cloth.

As the century progressed the skirt of the riding habit became fuller and longer, and the problem of retaining one's seat and one's modesty was a very

71. Petticoats but no pants. 1795–1800.

real one in anything like a stiff breeze. The trousers certainly helped, but did not offer the complete solution. As early as 1806, a French writer had said:

> The wind is sometimes indiscreet and agitates the skirts of a lady on horse-back. Rest assured, Madam, two ways of overcoming this have been up to the present time tried out. The first, conceived by the English, is to gather all the skirts together under a leather strap which, passing beneath the rider's

thighs, is naturally most uncomfortable; the other, much simpler, but which is also less secure, is to fasten the skirts one to the other with pins.

L. H. de Pons d'Hostun. *L'Ecuyer des Dames*, 1806.

The latter method also was practiced in England:

. . . when the lady is seated, the groom fastens the habit below her left foot, either by pins or a brooch. Vizetelly, *The Young Ladies Book*, 1832.

That seat and modesty were both lost on occasion is without question, as Rowlandson's drawing shows (Fig. 71). Some people maintain that the stretch of Epping Forest now known as "Fairmead Bottom" originally bore the name of "Fair Maid's Bottom" on account of the unhappy up-ending of a lady whose horse threw her in that spot. (This, however, may be only an argument *a posteriori*). It was a pity that neither of these ladies sported "white trousers, the legs made of florentine, confined above the knee and shaped under the foot" to cover their confusion.

72. Riding habit of waterproof cloth, bodice decorated with buttons: gigot sleeves. Collar, cuffs and petticoat of cambric trimmed with lace. Black beaver hat trimmed with ostrich feathers and green veil. Black half boots. 1835.

Riding habit bodices of the 1830s were fashionably cut waist length with a point at the front (Fig. 72), tight fitting, often ornamented by two or three rows of buttons, with or without braid trimming across the front. Fastening was generally by means of hooks and eyes, covered by the centre row of buttons when these were present. Skirts were long and full. An example in the London Museum has a slight flare given to each side.

In some instances bodice and skirt were of contrasting colours, worn with a wide belt around the waist, giving a blouse and skirt effect. A short, wide, shoulder cape was also a feature of the 1830s. Such an outfit is to be seen at the Gallery of English Costume.

Half-boots were commonly worn, and the tall beaver hat with a flowing veil was popular.

The 1840s saw a revival of the long-skirted coat with collar and lapels like a man's: with this was worn a habit-shirt (a short shirt like garment to fill in the front of the coat). The short jacket bodice was either open in front like the coat and worn with a habit-shirt, or closed to the neck with a small turn-over linen collar; a large bow was generally worn at the neck (Figs. 73a, b).

The skirt was full and now had a slight train. Trousers or pantaloons were worn strapped under the foot. The beaver top hat remained in favour: other styles were the cavalier-like broad-brimmed hat with a feather, a small round beaver also with a feather and varieties of straw hats. Half-boots were of kid, or even of silk with kid toes. Fur boas, popular at this time, may have been worn on horseback:

> the queen's, or riding boa . . . it is made flat about a yard and a half long and of fur on both sides: it is worn with gauntlet cuffs.
>
> *The Family Herald*, 18th November, 1849.

Riding as a recreation had been becoming steadily more popular among women, and the 1850s saw several new developments in their attire. The jacket bodice or corsage, form-fitting and close buttoned, persisted, but the longer coat style noted in the 1840s became increasingly popular. In place of the cotton pantaloons riding trousers of stout cloth or chamois leather were introduced. These latter had black cloth feet: later they were made from the knee downwards of the same material as the skirt.

The London Museum has a dark blue face cloth habit and trousers of about 1855. The trousers are chamois to the knee, the lower leg of cloth; they fasten by a button-fly in front and have three buttonholes at the waist—presumably to button on to the stays. The skirt is slightly trained, on a waist band with a draw-string and hook-and-eye fastening: there is a pocket inset at the placket and a button and hook to attach the jacket at the waist. This skirt shows a new feature—as light pouch-like shaping at the right side to accommodate the knee when mounted. The skirt has a circumference of three yards at the hem.

The bodice is a close fitting waist length jacket with rudimentary tails, fastening with hooks and eyes and with fifteen false buttons and braiding to decorate the front edge: braiding is also applied to the waist and sleeves. The sleeves end in four-button false cuffs. The bodice is shaped by darts and circular stitching of the lining at the bust and there are three bones in front. The collar is a small standing band. This habit bears the label of W. C. Taylor 53 Baker Street (Plate 20).

73. Riding habits (*a*) bodice like a man's coat with deep 'Polka' skirt: habit-shirt, black cravat: "Cavalier"-style hat: gauntlet gloves (*b*) tight, short bodice with vestigal tails: Beaver top-hat with veil. Both habits have long, full skirts, slightly trained. 1843.

During the mid-century years various modifications were made to the side-saddle, including the addition of a third pommel, which had their effect on the "sit" of the skirt when the wearer was mounted and the primitive shaped pouch or cup in the skirt referred to above is a forerunner of the complicated cutting and tailoring which developed and led to the specialization of many tailors as habit makers (Fig. 75).

The 1860s saw "Skittles" riding in the shires and Lucy Glitters riding in Surtees clad in pork-pie hats worn over jewelled hair nets, ribbon bows at the neck of the habit and skirts as full and seemingly shapeless as ever:

> a woman . . . wore a habit that fitted like a glove, and a bit of cherry ribbon round her neck. *c.* 1860.
>
> Sir Willoughby Maycock, *Annals of the Billesden Hunt.*

(This was the celebrated "Skittles", who was overheard to remark to her companion that after such a ride a certain portion of her anatomy would be as red as her ribbon, despite, no doubt, the

> pair of riding trousers . . . made entirely of cloth, or strapped with doeskin dyed,

for which

> the prominence of the hips will be sufficient to keep the trousers up, as the waist is cut rather tight.
>
> *Minster's Gazette of Fashion*, September 1861.)

> Smiling cantering bevies of beauties, with their shining hair in gold and silver beaded nets, and party-coloured feathers in their jaunty little hats.
>
> Surtees, *Plain or Ringlets*, 1860.

There was a vogue for the fashionable bell sleeves at this time, and some habits had no collars: the skirt of the jacket in some models disappeared completely. The favourite fastening was still hooks and eyes concealed by braiding or rows of ornamental buttons. Some sleeves were puffed at the shoulder. Quilting or horsehair interlining was used to advantage:

> A thin horsehair is put through the body and back and has a very good effect by giving a roundness to the figure.
>
> *Minster's Gazette of Fashion*, April 1861.

An effect much sought after by the mid-Victorian miss.

Despite the advice of a writer in 1870:

> a lady's riding habit should be simple . . . showing eccentric innovations are in bad taste . . .'
>
> *The Young Lady's Book*, Ed. Mrs C. Mackarness, 1870.

the prevailing tendency in the 1870s for elaborate ornamentation in women's clothes did not pass the riding habit by (Fig. 74); nevertheless the serious horse-woman kept to a plain costume of some dark colour:

> . . . the Miller's daughter . . . dressed in a dark riding habit . . . and a black jaunty pretty hat with a black feather . . .'
>
> *Kilvert's Diary*, 1870.

74. Riding habit with military-style braiding on bodice: very long trained skirt: trousers just showing. Top hat and veil.

Ever since the acceptance of trousers the number of petticoats worn when riding had been decreasing and the effect began to be seen as a more slender line of the skirt and less fullness at the hips. In the year 1875 the first "safety" skirt was worn by a Mrs Arthur of Market Harborough, and this was the forerunner of many patent garments of a similar type. These skirts had a slit behind, fastened with hooks or press studs when dismounted, and opened when on horseback; the principle was that in the event of losing one's seat the danger of being caught up by the skirt was obviated.

During the 1860s and 1870s the skirt, or train as it was also known, had gradually become shorter; in 1879:

> They are still short and narrow, and cut in so complicated a manner that any attempt at home and amateur-making must be failures; the two sides of the skirt being quite different, in order to give ample room to the right knee over the pommel.
>
> *Cassell's Family Magazine*, 1879.

A reversion to the riding dress of the beginning of the century also appeared, a princess pattern of bodice and skirt all in one.

The bowler-hat was now appearing on women riders, either with or without a veil, and the tall hat, now of silk, tended to be less tall than hitherto.

Some jacket bodices were so tight that the rider had to mount unbuttoned, and fasten herself up in the saddle.

Fashionable colours at the end of the decade were dark brown, green, blue, and claret. Sometimes a buttonhole of fresh flowers was worn, sometimes a coloured-bordered handkerchief was tucked into the front of the bodice with one corner showing.

75. Riding habit with jacket bodice and wrap-over skirt with knee-recess. "when putting on the skirt . . . raising the right knee . . . the part which is cut to fit it will fall into its place." 1893.

In 1884 the *Tailor and Cutter* commented that the latest habits had short basqued bodices, the train short and with as little width as possible; and by this date

> The only difference between a woman's and a man's trousers is that ladies' waists being small, cuts have to be taken out of the waist.
>
> *The Ladies' Tailor*, August, 1885.

Presumably the same pattern would be used.

Miss Ada Ballin recommended that

> the habit should invariably be lined with flannel . . . the trousers as well as
> the jacket may be thus lined throughout, and when this is done, all the under-
> clothing that is required is woollen combinations, with perhaps the belt as
> described, or the belt and stays in the case of those inclined to *embonpoint*.
>
> Ada S. Ballin, *The Science of Dress*, 1885.

76. Riding habit with double-breasted jacket   77. Woman's riding breeches worn with
bodice. Flat-topped round felt hat. 1897.   very long coat. 1909.

The belt mentioned is desirable to support the abdomen during "horse-
exercise" and may be made of flannel and fastened like a baby's binder, or
crocheted out of coarse wool, or of silk elastic with three whalebones.

Miss Ballin condemns the "chimney pot" hat and is all in favour of the
bowler—preferably with a ribbon rosette in front, or a flat crowned felt, with
the sides tapering towards the top, also trimmed with ribbon (Plate 21).

The jacket bodice was regaining a masculine appearance, sometimes
double-breasted, and by the 1890s had quite deep skirts, some with pockets at
hip level. A vest or waistcoat was worn beneath the bodice (Figs. 75, 76).

Trains are still made very close fitting, and as regards length, cut just long
enough to cover the boot, or only just show the front part.

The Ladies' Tailor, 1892.

Underneath the skirt or train trousers had been giving way to breeches;

Trousers are quite the exception now, the general rule for nether garments,
being breeches cut fairly long, and top boots.

Ibid.

So by the 1890s women, who started the century wearing "trousers"
coped from the stern sex, but showing feminine influence by frills or lace at
the foot, had progressed through the stage of riding trousers no different
from a man's except in size, to the ultimate of adopting his breeches.

78. Riding habit of jacket, waistcoat, apron
skirt and breeches. Bowler hat and riding
boots. Man with loose jacket with half belt.
Early 20th century.

The increasing emancipation of women during the last three decades of the
century had created the right climate of opinion for the reintroduction of the
astride saddle which a few daring spirits adopted clad in divided skirts of
suitably ample proportions. An alternative to the divided skirt for the astride
seat was a calf-length coat worn with the breeches and successfully concealing
most of the rider's legs when in the saddle (Fig. 77).

But these fashions were still-born and, until after the Great War, when
women's legs like many other things came out of hiding and the astride seat
with breeches and jacket of a masculine cut was fully accepted, the generality

of horsewomen adopted the apron skirt, introduced at about the turn of the century, and retained the side seat. The apron skirt was just that: it hung, when mounted, straight and square from the knee, open behind; when the wearer was dismounted it fell back to make an incomplete skirt (Fig. 78).

The favourite head-gear for women riders was the bowler, the silk "topper", and less fashionable, a variety of felt hats. Riding boots, similar to a man's, no longer with "tops" were worn.

The riding cane or whip, which started the century in ladies' hands in the form of a light and elegant switch became through the years more workmanlike until the equestrienne of the nineties was wielding a hunting whip or crop as formidable as her male companion.

79. Tropical riding habit of drill jacket worn with normal cloth skirt. Pith helmet.

Macintoshes, waterproof and other coats similar to the male variety were worn by women riders throughout the period. Light drill jackets, worn with the normal skirt, were recommended for the tropics (Fig. 79).

There was little to distinguish the early nineteenth-century man on a horse from his brother on foot. Both wore a tail-coat, cut or sloping away in front, generally single-breasted (Fig. 80). For riding, gilt buttons were favoured. Waistcoats were usually single-breasted, cut straight across with a short waist;

buff or pearl grey or striped horizontally. Vertical striped waistcoats known as "jockey waistcoats" appeared in 1806. Shag (a mohair or silk mixture), Kerseymere, and toilenette were favourite materials. Riding breeches were high waisted, long and tight fitting, closed up the front by whole or small falls. Bedford cord was often the material used (hence "cords"), and from about 1809 leather came into fashion.

80. Man in tail coat and wide loose trousers known as "Cossacks". Wellington hat (widening towards the crown) and Wellington boots with spurs.

Pantaloons and trousers could also be worn when riding, (Fig. 80). Top-boots, with or without spurs distinguished the horseman with breeches; for pantaloons Hessian boots, or if the pantaloons extended over the feet, per-haps half-boots, reaching just above the ankles; with trousers, from 1817 on, the Wellington boot. With trousers and pantaloons shoes were sometimes worn instead of boots. Shirt collars were high at the beginning of the century, and were worn with a neckcloth—either a cravat, which was wrapped around the neck and the ends tied in front, or the stock, a made up neckband usually fastened behind by a buckle.

Outer garments were generally either the waist-length spencer or a long single-breasted great-coat.

By the 1820s the frock coat, where the skirts were not cut away, but were full knee length and flared from the waist became the normal type of coat for riding (Fig. 81); in 1825 a short version of this type appeared (Fig. 82).

81. Man in frock coat and tight trousers strapped under Wellington boots with spurs screwed into the heels. Top hat. 1817.

Top-hats of beaver or silk were the accepted head-wear.

The "dress" riding suit was one where a tail-coat was worn with pantaloons or trousers and shoes.

The short frock of 1825 had become known as the "Newmarket" or Riding Coat by 1838, and the full front skirts were sloped away. It could be single or double-breasted and might have flapped pockets.

Green was a popular colour for riding coats:

> The riding dress of a gentleman is green with gilt buttons, a velvet collar. . . .'
> *The World of Fashion*, July, 1824.

Some dashers wear white moleskin [a course twilled fustian] pantaloons, a green coat buttoned up, a black velvet collar and an high pointed crown hat. . . . '

Gentleman's Magazine of Fashion, April, 1830.

Seymour's illustration of Mr Winkle about to mount for the ride to Dingley Dell, drawn in 1836, shows the sporting Pickwickian clad in frock-coat with flapped pockets at the waist, breeches, and long gaiters, reaching above the knee, buttoned on the outside. His shirt has a high-pointed collar: he wears a check neckcloth and a tall white beaver hat.

82. Riding frock coat, faced with velvet: pantaloons: hessian boots: tall top hat. 1829.

Breeches became unfashionable in the 1840s; trousers and pantaloons, sometimes known as tights, were the common wear. (Breeches were often referred to as "shorts" or "small clothes" in the nineteenth century). The Newmarket coat, or a frock-coat, now beginning to be known as a "surtout", and waistcoat, were the usual upper garments, although the Dress Riding Suit was still worn on occasion (Plate 22). In the winter a short, waisted, over-

PLATE 21

Original specimen of habit. Brown twilled woollen cloth. Short bodice lightly boned.
Wrap-over skirt. Brown "bowler" hat trimmed with brown silk ribbon. 1880–90.

The Gallery of English Costume, Manchester.

PLATE 22

Dress Riding Clothes. Tail-coat, double-breasted waistcoat,
trousers strapped under boots, neck scarf, top-hat. 1843.

Drawing by Count D'Orsay. 1843.

coat known as a "paletot" might be worn; or some form of waterproof (Fig. 83).

Mr Macintosh had patented his "Indiarubber cloth" in 1823, and from the 1830s references to garments made of it occur—mostly not very complimentary:

> Such of my readers as recollect the first introduction of Macintoshes, will doubtless remember that the earlier specimens of the race differed very materially in form from those which are in use at the present day. The one we were now inspecting was of a whity-brown colour, and, though it had sleeves like a coat, hung in straight folds from the waist to the ankles, somewhat after the fashion of a carter's frock, having huge pockets at the side, and fastening round the neck with a hook and eye.
>
> Frank Smedley, *Frank Fairlegh*, 1850.

83. Riding macintosh, light blue with blue velvet collar and cuffs. "A sort of smock frock of Mackintosh's India rubber cloth." 1839.

(The scene, however, is set in the "old days when railroads were unknown" —sometime presumably before about 1829.)

The chief objection was the smell—again *Frank Fairlegh*:

. . . he applied his nose to it. The result of this was an indescribable exclamation, expressive of intense disgust. . . .'

In the 1850s the Newmarket began to be referred to as a "cutaway", and a looser-bodied and larger-skirted variety was introduced as the Doncaster Riding Coat, together with a double-breasted coat of similar cut (Fig. 84).

During the 1860s and 1870s breeches began to return to favour, although trousers continued the fashionable wear in town. The breeches were often cut loose and rather shapeless (Fig. 85).

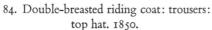

84. Double-breasted riding coat: trousers: top hat. 1850.

85. Lounge jacket: loose breeches: ankle boots and gaiters. Bowler hat. 1865.

. . . I surveyed the smart old gentleman with his Oxford mixture coat, buff waistcoat, nice Kerseymere continuations,[1] and top boots . . .

"Ay, you may look," said he, "this is the costume of an English horseman. I should as soon think of riding in the character of a sans-culotte as in a pair

[1] One of the many nineteenth-century euphemisms for "breeches".

of trousers. I am obliged to put on such abominations sometimes in an afternoon, but I never do it without a feeling of degradation.

Routledge's *Every Boy's Annual,* 1866.

In place of top-boots, ankle-boots were sometimes worn with leggings of
cloth or leather.

During the 1860s the terms Riding coat and Newmarket coat dropped out,
and the garment became known generally as a "Morning Coat." At about the
same time the "lounge" or "lounging jacket" was becoming popular. There
were several styles; single-breasted was most popular, generally fastened at the
top button only (Fig. 85).

> The length and width of this coat varies according to taste. Generally made
> from fancy coatings and coarse tweeds.
>
> *Tailor and Cutter,* 1869.

This jacket, generally with a back vent, became increasingly in use on horseback during the 1870s and 1880s, although the morning coat with trousers
was the correct wear in town; the trousers sometimes close fitting below the
knee and buttoned at the side.

During the 1890s breeches became more and more common and were
accepted for wear in Rotten Row: they were cut with a better shape, full to
the knee, and often "strapped" with leather on the inside of the thighs.
Breeches were sometimes made with fly-front opening in place of the "falls".
Buttoned cloth leggings or gaiters were popular. Lounge jackets or morning
coats were worn with waistcoat, collar and tie, and a top-hat or bowler
(Fig. 86).

In the latter half of the nineteenth century various types of over-garment
were developed for wear in the saddle. As well as the Macintosh, coats of
more or less waterproof material were worn, depending either on thickness
and closeness of weave, or using woollen cloth retaining a large degree of
natural oil, or impregnating the cloth with chemicals:

> When the coat, skirt, or suit is made, the final "waterproofing" is to be done
> thus. In, say, two gallons of distilled or very soft water, half a pound of sugar
> of lead and a piece of alum the size of a large egg (crushed to powder) should
> be mixed. The garment should lie in this preparation till thoroughly soaked
> through.
>
> *The Housewife,* 1896.

During the 1850s and 1860s a long weather-proof overcoat known as a "Siphonia" flourished—a short, light, variety was known as a "Pocket Siphonia" and could be rolled up and carried. Taglioni overcoats, sometimes

86. Morning coat: cord breeches with leather "strapping" inside legs: buttoned gaiters: silk hat. 1890.

of waterproof material, and the old-fashioned spencer, which in the 1840s merged into the "pea-jacket", generally gave way to the covert coat from about 1880 on.

> . . . fussy gentlemen in taglionis, macintoshes, siphonias and reversable coats, etc. . . .
>
> J. S. Surtees, *Handley Cross*, 1857.

> Covert Coats in various shades of Drab and Brown. Venetians and Covert clothes.
>
> Advertisement, 1897. (Fig. 111).

Soft cloth caps began to appear on riding heads towards the end of the century, and by the early 1900s vied with the bowler-hat for informal wear.

In the early twentieth century the breeches had become better cut, tight over the knee, with buttons or laces, and wide with a well developed "wing" above (Fig. 87). The jacket much resembled the ordinary lounge of the day, with a flare and back vent in the skirt. A stock or collar and tie was worn, and leather leggings and ankle-boots were often substituted for riding boots.

87. Riding jacket, flared skirt, centre back vent, three flapped pockets: breeches cut with pronounced "wings", leather strappings. Ankle boots with leather gaiters and bowler hat with safety cord. 1912.

Boot garters, a leather strap attached to the back of the riding boot and buckled below the knee, and spur rests of leather on the heel were commonly present in riding boots.

Bibliography

Bloodgood, Lida Fleitmann. *The Saddle of Queens.* J. A. Allen and Co, 1959.

Cunnington, C. W. & P. *Handbook of English Costume in the nineteenth century.* Faber and Faber, 2nd ed., 1966.

Hayes, Alice M. *The Horsewoman.* W. Thacker and Co., 1893.

Surtees, R. S. "The novels". Various dates and editions.

Woodforde, Rev. James. *Diary, 1758–1803.* Ed. John Berisford, Oxford University Press, 1924.

CHAPTER 8

RACING, DRIVING AND POLO

BY ALAN MANSFIELD

I. RACING

When weighed and mounted, 'twas my pride
Before the starting post to ride;
My rivals drest in red or green,
But I in simple yellow seen.   "Songs of the Chase" 1810.

Horse-racing, today largely a professional and commercial undertaking, evolved naturally from the sporting instincts of owners of horses in ancient times who matched their favourites, normally employed in workaday tasks, against each other in trials of speed and endurance.

In England horse-racing became a favourite practice in early days and by the sixteenth century "running horses" bred and kept for racing were well established.

Henry VIII's accounts note payments made for

> doublets of Bruges Satin for the boyes that runne the gueldings.

and for

> Ryding cappes of black satin lyned with black vellute [perhaps velvet, or an imitation velvet].
> Quoted in Cope's *Royal Cavalcade of the Turf,* 1953.

Unlike the clothes of the huntsman, the jockey's have no protective function; worn for short rides at high speeds, weather-resisting properties appropriate to the hunting field are unnecessary. Also, a minimum of weight is essential; the jockey himself is a lightweight, and so should be his clothes.

The method of achieving the required lightness in a jockey is described by a visitor to Britain in the early nineteenth century:

> He would go out in the greatest heat, dressed in three or four greatcoats, ride a certain distance at a hard trot till the sweat streamed off him in torrents, and he almost sank from exhaustion.
> Letter of Prince Puckler-Muskau, 1826.

If this exercise brought down the jockey's weight too much for the horse's handicap, then weights would be added. In the seventeenth century these were carried on the man, not the horse.

> If you are so light that you must carry weight, let it be shot, equally quilted in your waistcoat. . . .
>
> Richard Blome, *The Gentleman's Recreation*, 1686.

In an illustration to Matthew Walbancke's *Annalia Dubrensia* of 1636 we see among other diversions of the Cotswold (or Dover's) Games, a horse-race. This is a country meeting, and the riders wear the normal clothes of the day—doublet, wide breeches, wide brimmed hat, and a deep "falling band" (a wide collar) spread across the shoulders (Fig. 88).

88. Dover's, or the Cotswold Games. Racing, wrestling, etc. in
doublets and breeches. See text. 1636.

In 1687 Francis Barlow published the first racing print, of Charles II watching a race at Dorset Ferry, near Windsor, in 1684. The jockeys in this scene are clad in apparently identical vertically striped breeches and doublets, or jackets. They wear peaked caps and spurs and carry whips: in two cases neckerchiefs or cravats can bee seen. There appears to be no differentiation by colour or other means of the contestants (Plate 23).

A contemporary sporting writer had this to say of a jockey's dress:

> Your clothes should be of coloured silk, or of white Holland, as being very advantageous to the spectators. Your waistcoat and drawers must be made close to your body, and on your head a little cap, tied. Let your boots be gartered up fast, and your spurs must be of good metal.
>
> R. Blome, op cit.

Barlow's jockeys' clothes are certainly made closer to their bodies than are those of the horsemen in Dover's race.

Blome's use of the words "waistcoat" and "drawers" indicates the under-garment-like nature of the costume—silk or Holland in place of cloth or skin for the breeches, and a close fitting jacket of the same material in place of a stout cloth coat. (Sleeved waistcoats were worn at this time and were some-times worn indoors without the coat.)

Barlow heads a long line of English sporting painters which flourished during the eighteenth and nineteenth centuries. These artists did not neglect the race-horse nor the race-course and from their pictures we can see how the jockey, amateur or professional, was attired. By the early eighteenth century the jockeys had adopted Blome's advice and pictures of them show waist length tight fitting jackets, white breeches, short top-boots, and peaked cap with a bow in front. The cap was generally plain black, but the "coloured silk" of the jacket was now chosen according to the fancy of the horse's owner for easier identification by the spectators. Horses at exercise would be ridden by stable lads or grooms dressed in the owner's livery.

By this time, also, the term "jockey cap" was applied to the peaked velvet or silk cap, and "jockey boots" was the name applied to the lightweight top-boots of fine leather.

The Jockey Club was established at Newmarket in about the year 1750, and racing colours were first mentioned in 1762. That these colours were recognized as official identification before this date, however, seems to be shown by the judges' decision in 1757 of "Brown-and-black cap first".

A picture by W. Mason of 1786 *A country race-course with horses preparing to start* shows two jockeys in the foreground. One wears horizontal, and the other vertical stripes, on jacket and cap. The jackets are short, tight fitting, buttoned down the front to the hem, the top two or three buttons are un-done, disclosing a cravat. The jackets have small stand collars, and are not unlike sleeved waistcoats, as mentioned a century earlier by Blome. The men wear top-boots "gartered up fast" above the knee.

Such a jacket was worn at about this time by George Morland at Margate, according to a letter to a friend:

> I was sent for to Mount Pleasant by the gentlemen of the Turf to ride a race for the silver cup, as I am thought to be the best horseman here. I went there and was weighed, and afterwards dressed in a tight striped jacket and jockey's cap. . . .
>
> George Morland: quoted in *British Sporting Artists*,
> W. S. Sparrow, 1965 edit.

A picture by Ben Marshall of 1810 shows a jockey in an, apparently, silk jacket with a stand collar, the neck open to reveal shirt collar and cravat. His jockey cap has a large bow of a light colour in front. The breeches are fastened at the knee at the side and have small falls.

In the early nineteenth century breeches were generally white or buff in colour.

A sketch of three jockeys made by the same artist in about 1818 shows high shirt collars, large cravats, and loose fitting stand collars to the jackets; which are unbuttoned at the neck. The soft jockey caps have large peaks and bows tied in front. One of the subjects is Sam Chifney junior (Fig. 89), who,

> in 1802 . . . mounted the magnificent "purple jacket with scarlet sleeves, and gold-braid buttons, and black cap with gold tassell" of the Prince for the first time. . . .
>
> *The Post and the Paddock*, by The Druid, 1856.

During the first half of the nineteenth century the jacket became easier in fit, creating a somewhat blouse-like effect, and the simple stand collar was sometimes replaced by a "stand-fall", or turned over collar (Fig. 90).

Steeplechasing evolved from the hunting field in Ireland about the middle of the eighteenth century and reached England about forty years later. At first the competitors rode in ordinary hunting kit—the first time racing colours were worn is said to have been in 1804. As late as 1829 Alken depicted the Grand Leicestershire Steeplechase being ridden in top-hats and red hunting coats; and twenty years after that Surtees could write of a local meeting:

> . . . some of them are attired in the miscellaneous garb of hunting and racing costumes.
>
> R. S. Surtees, *Mr Sponge's Sporting Tour*, 1849–51.

89. Jockey wearing jacket with sleeves of differing colour: large cravat: jockey cap with ribbon bow. See text, *c.* 1818.

However, in 1826 Captain Ross rode his steeplechaser dressed in normal jockey's garb and in 1831 Mr Jesset was painted on the horse "Moonraker". He wore long tight breeches, jockey-boots, jacket, high shirt collar and dark cravat, and a black jockey cap.

From mid-century onwards it was normal to wear racing jackets rather than hunting coats when riding in steeplechases. When Captain Beecher (of the Brook) died in 1864, among his effects were seven silk racing jackets.

There is little apparent change in the design of racing jackets during the latter half of the nineteenth century, but the fashion of wearing the top buttons open to show a large cravat gradually died out and by the 1870s jacket collars tended to be smaller and closer fitting. In the 1880s and 1890s stiff wing collars and ties were fashionable (Fig. 91). The jacket was sometimes worn tucked into the breeches, shirt fashion: this occurred from quite early in the nineteenth century (Fig. 90).

90. Jockey with jacket worn inside breeches: saddle carried on back. *c.* 1820.

91. Jockey wearing wing collar; tie; silk jacket with small stand collar. *c.* 1890.

In the paddock the jockeys of the 1890s might wear a covert coat over their "silk"—the name of the racing jacket, taken from the material from which it was made (Fig. 92).

92. Jockey wearing covert coat. *c.* 1890.

By the opening years of the twentieth century the jacket had reverted to a narrow stand collar and the shirt was worn with collar and tie, or else a stock (Fig. 93).

The London Museum possesses a jacket dated 1904–5: it has a round neck, stand collar, six buttons at the front. The garment is not shaped, and is made

93. Jockey with jacket tucked into breeches. Early 20th century.

of alternate horizontal bands of yellow and pink satin sewn together. The sleeves fasten at the wrist with a button and are made in two sections. The length is 28 inches and the shoulder width 18 inches. Inside the neck is a label, "Gilbert, Saddler, Newmarket". A further, handwritten, label indicates that the owner of this jacket was the jockey of Cicero, Lord Roseberry's 1905 Derby winner. It is altogether a dainty garment conjuring up the glamour, the excitement and the general jollification of Derby day: but let our closing thoughts be with the poor jockeys as they "sweat it out" in training for the great event:

After breakfast, having sufficiently loaded themselves with clothes, that is, with five or six waistcoats, two coats, and as many pairs of breeches, a severe walk is taken, from ten to fifteen miles.

Nimrod, *The Chace, The Turf, The Road,* 1843.

2. DRIVING

What can Tommy Onslow do?
He can drive a phaeton and two.
Can Tommy Onslow do no more?
Yes—he can drive a phaeton and four.

Anon. Early nineteenth century.

Driving as a recreation seems to have originated in the eighteenth century among outside passengers of stage coaches. For a consideration the coachman allowed certain favoured individuals to "handle the ribbons" for part of the journey; and with the improved roads of the latter part of the century allowing the use of lighter vehicles, the fashion for owner-driving began. During the middle years of the nineteenth century there was more than one "gentleman coachman" owning and driving public coaches, running over scheduled routes. With the improved roads of Telford and Macadam the one- or two-horsed private carriages introduced in the latter half of the eighteenth century rapidly gained popularity.

The admiration excited in the hearts of amateur drivers by the feats of the professional coachmen led to an emulation of the latter's style of dressing. As early as 1758 we hear of

gold laced hats slouched in humble imitation of stagecoach men.

London Evening Post, 1758.

And writing of the early years of the nineteenth century:

When I was young coaching was at its height. It was the most fashionable amusement of the British youth. He loved not only to be "the Coachman" but he endeavoured to look like him. . . .

Bailey's Magazine of Sports and Pastimes, March, 1861.

In 1839 "Craven" wrote that

In very cold weather the chin should be protected by a shawl, and the knees by thick cloth knee caps. In very severe weather, the breast should be protected; for which purpose hare-skins are now manufactured, and are getting into use on the road.

Walker's Manly Exercises, revised by "Craven", 1840.

Similar chest protectors made from small mammel skins are still in use on the Continent.

94. Coachman: greatcoat with triple capes: low crowned round hat.
See text. 1786.

One of the distinctive features of a coachman, professional or amateur, was the multi-cape-collared greatcoat (Fig. 94); multiple collars seem to have been a sign of sporting interests from the mid eighteenth century:

> His great ambition was to be deemed a jemmy fellow . . . he appeared always in the morning in a Newmarket frock, decorated with a great number of green, red, or blue capes.
>
> Francis Coventry, *Pompey the Little*, 1751.

The round-, as opposed to the three-cornered, hat was introduced in the 1770s for riding and driving (Fig. 95):

> One of the highest phaetons I had ever seen rattled up to the gate, out of which jumped a complete Buck in his round hat and leather breeches.
>
> *Gentleman's and London Magazine*, 1776.

Hats for driving often tended to be low crowned and wide brimmed.

> These had been an age of stout broad shouldered, red-faced men, top booted and low-crowned hatted . . . whose souls delighted in many-folded capes and cheese plate buttons.
>
> *Bailey's Magazine*, March 1861.

> A hat three inches and a half deep in the crown only, and the same depth in the brim exactly.
>
> *Morning Post*, 1808, quoted in Ashton, *England 100 Years Ago*.

95. Gentleman dressed for driving. Frock with skirts sloping away: breeches and English top boots with boot garters: "Newmarket" striped waistcoat: round hat: long whip.
c. 1788.

Various Clubs for gentlemen coach-drivers and for owner-drivers were established, including the famous Whip Club, later known as the Four in Hand Club. At a typical meeting of the Whip Club at Park Lane in 1808:

> Costume of the drivers: A light drab colour cloth coat made full, single breast, with three tiers of pockets, the skirts reaching to the ankles: a mother of

pearl button of the size of a crown piece. Waistcoat, blue and yellow stripe, each stripe an inch in depth. Small cloths [*sic*] corded with silk made to button over the calf of the leg, with sixteen strings and rosettes to each knee. The boots very short, and finished with very broad straps, which hung over the top and down to the ankle. [Hat as described above]. Each wore a large bouquet at the breast.

Ibid.

An account of the Four in Hand Club in the following year speaks of a long waisted blue single-breasted coat with brass buttons engraved "Four in Hand Club", striped waistcoats as before, white corduroy small clothes

made moderately high, and very long over the knee, buttoning in front over the shin bone. Boots very short, with long tops, only one outside strap to each, and one to the back; the latter were employed to keep the breeches in their proper longitudinal shape. Hats with a conical crown and the Allen brim; box or driving coat, of white drab cloth, with fifteen capes, two tiers of pockets, and one inside one for the Belcher handkerchief; cravat of white muslin spotted with black. Bouquets of myrtle, pink, and yellow geraniums were worn.

Morning Post, 1809, quoted in Ashton op cit.

Coins, such as shillings, or even crown pieces, were also popular as buttons at this time.

96. Tommy Onslow, with multi-caped greatcoat: high-crowned round hat: hay bands around ankles. See text. *c.* 1802.

The last Horse Race
Run before
CHARLES the Second of
Blessed Memory
By Dorsett Ferry
near
Windsor Castle.

PLATE 23

Charles II at the Races. Jockeys in jackets or doublets and peaked caps. (See text.) 1684.

Print after Francis Barlow's etching, published 1687.

PLATE 24

Trotting: green jacket, drab trousers, tall white beaver hat. 1831.

Mr Osbaldeston's "Tom Thumb" engraving by Ackermann. 1831.

One of the most enthusiastic drivers at the beginning of the nineteenth century was the Tommy Onslow (later Lord Cranley) of our chapter heading (Fig. 96). The hay-bands round his ankles were a substitute for gaiters favoured by countrymen and those working among horses:

> . . . snow having fallen . . . those who had no leggings went to the stable and wound wisps of hay round their ankles to keep the insidious flakes from the interior of their boots.
>
> Thomas Hardy, *Under the Greenwood Tree*, 1872.

> Mr. Barker [assistant waterman on a hackney coach stand] . . . seated . . . near the curb stone, . . . his ankles curiously enveloped by hay-bands.
>
> Charles Dickens, *Sketches by Boz*, 1836.

97. Box-coat: very long with large mother-o'-pearl buttons: bouquet on breast: low-crowned round hat with broad brim. 1809-10.

Those owner-drivers who did not ape the professional wore, generally, the usual garb of their day, or at least eschewed multiple capes to their box-coats (Fig. 97).

In the 1840s the Box-coat became known by the alternative name of Curricle coat.

As the century progressed driving dress, as dress generally, for men became quieter, and dark coats with top-hats or, later, bowler-hats, became general.

Hunting was a winter pastime, and the clothes worn were of necessity stout, warm, and as far as possible waterproof.

98. Trotting: morning coat: trousers: jockey-cap. 1863.

Rugs were generally worn around the legs in winter. By the early twentieth century a tweed suit and bowler hat, or straw hat in summer, could be worn when driving.

Ladies who drove made little concession to the fact, and normal fashions were the rule. The Lady's Phaeton, as opposed to the male version of that vehicle, was made exceptionally low to allow of mounting and dismounting encumbered by a multitude of spreading petticoats in the 1840s and 1850s.

At the commencement of this century a woman could

> . . . "look smart and sportsmanlike in the costume suitable for the season. In winter the fur-lined coat is indispensable, and the smart three-cornered hats of white or black beaver make ideal headgear. In the summer white panama hats are delightful." Gloves "for riding and driving, especially in cold weather, should be at least two sizes too large".
>
> Mrs Eric Pritchard, *The Cult of Chiffon*, 1902.

Trotting, in a light carriage little more than a skeleton seat on two large wheels, was indulged in, racing either against the clock or other horses. For this sport, coat, trousers rather than breeches, and top-hats, later replaced by jockey caps, were the recognized wear (Plate 24 and Fig. 98).

3. POLO

O saddle me my milk-white steed,
And go and fetch me my pony, O!

Anon.

99. Polo in pill-boxes. Striped jerseys; breeches with adjusting strap
at back waist. 1873.

Polo, although one of the oldest of games, has only a short history in this country, having been introduced about the year 1869 by a cavalry regiment home from the East.

Called by an undiscriminating public "Hockey on horseback", the game was played in the 1870s at Aldershot and London by regimental teams clad in striped shirts or jerseys and pill-box hats (Fig. 99).

In the 1890s and early years of this century self-coloured shirts, with short sleeves, or rolled up long sleeves, white breeches, plain riding boots, and a cricket-style cap was the most common wear. Club badges were sometimes embroidered on the shirts, and the caps might be quartered in club colours. Shirts sometimes had a stand-fall collar, open at the front, and worn with a bow tie (Fig. 100). Jerseys were sometimes worn in place of shirts (Fig. 101).

100. Polo: cricket cap: shirt with turn down
collar and shoulder straps: bow tie. 1891.

The Hurlingham Club laid down that the club colours were light blue shirts, the second team white and red. For internal club matches red or blue waistcoats, supplied by the club, were worn over white shirts or jerseys. The rules were incorporated in the Club By-Laws of 1903.

The material for breeches was preferably a light-weight white washing fabric, and brown boots with blunt spurs were judged correct, although other cloth for breeches and also black boots were acceptable.

In 1905 the polo cap, invented by Mr Gerald Hardy was recommended as being the smartest type of headwear, as well as being a crash-helmet in case of an accident.

In India the sola topee was the usual head-gear and light coloured boots were worn; umpires would wear dust-coats. Such a garb is mentioned by Kipling in 1898.

In London in 1873 an umpire is depicted in a dark suit and top-hat.

Ladies, in small numbers, took up the game, and members of the "Rainbows" were photographed at Ranelagh in 1905 wearing dark habits with a coloured sash over one shoulder and with straw "boaters" on their heads. They were, of course, riding side-saddle. In 1913 an American women's

101. Polo: knitted jersey with short sleeves, worn over breeches. 1891.

team, visiting this country, were clad in breeches, long coats, and polo caps: they rode astride.

Bibliography

Blome, Richard. *The Gentleman's Recreation*, 1686.
Dale, T. F. *Polo Past and Present.* Country Life, 1905.
Mortimer, Roger and others. *A History of Steeplechasing.* Michael Joseph, 1966.
"Nimrod" (Appleby, Charles James). *The Chace, the Turf, and the Road.* John Murrey, 1843.

CHAPTER 9

HUNTING

BY ALAN MANSFIELD

> The Master of Harriers wears a green coat
> The Master of Foxhounds a pink 'un,
> But the Devil he cares
> Not a damn what he wears
> When he's hunting the people of Lincoln.   Anon.

The hunting with horses and hounds of the deer and the hare has a long history—that of foxes a shorter one, starting seriously somewhere about the beginning of the eighteenth century. Today the hare is also hunted on foot by packs of beagles, the mounted hunts adopting the name of Harriers. The beagler, and the otter hunter, also a pedestrian, will be considered later.

The clothes worn in the hunting field were the usual riding clothes of the day adapted as necessary for convenience and efficiency. In the case of hunting social convention came to play its part, also, in dictating the style of costume adopted.

An illumination to the Bibliotheque Nationale manuscript of *The Master of Game* (1500) shows a mounted huntsman pursuing a fox. He wears a gown with, apparently, a fur collar and hanging sleeves, from which emerge the doublet sleeves. He wears hose and high shoes with enormous spurs. His head-gear is a soft bonnet or cap, and he carries a long stick or pole.

Henry VIII is said to have had a preference for green as a hunting colour; Elizabeth was apparently less conservative, and traditionally she hunted in Enfield Chase in 1557 accompanied by twelve white satin-clad ladies. In Turberville's *Booke of Hunting* we see her in a fashionable gown, wearing a tall hat ornamented with feathers standing up at the back, and carrying a pair of gloves. The attendant huntsmen and courtiers wear doublets and bombasted trunk hose (Fig. 252). Some carry crescentic hunting horns slung across their shoulders. Although they wear shoes, Turberville recommends boots

> for I have lent a Foxe or Badgerd ere now a piece of my hose, and the skin and fleshe for companie, which he never restored again.
> *Noble Arte of Venerie or Hunting*, 1576.

The huntsmen whose pictures illustrate the *Booke of Hunting*, shown in company of a succession of benign and half-witted dogs, wear boots or shoes indiscriminately. All, however, carry a short sword and the half-moon hunt-ing horn. They wear doublet, hose, and tall, wide-brimmed hats (Fig. 102).

102. Huntsman. Slashed jerkin with short sleeves: doublet: close fitting hose of old fashioned type: long boots rolled down: wide brimmed tall hat. 1575.

In about the year 1610 Henry, Prince of Wales, was portrayed with the young Lord Essex at the kill of a stag. Both wear doublets, Venetians (breeches) and top-boots turned down exposing boot-hose inside. Swords and hunting horns are slung from their shoulders. (Painting attributed to Robert Peake, in the Royal Collection) (Plate 25).

Francis Barlow's picture of *c.* 1671 "Coursing Fallow Deer" (Plate 26) shows mounted men wearing loose coats with side and back vents, possibly "jumps", wide-brimmed hats with large bows, and high boots with boot-hose. One pair of boot-hose appears to be lace-edged, and the owner of these wears a short straight sword. Another man, on foot, similarly clad but with boot-tops turned down, carries a long pole and wears, as does another mounted man, a short, broad bladed, curved sword or falchion; he also carries a hunting horn. The sportsmen in "Hare-Hunting" by the same artist, are similarly clad, but carry no weapons, except the men on foot who weald long poles—from one of which a hare is slung by its hind legs.

Randle Holme's *Academy of Armoury* has several crude figures depicting various kinds of huntsmen:

> A Hunter or Huntster, his horn by his side and Staff upon his shoulder . . . clothes Azure . . . Some term this a Courser, but then he hath no horn.
>
> *Academy of Armoury*, 1688 (Fig. 103).

103. Huntsman in doublet and breeches, with shoes and stockings. See text. *c.* 1620–40.

The statement about coursers having no horn is at variance with Barlow's picture described above. Although published in 1688 Holme's illustrations portray the doublet and breeches of an earlier date, about 1620–40.

An unknown seventeenth-century author is quoted by the Rev. W. B. Daniel:

> The Ladies of Bury in Suffolk that used Hawking and Hunting, were once in a great vaine of wearing Breeches.
>
> Quoted in *Rural Sports*, Vol. I, 1801.

A painting by Robert Byng in 1706 shows a mounted man clad in a normal coat and wearing a wig and three-cornered hat. A dismounted figure wears a coat, buttoned at the waist only, and a belt. One figure can be seen wearing what appears to be jockey boots (later known as top-boots).

At the commencement of the eighteenth century such packs of hounds as there were belonged to individual landowners and tended to confine their hunting to the owner's land. As the century progressed the Hunts became more public, hunted over wider country and raised subscriptions for their support on the principle of a club. This century also witnessed the rise of the great school of English sporting artists and the dress of the contemporary hunting man is portrayed in detail by Tillemans, Seymour, the Sartoriuses, Woolton, Stubbs, and a host of others. Red seems to be a predominant colour for coats, though by no means universal. From about 1730 the frock with its small flat collar, often of a different colour, became the common garment. Coats or frocks were sometimes embroidered with emblems of the chase (Plate 32). Breeches were generally of leather, buckskin being a favourite. From about 1760 the front verticle button opening was replaced by falls—by this time the waistcoat had become much shorter.

Coat- or frock-buttons were often of brass or plate and could bear sporting designs. Belts were often worn round the waist, over the coat.

Hats were, at the beginning of the century, the three-cornered cocked type for gentlemen, and jockey caps for hunt servants. Later the jockey cap spread to the gentry, and also the round hat was worn (Fig. 104).

The jockey or top-boot was most usually adopted for hunting, a specially elegant and light variety was known as a "jemmy boot".

> I was dressed in my blue riding-frock with plate buttons, and a leather belt round my waste, my jemmy or turn down boots, my brown scratch wig and my hat with the narrow silver lace cocked in the true sporting fashion.
>
> *The Connoisseur*, November, 1754.

> When I hunt with the King . . . I'll on with my Jemmy's . . .
>
> Foote, *Englishman in Paris*, 1753.

Ladies wore the contemporary habit, sometimes in hunt colours—the Countess of Conningsby (Fig. 67) was painted by Stubbs about 1759–60 in the blue uniform of the Charlton Hunt, wearing a black wide-brimmed hat trimmed with feathers and carrying a long thonged whip. Another painting by Stubbs, about 1752–4 shows Mrs Wilson, of Tranby Croft, Yorkshire, at a hare hunt wearing a brown habit, the bodice unbuttoned to show a long waistcoat (or waistcoat-front) beneath. She wears a jockey cap. Her husband wears a long grey frock with large buttons, breeches buttoned at the knee on the outside, jockey boots and a jockey cap.

104. Gentleman in frock, full cut, with side pleats: jockey cap: breeches and jockey or top-boots. 1780–90.

Rowlandson's "Death of the Fox" (1787) shows frocks of less generous proportions with cuffs buttoned "a la mariniere", open at the neck to show the neckcloth, high turned down collars, and waist belts: top-boots and jockey caps. The riders carry long whips: the huntsman has a circular French hunting horn. An elderly gentleman in a bushy toupée has a long waistcoat and a round hat (Fig. 105). A Zoffany painting of about 1790 "A Group of Sportsmen" shows long waistcoats, one with the top buttons undone showing the neckcloth or cravat; the other figures with the frocks buttoned to the neck.

The stock, which fastened at the back of the neck by a buckle, instead of being tied in front, came in during the first half of the century.

> The stock, with buckle made of plate,
> Has put the cravat out of date.   Whyte's Poems, 1742.

Energetic pursuit of the fox, or other game, precluded the wearing of top-coats and the hunting coat or frock was ideally constructed of a weatherproof material to keep, with the aid of leather breeches and stout top-boots, the hunter as well protected as possible from the English elements.

> Hunting season. New patent waterproof cloth in scarlet and other colours. Effectually repels humidity as to occasion the rain to run off its surface.
>
> Advertisement, *The Times*, 3rd October, 1798.

105. Two hunters—man in dark coat possibly a clergyman. The other in riding frock sloping back from waist and with Star of an Order on left breast. 1787.

Hare hunters still carried poles,

> ... the huntsman getting forward, threw down his pole before the dogs ...
>
> *Spectator*, 13th July, 1711.

and continued to do so at the commencement of the nineteenth century.

> The Huntsman's dress should be light and he should have a pole in his hand ...
>
> Rev. W. B. Daniel, *Rural Sports*, 1801.

In the early years of the nineteenth century red-coated huntsmen mingled with those clad in coats of other hues—blue, green, brown, buff and black. These coats were the ample, deep-skirted frocks, or frock-coats as they became known, waisted and closer fitting than the eighteenth-century garment (Fig. 106). These gave way later to the Newmarket, or morning-coat, and the dress-coat, with no skirts, but short tails.

By the late 1820s the hunting frock-coat had become much shorter, and had flapped pockets at the waist.

White or pale buff breeches, cut long in the leg, generally of leather or Bedford cord, and top-boots, were almost universal, but the 1840s and 1850s saw a brief appearance of pantaloons or trousers on some hunters' nether limbs. Leather trousers have been hinted at.

106. Two gentlemen in red sporting frocks, one with M-notch in collar, one with V-notch, and lapels. Huntsman in jockey cap and red frock with small turn-down collar and no lapels. 1823.

Gaiters with pantaloons had sometimes been worn in the 1820s—Dr Syntax wore a knee-length pair when hunting with "his kind lady friend", during his Tour in Search of a Wife—but by 1830

> Fashionable hunting men no longer wear gaiters, but the pantaloons made "en guetre" and buttoned above the ankle.
>
> *Gentleman's Magazine of Fashion*, 1830.

The top-hat in the early years of the century ousted other forms of head-gear almost completely, and the jockey cap was again worn principally by the hunt servants (Fig. 106).

The High Priest of Hunting in the mid-nineteenth century was R. S. Surtees, and his novels abound in descriptions of contemporary sporting costume: and Surtees was a countryman and a hunter as well as a keen observer and vivid writer. Who would not be as astonished as the Yorkshireman to meet in Covent Garden at 7 a.m.

> . . . a man in a capacious, long, full-tailed red frock coat reaching nearly to his spurs, with mother o'pearl buttons with sporting devices—which afterwards proved to be foxes done in black—brown shag breeches . . . and boots . . . tied round the knees with pieces of white tape, the flowing ends of which dangled over the mahogany coloured tops.
>
> *Jorrocks' Jaunts and Jollities*, 1831–4.

Mr Jorrocks was also wearing a broad-brimmed low-crowned hat anchored to his waistcoat by a green cord.

For hunting the stag Mr Jorrocks was equally prepared.

> He was dressed in a fine-flowing olive-green frock (made like a dressing gown), with a black velvet collar, having a gold embroidered stag on each side, gilt stag buttons with rich embossed edges; an acre of buff waistcoat and a most antediluvian pair of bright yellow-ochre buckskins . . .
>
> Ibid.

The white tape tied round Mr Jorrocks' knees was to keep the boot from working down the leg and was a variation of the leather boot garters: a short strap on the boot and a button on the breeches-knee also achieved the same object.

White neckcloths were normal, but mid-century saw a number of coloured ones, and also coloured striped shirts:

> Once at the meet . . . he sported a shirt collar with three or four blue lines . . . a once round blue silk tie, with white spots and flying ends. . . .
>
> Surtees, *Mr Sponge's Sporting Tour*, 1853.

The jockey-style hard cap was also becoming popular and was not confined to hunt servants, although for them it became part of their uniform replacing the earlier soft jockey cap (Fig. 107). Masters took to this form of head-gear: speaking of the 1870s:

> The farmer said he knew it was the Master and Whips, as they had on caps.
>
> "A Melton Rough rider" *Rum 'Uns to Follow*, 1934.

But the Roughrider goes on to say a dozen members of the hunt (the Quorn) were also wearing caps.

The spread of railways had opened up the hunting countries to those town dwellers who, in past years, had been unable to make a lengthy expedition into the shires to indulge in the sport. It was possible, by means of the train, to spend a day hunting on a borrowed or hired horse, or even on your own, travelling with you in a railway horse-box.

107. Short hunting frock coat: breeches: top
boots: jockey cap. 1850.

b

An anonymous author in 1859 advises his readers:

> For hunting . . . cord breeches and some kind of boots are indispensable. So are spurs, so a hunting whip or crop; so too, if you do not wear a hat, is the strong round cap that is to save your valuable skull from cracking if you are thrown on your head. Again I should pity the man who would attempt to hunt in a frock-coat or a dress coat; and a scarf with a pin in it is much more convenient than a tie. But beyond this you need nothing out of the common way, but a pocketful of money. The red coat, for instance, is only worn by regular members of a hunt . . . In any case you are better with an ordinary

riding coat of dark colour . . . your "cords" should be light in colour . . .; your scarf of cashmere, and fastened with a simple gold pin; . . . and your cap of dark green or black velvet, plated inside, and with a stiff peak, should be made to look old.

Anon., *The Habits of Society—a Handbook of Etiquette*, 1859.

Nevertheless the nucleus of the hunt was always the "regular member" and Sir John Astly, writing of the Brocklesby in the 1860s recalled that:

About fifty yeomen used to hunt in pink . . .

Sir J. Astly, *Fifty Years of My Life*, 1894.

108. Lady in riding habit with close fitting bodice with tails, flower tucked in from opening: "Narrow" skirt: top hat. 1884.

The convenience of getting about the country offered by the railways was also bringing more ladies into the hunting field (Fig. 108).

Mrs Somerville re-entered attired for the chase . . . she had on a smart new hat with an exquisitely cut eight-guinea habit braided in front, and beautifully made chamois leather trousers with black-cloth feet . . . She had on a pair of smart new primrose-coloured kids [gloves] that fitted with the utmost exactitude. She had got a beautiful gold-mounted whip down from London with a light blue silk tasselled cord through its ruby-eyed fox head handle.

> Surtees, *Mr Facey Romford's Hounds*, 1865.

But not always are the smart ladies' clothes up to the rigour of the hunting field. Miss de Glancey in her wide-awake hat and feather, her light green habit of exquisite fit and the straw coloured ribbon at her neck, after a run ending in a thunderstorm

> is as drenched as if she had taken a shower bath. The smart hat and feather are annihilated . . . down comes her hair . . . the crinoline and wadding dissolve like ice before the fire: and . . . she has no more shape or figure than an icicle.
>
> Surtees, *Ask Mamma*, 1858.

But then Miss de Glancey was a husband-hunter rather than a fox-hunter.

As a red coat was the hall mark of a fox-hunting man, so was a green one that of the hare-hunter:

> His Lordship, who, in addition to boots and breeches, was attired in a smart new pea-green cut-away . . . detailing for the third time the splendours of a hare hunt he had been engaged in.
>
> Surtees, *Hawbuck Grange*, 1847.

Speaking of a macintosh, with which the truant Lawless hoped to deceive his Tutors:

> The harriers meet there at eleven, and this will be the very thing to hide the leathers, and tops, and the green cut-away.
>
> Frank Smedley, *Frank Fairlegh*, 1850.

But despite this already established distinction the middle years of the nineteenth century saw a wide selection of colours on hunting men's backs. At the opening meet at Tantivy Castle:

> The great flood of company now poured into the hall, red coats, green coats, black coats, brown coats. . . .
>
> Surtees, *Ask Mamma*, 1858.

And at less serious meets one even saw

> the rest of the field in shooting-jackets, tweeds, antigropolos, and other anti-fox-hunting looking things.
>
> Ibid.

PLATE 26

(*a*) Coursing Fallow Deer. Men in "jumps" and round wide-brimmed hats. (See text.) *c.* 1671.

Francis Barlow, engraved by W. Hollar.
Photo by J. R. Freeman & Co. Ltd.

(*b*) Stag hunter in frock embroidered with stags' heads: gold laced "tricorne" hat. 1747.

Francis Cotes, "Portrait of a Gentleman".
1747. Leicester Museum.

('Antigropolos' were high leather gaiters fastening by a spring at the back.) This type of dress later became known as "Ratcatcher", an expression derived from a remark attributed to King Edward VII.

In 1866:

> Some gentlemen now wear their breeches fuller in the thigh than formally, even when made of leather. They however always fit close to the knee and are cut long . . . fly front is the usual style.
>
> *Minsters' Gazette of Fashion*, January 1866.

But in 1868:

> Hunting breeches cut in full fall style . . . and made of Bedford cord.

Also

> Hunting coats are now made in the regular Frock-coat style, double breasted and very short in the skirts . . . to button to the top, . . . five club buttons on the front and two behind . . . and large pockets across the skirt facings, put high . . . Scarlet cloth, velvet collar.
>
> *The Tailor and Cutter*, October, 1868.

In the 1870s bowler-hats were being worn in the hunting field.

Despite the statement of the *Tailor and Cutter* in 1868 hunting coats during the 1870s and 1880s appear to have been, on the whole, single-breasted (Fig. 109) and this style persisted in popularity throughout our period (Fig. 110).

Ratcatcher, antigropolos, and breeches "so very tight in the knee" were worn by harriers in 1884 and that same year the *Tailor and Cutter* was noting:

> Hunting vests with buttons carved in ivory representing the heads of distinguished members of the canine family. As each button costs from one to two guineas, not many can indulge in the fancy.
>
> *The Tailor and Cutter*, September, 1884.

In 1889 members of the West Norfolk Hunt escorted the Queen from Wolferton Station to Sandringham:

> twenty four members of the hunt in black cut-away hunting coats, white leather breeches and top boots, riding four abreast. Behind these rode thirty two more members of the hunt, also four abreast but in scarlet coats. . . .
>
> Quoted in Alan Ball, *Our Fathers*, 1931,
> (probably from *The Graphic*).

In 1894

> the full skirted frock is still the leading style. The breeches are still worn very full.
>
> *The Tailor and Cutter*, 1894.

But "full dress hunt coats" were still worn by some, and with their tails and lack of front skirts,

> these coats require great care in cutting and trying on. The latter I always do in the saddle.
>
> Ibid, article by a First Coat Cutter.

109. Red morning coat: tight breeches: top boots: top hat. Stiff wing collar. 1888.

In the early 1900s there was more interest shown in the dress-coat:

> The revival of the dress coat for hunting marks a distinct departure from the ordinary well-known garments hitherto worn in the field.
>
> Whether the dress coat will remain permanently fashionable is very much open to question, the main objection appearing to be that the meagre skirts

prove but a poor covering against the rough weather invariably met with in the field.

Many no doubt will stick to the frock coat with its ample folds of cloth, or the more primitive but no less acceptable morning coat.

West End Gazette, 1905.

110. Red single-breasted frock coat: top hat with hat-string. 1890.

Apparently the revival did not catch on; in 1906 novices were advised to wear:

a black or iron grey frock coat—with the former cloth breeches slightly lighter in colour, and with the latter breeches to match . . .

Charles Richardson, *Practical Hints for Hunting Novices*, 1906.

Richardson goes on to advise black jackboots and a bowler or top-hat. No novice, he says, should begin with scarlet coat and leather breeches. After a year he may come out in top-boots and white breeches, and after a second year may graduate to scarlet.

As well as leather breeches white twill or cord were also popular, and fly-fastening was again common.

Despite the disadvantages of a top-coat and the weatherproof qualities of the hunting frock-coat there had always been a number of over garments available—besides the macintosh very long belted Ulsters were advertised in the 1870s and from the eighties the short, side-vented covert coat was seen on both men and women (Fig. 111).

111. Short top-coat known as a "covert" coat: tweed breeches: buttoned cloth gaiters: bowler hat. ("Ratcatcher"). 1897.

During the latter half of the nineteenth century women's hunting habits had become less voluminous in the skirt and less ornate and more masculine as to the bodice, which began the twenieth century much on the lines of the man's coat.

> Dark grey and black are, perhaps, the most sporting, but light brown and drab are conspicuous and become shabby much sooner than the dark colours. I have seen a habit . . . green with white spots all over it, and . . . a girl in a purple hunting costume; but my advice is to stick to the dark, quiet colours. . . .
>
> Ibid.

One or two daring ladies about 1890 ventured out in scarlet habits, but these were denounced as loud and never caught on.

Top- or bowler-hats were *de rigeur* for both sexes, but children were allowed cloth caps if boys or Tam o' Shanters if girls.

Girls up to sixteen or so might ride astride in the days before the Great War, either in a divided skirt or breeches and a long coat coming down to the top of the boots (Fig. 112).

Leather gloves and hunting whips or crops with a thong, collars and hunting stocks were worn by both sexes.

For cub-hunting, varieties of ratcatcher were permissable; brown boots, Norfolk jackets, knickerbockers, puttees, shooting boots, cloth caps, all made their appearance on those who after November 1st would only venture out in the most orthodox of kit.

112. Young woman riding astride: long coat covering knees: breeches: black "butcher" boots: wide brimmed felt hat. Early 20th century.

The fox-hunter, stag-hunter, and harrier have always presented a more glamorous image than their more humble pedestrian brothers the beaglers and the otter-hunters, and this glamour largely derives from the riding clothes worn by the former categories. The conditions of pursuing the quarry on foot across plough-land or along muddy streams dictate less sartorial elegance than that possible when elevated upon a horse.

Francis Barlow's seventeenth-century hare-hunt embraced men on foot and also men on horses—by the mid-nineteenth century the Harriers retained the horse and the Beaglers went a-foot.

There is little known of foot beaglers before the middle of the nineteenth century; "Stonehenge" writing in 1857 speaks only of the mounted chase. The harrier and the beagle he says are so interbred that it is impossible to say what are harriers and what are beagles. Courtney Tracey, who was significantly an otter-hunter, hunted a beagle pack in Cambridgeshire in 1863 or 1864. They had no hunt uniform. In 1867 the Trinity Foot Beagles was founded in Cambridge and the name would indicate that hare-hunting on foot was not usual at that time. The Colchester Garrison Beagles were founded as a private pack in about 1863.

As in the case of Harriers the beagle hunts adopted a uniform of green coat and white breeches. This normally was worn by the Master, huntsman, and perhaps whippers-in and any hunt servants employed, with a velvet cap (Fig. 113). The field generally wore convenient clothes—trousers and boots and

113. Master of Beagles. Green jacket: white breeches, buckled over green stockings: shoes: black jockey or riding cap. 1902.

gaiters, or running shoes, breeches, knickerbockers, riding jackets, shooting jackets or just lounge jackets. Lady followers generally chose a tweed coat and skirt. Unlike the devotees of the seventeenth century they did not carry poles.

Otter-hunting, unlike other forms of the chase, is a summer sport, and one which by its nature can only be pursued on foot:

> . . . the legs are constantly called into play . . . and long waterproof boots would be beyond measure annoying . . . the season is a warm one . . . therefore, india-rubber is tabooed. Flannel is the article . . . and should be worn all over the body. No linen should touch the skin, but fine Jerseys should be worn over the upper half of the body . . . covered by a Tweed

shooting-coat . . . plain white flannel trousers . . . strong shooting shoes
. . . and good woolen socks.

Stonehenge, *Manuel of British Rural Sports*, 1857.

Later breeches tended to replace white trousers and shirts the jerseys. Ladies
dressed much as for beagling: in the 1890s and early years of this century they
are sometimes portrayed in skirts and blouses and large brimmed hats.

As in beagling the Master, etc., might wear a hunt uniform. Otter-hunters
did carry a pole (Fig. 114).

114. Otter hunting. Lady in coat and skirt:
shirt-blouse with stiff collar, tie: straw
"boater". Early 20th century.

We will take leave of our hunting men as they enter for the annual Hunt
Ball or club dinner; whether soberly clad in black coat and trousers, gilt
buttons with a letter L and a fox, and white waistcoat of the early nineteenth-
century Lambton evening dress, or dazzlingly dressed in the

> full-dress uniform of the Handley Cross Hunt—sky blue coat, lined with
> pink silk; canary-coloured shorts, and white silk stockings . . . large
> gold-buckled, patent leather pumps . . .
>
> Surtees, *Hillingdon Hall*, 1844.

with which Mr Jorricks threw the Duke of Donkeyton so completely in the
shade. And however clad, we will join with them and old John Jorrocks in
their toast, with three times three and no heel-taps,

"The Noble Sport of Fox hunting."

Bibliography

"A Melton rough Rider". *Rum 'Uns to follow*. Country Life, 1934.
Richardson, Charles. *Practical Hints for Hunting Novices*. Horace Cox, 1906.
Surtees, R. S. "The novels". Various dates and editions.

CHAPTER 10

ARCHERY

BY PHILLIS CUNNINGTON

A point that is emphasized throughout the history of toxophily is that an archer's costume must be green, both for men and women. This, for example, was the colour worn by the famous Scottish Royal Company of Archers, founded in 1676:
A popular song of the 1830s underlines this fact.

> The archery meeting is fixed for the third;
> The fuss that it causes is truly absurd;
> I've bought summer bonnets for Rosa and Bess,
> And now I must buy each an archery dress,
> Without a green suit they would blush to be seen
> And poor little Rosa looks horrid in green!
>
> Thomas Haynes Bayly, *The Archery Meeting*, 1830–6.

When guns began to replace bows and arrows as weapons of war, and in the hunt, archery continued to flourish as a sport, and archery pageants on a grand scale were often organized in the sixteenth century. The convention of wearing "Robin Hood Green" for the sport presumably stemmed from the fact that green was the natural colour for a hunter to wear in the forest. Even green leaves were sometimes worn in the hat in true camouflage style.

> Among the old descriptions of her progress (Queen Elizabeth) [when she hunted the Hart from West Lodge, Enfield Chase, Herts.] we read that she rode with a retinue of twenty yeomen clad in green on horseback. On entering the Chase she was met by fifty archers in scarlet boots and yellow caps, armed with gilded bows, one of whom presented her with a silver-headed arrow winged with peacock's feathers.
>
> Advert. leaflet of West Lodge Park Beale Hotels Ltd,
> Hadley Wood, Barnet, Herts.

Peacock's feathers were traditionally used by Robin Hood.

115. Instructor in long gown. Figure with bow: Doublet with sleeves puffed out above, long tight hose, small hat with turned up brims, very broad toed shoes. *c.* 1510.

How characteristic was the traditional dress of an archer is shown by the following account of its use in a hoax.

The King, some time after his coronation, he came to Westminster with the Quene, and all their traine, and on a tyme being there, his grace therles of Essex Wilshire and other noblemenne, to the number of twelve, came sodainly in a mornyng into the Quene's chambre, all appareled in short cotes[1] of Kentish Kendal,[2] with hodes on their heddes and hosen of the same, every-

[1] Short-sleeved or sleeveless jerkins.
[2] A coarse woollen fabric, coloured green.

one of them his bowe and arrowes and a sword and a bucklar, like outlaws, or Robin Hodsmen.

E. Hall, *Chronicle*, 1548.

Henry VIII himself appears to have enjoyed archery as a spectacle as well as in practice. Holinshed informs us that in 1515:

> . . . the King and Queen, accompanied by many Lords and ladies, rode to the high ground of Shooter's Hill to take the open air; and as they passed by the way they espied a compnay of tall yeomen, clothed in green hoods, and bows and arrows to the number of two hundred. Then one of them which called himself Robin Hood, came to the King desiring him to see his men shoot, and the King was content. Then he whistled and all the two hundred shot and tossed at once; and then he whistled again, and they likewise shot again. Their arrows whistled by craft of their head so that the noise was strange and great and much pleased the King and Queen and all the company.
>
> All the archers were of the King's guard, and had thus apparelled themselves to make solace to the King.
>
> Holinshed, *The Chronicles*, Vol. III, Ed. of 1587.

The whistling arrow had a special mechanism fitted to its head.

Celia Fiennes in 1696 mentions the importance of green suits for New Forest archers.

> I think it fellony for any to kill the King's dear; there are several Rangers of the Forrest and 6 Verderers that are their justices or judges of all matters relating to the Forrest, these ought allwayes to reside in the Forest and are to attend the King when he comes into the New Forest, clothed in green. . . .
>
> *The Journeys of Celia Fiennes*, 1662–1741.

Certain accessories of dress have always been important in archery. A *belt* was worn into which the arrows were thrust, (with or without some pendant protection for their tips) which served as a quiver. The belt was often tied in a bow to avoid the use of a buckle and thus became a *sash*. The *bracer* and *glove*(s) were further necessities.

In *Toxophilus* or *The Schole of Shooting*, a text book on archery by Roger Ascham, 1545, he states that it was

> necessary for the archer to have a bracer, or close sleeve, to lace upon the left arm, made of a material sufficiently rigid to prevent any folds which might impede the bowstring when loosed from the hand, and a shooting glove, for the protection of the fingers.

He also advises his pupil to follow the precepts of "Leo the Emperour" who

> would have al Archers in war to have theyre heades pouled and theyr berdes shaven leste the heare of theyr heades shuld stop the syght of the eye, the heere of theyr berdes hinder the course of the strynge.

Schoolboys often practised archery and these are the actual words of John Lyon the founder of Harrow School in 1571.

> You shall allow your child at all times a bow, three shafts, bow strings, and a bracer to exercise shooting.

In 1629 the Executors' accounts for Nicholas Hartley, a schoolboy of eight, include "pd. for bows and arrowes 1s.".

116. Note the two bracers tied to the archer's left arm, and the right hand glove with two fingers protected by goose quills or extra leather. See text. p. 174.

The important accessories are fully described by Gervase Markham in 1634, and are shown in Fig. 116:

> (1) *The Bracer* serveth for two purposes, the one to save the arme from the stripe of the string and his doublet from wearing, and the other, that the string glyding sharply and quickly of[f] the bracer may make the sharper shoote, for if the string should light vpon the bare sleeve, the strength of the shoote would stop and dye there . . . In a Bracer, a man must take heed of

three things; First that it have no nayles in it, then that it have no buckles, and lastly that the laces wherewith it is fastened be without tags or aglets [ornamental metal tags] for the nayles will sheare the string in sunder before a man be aware, and so put his bow into hazard, and the Buckles, Tags or Aglets, will (when a man least suspects it) raze and scratch his Bow, a thing both vncomely to behold, and dangerous for the weapon.

These Bracers are made for the most part of Spanish leather, the smooth side outward, sometimes of Spanish leather and the flesh side outward, and they are both good and tollerable, and others are made of hard stiffe but smooth bend-leather, and they be the worst and most dangerous, and thus much is spoken of the *Bracer*.

(2) *A Shooting-glove* is a necessary armour or defence for the hand, to preserve it from hurting or galling so that a man may be able in his fingers to beare the sharpnesse of the string to the vttermost of his strength . . . Leather if it be next a man's skin will sweate, wax hard and chafe; therefore scarlet [a rich soft fabric] for the softnesse is best to line the glove withall; but if you find that it helpeth not but still the finger hurteth, it is good then to take a searcloth made of fine virgin waxe and Deere suet, and putting it next your hand draw on your Glove; if you feel your finger pinched, then forbeare shooting . . .

A new Glove plucks many shoots, because the string goeth not freely off and therefore the fingers of the Glove must be cut short, and trimmed with some sweete oyntment, that the string may glide smoothly away.

There be some, that with holding the nocke[1] of their shaft too hard, rub the skin off their fingers which is an errour, yet there is for it two remedies, one to have goose quils spirretted and sewed against the nocking, betwixt the lyning of the Glove and the Leather, which both openeth the fingers, and helps the shoote. The other, is to have a rowle of leather sewed betwixt his fingers at the setting on of the finger-stals, which will so keepe his fingers asunder, that by no meanes he shall hold the nocke so hard, as before he did.

The shooting-glove should always have a purse on the backe of the hand, wherein the archer shall ever carrie a fine linnen cloth and waxe, two necessary things, for any man that vseth shooting; some men use gloves or the like on the bow hand, for feare of shafing; because they hold so hard. But that errour happeneth (for the most part) when a bow is not round but a little square, therefore fine tempered waxe shall do well in such a case to lay where a man holdeth his bow; yet I do not condemme the wearing of a fine thin cut fingerd-glove, which albe, they are but trifles in a generall opinion. . . .

[1] The notched end of an arrow, which, rests on the string.

In addition to these two items, Markham advises archers to carry a *pouch;* since if an arrow head sustains "a stripe against a stone . . ." it will be damaged,

> which to repaire . . . I would have our archer to carry by his side, a fine short close compact powch, in which he should have a fyle, a stone, a hurfish-skin and a cloth to wipe his shafts clean vpon every occasion.
>
> Gervase Markham, The Art of Archerie, 1634.

117. Archer in the fashion of his day. He wears country boots called highlows. From his belt is suspended a container for his arrow tips. 1790.

Apart from these accessories, archers at this time wore the clothes fashionable for their date. The archer depicted in Markham's book, Fig. 116, wears a doublet, breeches trimmed at the knee, and boots showing boot-hose tops with similar trimming.

Archery as a recreational sport of skill, the shots being aimed at a target, developed rapidly all through the seventeenth century and after the Restoration became the general amusement. Charles II himself took great delight in it. After his death it began to decline in popularity and remained in abeyance until the end of the eighteenth century.

> Archery, though an exercise not much heard of, yet is not out of use. There are some men of fashion who still amuse themselves this way.
>
> *The World*, 6th July, 1787.

The formation of the Toxophilite Society in London in 1781 was the first indication of its revival and it continued to be practised with enthusiasm all through the nineteenth century.

As will be seen by the illustrations, both men and women still wore the clothes that were fashionable in their day, as regards cut, and almost without exception their heads were covered. Women appear never to have deviated from the fashion, however inconvenient, but men sometimes wore suits specified by the Archery Club to which they belonged; these were always green. Women indicated their club membership by special trimmings (Plate 27).

A picture of a meeting of the Hertfordshire Archers in 1792 shows their foundress, the Duchess of Salisbury, shooting. From her belt is slung a quiver of arrows and her hat is adorned with a conspicuous vertical feather. This wearing of plumes persisted as a fashion for all archers until at least the end of the nineteenth century.

With an illustration representing the same Society of Archers in 1791, the gentlemen's full bowman's costume is described thus:

> which shall consist of a green coat with white waistcoat and breeches, a black hat, green and white feathers, white stockings, half boots, a buff coloured leather belt with a pouch and green tassel, and black leather bracer.
>
> *Ladies' Pocket Book.*

In a picture (Plate 27) of the Meeting of the *Royal British Bowmen* in the grounds of Erthig, Denbighshire, on 13th September, 1822, the men wear cut-away tail-coats and trousers of bottle green, tall-hats with broad brims trimmed with tall vertical plumes in front. Their waistcoats are pink. The women are in dark green short-waisted belted frocks with sleeves having shoulder puffs slashed with pink, and the skirts are vandyked in pink, matching the colours worn by the men and representing a kind of uniform. Like the men, they wear large hats trimmed with feathers.

118. Lady wearing archery sash, and hat massively trimmed with feathers. 1790.

A sash for the quiver persisted:

> Cry'd Venus, her words sweetly kissing the air,
> Gift you your bold bowmen, whilst I gift the fair;
> And first of my cestus[1] each fair shall be queen,
> Who sports a gay sash of toxopholite green.
>
> Pierce Egan's Book of Sports, 1832.

Archery throughout the nineteenth century was still a very popular sport for women. A writer[2] in 1828 explains why!

[1] Girdle of Venus.
[2] Pierce Egan, *The Finish to the Adventures of Tom, Jerry and Logic.*

PLATE 27

(*a*) The Royal British Bowmen. 1822.

Detail from painting by J. Townsend. Lucas Collection. British Museum.

(*b*) Archers in green belted top-coats, white pantaloons (i.e. tights), brown boots, large black, feather-trimmed hats. 1828.

Detail from Pierce Egan, The Finish of the Adventures of Tom, Jerry and Logic, *edn. 1887.*

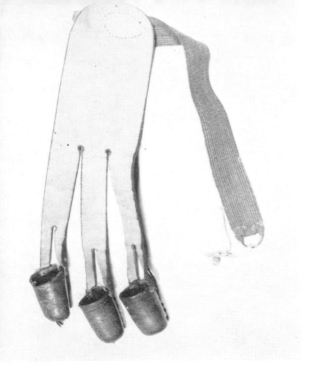
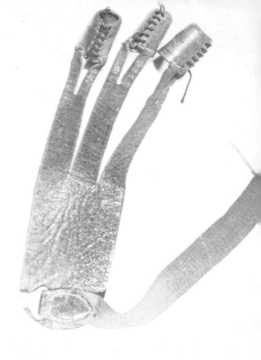

PLATE 28

(*a*) Gloves for archery, as described in the text, p. 178, early 19th century.

Original specimens in York Castle Museum. Photograph kindly given by the Curator.

(*b*) "Amazons of the Bow", very fashionably dressed and wearing bustles.

Detail from a drawing by Lucien Davis in the Illustrated London News.

Another advantage of attending the amusement of Archery is . . . that it is equally open to the fair sex, and has for these last thirty years, been the favourite recreation of a great part of the female nobility, the only field diversion they can enjoy without incurring the censure of being thought masculine . . . Of course the company of the ladies must prove a great attraction to the admirers of archery . . . but instead of hitting the target, their aim, I rather apprehend, is of a more tender nature—the hearts of the archers!

The handsome uniform of the men themselves is shown on Plate 27.

119. Archer in green coat and cap. White trousers. He has the archer's belt, bracer, gloves and tassel, with arrows in protective container. 1829.

Donald Walker in his book on Games and Sports in 1837 has this to say on archery accessories and clothes:

The Belt is usually made of stout leather, having on the right side a pouch [a substitute for the quiver (cf. Fig. 119)], somewhat resembling a small bucket, into which the heads of the arrows are placed, after passing through a leathern loop, which keeps them steady by the side.

The Tassel for the purpose of dusting the arrows, or keeping them clean, is usually made of green worsted, and is slung on the belt on the left side of the archer.

The Brace is composed of stout leather, polished externally to allow the string to glide over it freely. Its size depends upon that of the arm, and the manner of holding the bow; . . . It is generally made from six to eight inches in length, with two straps and buckles to fasten it on the arm. Its form is oval; its colour black or brown. . . .

For the hand are used—either the *Glove* which consists of three finger-stalls (projecting no more over the fingers than is necessary to protect them) fastened to back thongs, which by means of a cross strap, are buttoned round the wrist [Plate 28] being used with or without a proper glove;—or the tab, a piece of flat leather into which the fingers are let and which lies on the inside of the hand.

The leather for all these is dressed on that side which is used outwardly.

The *grease-box* hangs by the side of the tassel; and the grease contained in it, suet and bees'-wax in equal quantities, is to soften the fingers of the glove, and facilitate loosing. Women are advised as follows

Clothes should be made of strong materials, not so expensive as to make it of consequence if they should be spoilt in exercise. They should not be so tight as to constrain the motions, nor so large as to embarrass by their loose-ness. They should contain nothing capable of hurting. The shoes should be large. No band should confine the body or limbs: the shoulder-straps to stays should be loosened and it is better to wear neither sash, nor garters. Everything that may prevent freedom of action should be rejected.

The Exercise-Stays . . . are absolutely necessary in all exercises of the arms . . . for which they are constructed. Their pressure on every part of the chest is slight, and, by an ingenious contrivance of employing very elastic shoulder-straps, which are of greater length and fixed lower than usual, and which also play freely in the lateral direction under a transverse band on the back of the stays, the most perfect freedom of motion is ensured.

See Fig. 120.

Surtees's description in *Jorrocks's Jaunts and Jollities* of the gay James Green's archery costume, is probably fancy, but it is worth quoting:

His curly flaxen wig projected over his forehead like the roof of a Swiss cottage and his pointed gills were supported by a stiff black mohair stock, with a broad front and black frill confined with jet studs down the centre. His coat was light green with archery buttons, made very wide at the hips with which he sported a white waistcoat, bright yellow ochre leather trousers, pink silk stockings and patent leather pumps. (1831–4).

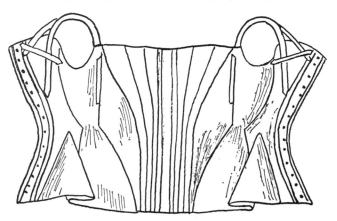

120. The Geary exercise stays worn for archery by women. 1837.

We are given a graphic description of lady archers in 1864 by a writer in *London Society*.

The bevy of fair dames [archeresses] engaged in the most graceful pastime . . . Ballroom costume was never so attractive and fascinating. What constitutes its peculiar charm . . . a Regent Street modiste might fail to tell. But it is charming. I, feeling myself quite incompetent to describe adequately the effect produced, . . . say nothing of the dainty scarfs and the wicked little hats which are decked with green leaves and set in a most provokingly coquettish way over neatly braided hair. Then there are the belts; what lady does not a waist-belt become . . . The costume of an archeress is all-important. Not only does it most materially affect the pageant, which from a spectator's point of view is a great matter, but it very nearly concerns the shooter. Hence have arisen the numerous attempts made by societies to adopt a distinctive costume . . . But a standard of grace cannot be fixed, and now ladies are left to follow their own taste, and the result is far more pleasant than any uniformity could be. "A good and practised archeress," says a lady, who is one herself, "knows that there must not be a string, a ribbon or a long curl, or a flying feather in the way of either bow or arrow." The same authority declares large crinolines to be very uncomfortable, and those who remember the whimsical effect produced at an important meeting a year or two ago, will readily endorse the assertion. It happened that the day of competition, on the occasion referred to, was tempestuous. The ladies—many of them with reluctance be it said—had adopted the prevailing fashion, and appeared in the archery field with an exuberance of skirt. Boreas did not neglect the opportunity, and the wind came sweeping over the ground, causing the skirts to touch the bows, and this occurring at the moment of loosing, made many an arrow from the bow of a clever archeress

"Be short—gone—and on either side, wide."

Not only were there the cases in which the bow was actually turned aside, but the fear that it would so unsettle the shooters, and promised to make the meeting very unsatisfactory, till a lady, more careful of her fame as an archeress, than of her appearance at the moment, very wisely made use of her cord, as captain of a target, to tie in the skirts of her dress. And then scarfs, and sashes and cords were impressed into the same service, and there was a field full of ladies whose skirts are said to have presented the novel appearance of so many sacks of flour tied in at the middle. But the reputations of the shooters were saved, and good scores, for a windy day, were made.

London Society, 1864.

Thus in spite of the difficulties involved in wearing unpractical clothes, fashion prevailed and ladies faced their targets dressed in the style of their day, knowing only too well that pretty dresses would attract and please the spectators (Plate 28(b)).

What causes young people . . . to wear Lincoln Green *toxophilite* hats and feathers, but that they may bring down some "desirable" young man with those killing bows and arrows of theirs?

W. M. Thackeray, *Vanity Fair*, 1848.

Bibliography

Ascham, Roger. *Toxophilus or the Schole of Shooting.* ed. by W. Aldis Wright, Cambridge, 1904 (first publ. 1545).
Burke, Edmund. *Archery Handbook.* Greenwich, Pawcett Pubns. 1954.
Ford, H. A. *Archery.* London, 1887.
Walrond, H. *Archery in Shakespeare's England* . . . ed. by Sir Sidney Lee and C. T. Onions, Oxford, Clarendon Press, 1916.

HAWKING AND SHOOTING

BY ALAN MANSFIELD

Of shooting then, let us partake;
What pastime is so pleasant?
The partridge gone, we'll change each gun,
And so proceed to pheasant.   Anon. Eighteenth Century.

The invention of gunpowder placed in the hands of the sportsman, as in those of the soldier, a deadlier weapon than hitherto available. Before the advent of the hand gun and its application to the chase, bows and arrows, cross-bows, and trained hawks were the methods most in favour for bringing down game birds and small ground game; even after this invasion of the quiet country-side by villainous saltpetre there were diehards who clung to the old ways. These conservatives may have felt that the new-fangled weapons were un-gentlemanlike and unsporting, or more practically, have preferred the old, tried ways to the erratic performance of the early firearms and ammunition. By the end of the seventeenth century, however, fowling-pieces had replaced falcons, and, apart from a dedicated minority, from that time onward the common reaction to the word "Hawking" was that of the Cockney visiting an Art Gallery who, pausing before a painting bearing that title, was heard to mutter "Gor'—wot abaht riding round on 'orseback flogging ruddy parrots for a living."

Falconry in the sixteenth century had, then, its greatest days and a long tradition behind it, but the dress of the contemporary hawker did not owe any more to fitness of purpose than did any other "sports" costume of that day. The elaborate clothes worn by both Queen Elizabeth I and her attendants (Fig. 121) contrasts strongly with the coat-hardie of the earlier, albeit humbler falconer of the Luttrel Psalter (Fig. 122). The only practical items are the glove, and bag or puch; both of which are common to the sport from medieval to modern times.

The glove, a gauntlet, was worn upon the left hand and afforded a perch for the bird, protecting the wearer from the hawk's talons. In training, the

121. Queen Elizabeth hawking. 1575.

birds were fed with a gloved hand. In early days, as in later, the glove was a simple and workmanlike affair (Fig. 122), but during the sixteenth and seventeenth centuries decorative features are noticeable: tassels were usual, hanging from the lower point of the gauntlet (Figs. 123, 124).

> . . . thick, strong leather glove, with a Button and Tassell at the lower part of it, on which he carrieth his Hawk to secure his hand from her Tallons.
>
> Randle Holme, *Academy of Armoury*, 1688.

The bag or pouch, worn at the girdle or belt, was used to carry the objects necessary to the sport—hood, leashes, etc. (Figs. 123, 124). It resembled, in

somewhat larger form, the pouch normally worn by men before the introduction of pockets in trunk hose and breeches (Fig. 125).

The pouch might be made of leather or silk, and was often decorated by
embroidery and, generally, by a fringe and, or, tassels. The method of closure
was a draw-string, also generally tasselled.

122. Hawking in the 14th century. Falconer's glove of a simple type.

The seventeenth-century falconers started the century clad in garments
similar to those of the preceding age (Fig. 124), but by the fourth quarter of
the century had changed as fashions changed, and had also taken to more workmanlike clothes generally, though it must be noted that with the advent of
Barlow and the other sporting artists, ordinary country squires and their
attendants began to be depicted at their sports, in contradistinction from the
Royalty and courtiers of Tudor days.

Plain coats, or jumps were worn, with knee breeches, stockings and shoes,
if on foot, or with boots and breeches if mounted. The usual head-wear was a
round hat, wide in the brim, which was cocked at one side, sometimes with

a bunch of ribbons. The pouch was now slung across one shoulder, not from a waist girdle (Figs. 126, 128).

The decline of falconry during the eighteenth century was such that in 1814 it was said:

> It is much to be regretted, at least by the sporting world, that this, one of the noblest and most pleasing of field sports, which calls into action the various powers of the horse, the dog, and the bird of prey, should in this age be discontinued. We believe that Yorkshire is the last county in England which has been the scene of this diversion.
>
> *Costume of Yorkshire,* 1814.

123. Falconer's glove and pouch. 1575.

This, perhaps, was too sweeping a statement, for it is reasonable to believe that the sport lingered on in more than one corner of the country despite the improvement of the fowling-piece during the century: indeed Osbaldeston in *The British Sportsman* published in 1792 devotes some space to it.

Sporting artists did not paint many hawking scenes, which held less appeal than the popular hunting and shooting prints; but the Romantic Revival of the early nineteenth century, with its renewal of interest in the "medieval", including falconry, led a number of painters to execute and publish views of the ancient sport as practised in contemporary fashionable circles.

The 1814 illustration to the *Costume of Yorkshire* shows a hawker on a horse, wearing a scarlet coat with green collar and cuffs, white breeches and a small round hat with a yellow band with a brace of feathers. The dismounted servants wear green coats and red waistcoats, and breeches with long gaiters.

124. Hawking: elaborately decorated glove and pouch. 1608.

Hawking by Henry Alken, published in 1820, shows a woman and several men on horseback. The mounted falconer wears a frock-coat, white round hat and long gaiters to the thighs: the gaiters are buttoned up the outside of the leg. Another mounted man wears morning-coat, black round hat, breeches and jockey boots. The lady is resplendent in a blue, high-waisted, riding dress with a décolletée neckline, and a small close-fitting hat decorated with such an enormous pair of bird's wings that one fears for her fate at the talons of the various hawks gyrating in the sky above her.

A servant in long gaiters, frock-coat and black top-hat carries a selection of hawks on a round perch slung from his shoulders on cross-over straps and encircling his waist. The mounted falconer wears a small pouch over the left shoulder: a foot attendant carries a large game-bag in a similar manner.

125. Pouch or bag, used before introduction of pockets. See text. *c.* 1530.

The costume (in every sense of the word) of the Duke of St Alban's, Hereditary Grand Falconer, at the Coronation of King George IV in 1821 can hardly be considered as typical, practical or sporting in the true sense of the word. It included plumed hat, green silk "tights", suede boots, and a symbolic glove. This confection in the Gothic taste is now in the Bath Museum of Costume.

In 1839 green coats were worn by hawkers and their servants, though the latter wore gaiters and the mounted gentlemen breeches and boots. Top-hats were general, with one servant in a peaked cap. Pouches are plain or tasselled at the lower corners, and a flap has superseded the draw-string. The falconer's glove is a plain white gauntlet (Plate 29).

The circular perches described above in the early nineteenth century re-placed the simpler straight perch of earlier days:

> Pearch = cross piece of wood or such like, lapt about with cloath or a straw
> robe; on which the Hawk rests when she is off the Falconer's fist.
>
> Randle Holme, op cit.

126. Falconer: doublet and breeches.
Early 17th century.

With the advance of the century hawking again receded in popularity and those sportsmen indulging in it dressed themselves in the increasingly sober taste of the day, the traditional pouch and glove remaining in varying degrees of elaboration.

The dress of bowmen is described in the Chapter on Archery, though for target practice as distinct from shooting game the archer tended to dress himself in more elegant clothes—nevertheless King Henry VIII on May Day, 1510, is said to have gone shooting in the woods, he and his gentlemen dressed

127. Hawking on horseback: "jump", lure (artificial bait to retrieve bird) slung over shoulder. 1686.

128. Hawking on foot: "jump", breeches, stockings, "sash" garters. 1670.

in white satin. Randle Holme gives us a picture of a seventeenth-century "Forester":

all in green with his steel bow on his right shoulder . . .

Ibid.

(Fig. 129.)

129. Forester with cross bow. Green doublet and breeches. Early 17th century.

Green seems to have been the accepted uniform for bowmen, as it is for foresters and shooters on the Continent today.

Shooters in this country did not bind themselves to the traditional colour of their bow-bearing predecessors, despite its associations and protective camouflage.

The sixteenth-century sportsmen who went out with their guns were most probably clad in doublet, hose or breeches, and with startups on their feet. These last were a variety of stout shoes and were certainly used for hawking at this time.

> For a payre of startups to hawke in.
>> Petre Archives (Essex Record Office), 1569.

130. Shooter: long skirted doublet: Venetians: See text, *c.* 1630.

Sir Thomas Southwell of Norfolk was painted in about 1630 with a retriever-like dog and an immense gun. He wears a plain, long-skirted doublet, wide lace falling-band and lace turned-up cuffs, Venetians (a wide knee breeches) and long boots with lace-topped boot-hose.

At his right side is a bag with draw-strings, and tassels on its lower corners, reminiscent of the falconer's pouch: on the other side of his belt is a shot or powder horn (Fig. 130).

In 1686 Francis Barlow depicted two men on horses "Shooting flying." Their guns are lighter than that of a half century earlier and they wear jumps, breeches and high boots, and round hats (Fig. 131). One carries a bag slung over the right shoulder, the other a falchion likewise. One of the hats has a bunch of ribbons in front and the brim turned up and buttoned at the back.

The shooter of the early 1700s wore the fashionable coat, with pockets low in the skirt, knee-breeches and shoes. The pouch or bag was on a waist belt, and powder flask slung (Fig. 132).

131. Mounted shooter: "jump" round hat, Falchion slung over shoulder. Foot man with pouch slung. 1686.

From about 1730 the frock, with its small turn-down collar, often of a contrasting colour, replaced the coat in the field (Plate 30). Colours were varied, brown, grey, blue, and red were popular. Double-breasted frocks were worn from about the middle of the century; and jackets, a hip-length coat with short side and back vents,

> a sort of garment in use among Country People,
>   Phillips *World of Words*, 1708.

also gained favour with the sportsman by the end of the century:

> To a shooting jacket £1. 10.—   Kent Record Office, 1798.

Breeches and stockings were the normal leg wear. In the first half of the century the stockings were generally rolled up over the breeches, but from about 1735 it was increasingly fashionable for breeches to be buckled or tied below the knee over the stockings. Shoes or calf-length laced boots known as "highlows" (Plate 30) were usual, although top-boots were sometimes worn.

132. Shooter: long coat with low-set pockets: breeches tied over stockings (a countryman's fashion at this date) shot pouch on waist belt: powder flask slung. Early 18th century.

Spatterdashes, or long gaiters, made of canvas or leather and fastened on the outside of the leg with laces, buttons, or buckles, were an added protection for the feet and legs, sometimes adopted by shooters (Fig. 133).

Round hats, generally uncocked, though sometimes turned up at the back were general, although the three-cornered cocked hat is sometimes seen. The round hat often had a bow or bunch of ribbon at the front.

Powder and shot flasks or horns were slung from the shoulder; and perhaps a bag or pouch, though this could also be worn on a waist belt, sometimes underneath the frock.

The frock might be made of cloth, fustian, serge, etc., and breeches of similar material.

In the early days of the nineteenth century the frock became more skimpy and the skirts cut away into "tails" (Fig. 133); at the same time the jacket gained popularity, as did the spatterdashes or gaiters:

> Many gentlemen in their morning walks have attempted to introduce a sort of shooting dress, parading in a short coat of any light colour, and with drab coloured cloth or Kerseymere gaiters coming up to the knees. . . .
>
> *Beau Monde*, 1807.

133. Shooter: sporting frock with front skirts sharply sloping away: round hat: spatterdashes. *c.* 1800.

The French Revolution and the wars of the late eighteenth and early nineteenth century allied to the influence of George Brummel produced a profound change in male fashions in England and one result of this was the emergence of a definite style and specialized garments for the sportsman. By the second decade of the century the shooter sallied out in workmanlike garments, spoilt only by the universal top-hat: although as early as 1802 the Rev. W. B. Daniel had warned wild fowlers that:

> a cap must be worn made of skin, instead of a hat; the fowl will not approach near the latter, and nothing so much or so soon shies them.
>
> W. B. Daniel, *Rural Sports*, 1802.

This same sporting parson also advises warm clothes,

> flannel shirt, drawers, and additional exterior and warm garments . . . thick
> yarn stockings, and over them what is termed *wads* by the Fishermen (*knit
> stockings* that come up to the middle, and, however inelegant in their
> appearance have their solid comforts to the wearer); and over these double
> defenders of the *legs*, a pair of waterproof *boots* will also be found indispen-
> sable.
>
> Ibid.

To make boots waterproof a receipt of the late Dean of Exeter's is given:

> If the *Boots* are new, half a pound of *Bee's Wax*, a quarter of a pound of
> *Resin*, and the like quantity of *Mutton Suet* or *Tallow*; boil them up together,
> and anoint the *Boots* well with the preparation lukewarm. Should the *Boots*
> have been used, *Beef Suet* is to be substituted for the *Mutton*.
>
> Ibid.

Wild fowling in estuaries and coastal marshes has always produced dangers
and discomforts unknown to the dry land shooter—not the least hazard being
that of sticking fast in the Essex or Hampshire mud flats. To assist his passage
across the mud the wild fowler

> . . . immediately puts on his *mud-pattens* (flat square pieces of board which
> the fowler ties to his feet, that he may not sink in the Ooze) . . .
>
> Ibid.

Henry Alken depicts a sportsman wearing just such mud pattens (or
"splashers" or "Mersea pattens" as the Essex fisherman calls them) (Plate 31),
and a modern pair is to be seen in Plate 32. In 1857 "Stonehenge" describes
them as:

> . . . a pair of mud boards, from 12″ to 16″ square, which are securely
> fastened to the ankles, when wanted, as follows:—Put the foot between the
> two loops with the heel against the loose line that is attached to both: then
> cross the line over the instep, and pass it under the loop, on each side, when
> bring it back to the instep again and tie.
>
> "Stonehenge", *Manual of British Rural Sports*, 1857.

The white night-cap and shirt of the man in the gun-punt in Alken's
picture is in contrast to the advice on dress given by Parson Daniel, and
accords more with John Mytton's habits:

He would sometimes strip to his shirt to follow wild fowl in hard weather, and once actually laid himself down on the snow in his shirt only to wait their arrival at dusk.

Nimrod, The Life of John Mytton, 1837.

But Daniel is vindicated, for

Dame Nature took offence at this and chastised him rather severely for his daring.

Ibid.

However, Mytton was hardly the type of the well dressed sportsman, for on one occasion he

followed some ducks "in puris naturalibus"—anglice, stark-naked—on the ice, and escaped with perfect impunity.

Ibid.

And we are told that his "winter shooting wear was a light jacket, white linen trousers, without lining or drawers, of which he knew not the use. . . ."

134. Shooter: jacket, pantaloons, hessian boots. *c.* 1831.

That other great sportsman, albeit a fictional one, John Jorrocks, dressed more appropriately:

Settling himself into a new spruce green cut-away gambroon[1] butler's pantry-jacket, with pockets equal to holding a powder-flask each, his lower man being attired in tight drab stocking-net pantaloons and Hessian boots with large tassels (Fig. 134).

R. S. Surtees, Jorrocks' Jaunts and Jollities. 1843
(though written 1831–4).

[1] Gambroon was a worsted and cotton mixture.

In the 1830s peaked caps were sometimes worn, and rather feminine looking straw-hats with a large ribbon bow, generally blue or red (Plate 34).

During most of the first half of the nineteenth century powder flasks were carried in the pocket and the shot in shoulder belts, which also often carried a dog whistle.

As well as a pocket for the powder flask another was provided for percussion caps, and two large "hare" (later known as "poacher's") pockets in the skirt linings.

In the 1850s jackets and trousers of waterproof material were worn, the trousers sometimes made tight in the lower leg and buttoned round the boots.

"Macintosh inventions" however were not recommended as they retained the perspiration. For grouse shooting "Stonehenge" recommends plain Scotch tweeds for jacket and trousers and waistcoat of heather pattern. In addition a flannel waistcoat and drawers and worsted stockings and waterproof cow-hide boots are necessary. The coat is to have leather patches on the shoulders and

> an outside pocket on the left side, for the shot pouch, and a similar one on the right side for the powder flask and wadding: a small pocket on each side above these, will contain the cap holder on the right side and the nipple-wrench on the left. You will not require any game-pocket, because, at the grouse season, no game will bear the heat of the body, without becoming speedily tainted.
>
> "Stonehenge", op cit.

"Stonehenge's" recipe for waterproofing boots is

Boiled linseed oil　1½ lbs.
Yellow wax　　　　3 oz.
Canada balsam　　1 oz.,

mixed over a slow fire and rubbed in alternately with neats foot oil.

The efficacy of these preservative measures is vouched for by "Craven":

> An old sporting associate . . . showed me a pair of shooting shoes, for which he paid Hoby two guineas, that he has had in constant work for sixteen years! No record has been preserved of the number of times they have had new bottoms.
>
> *Walker's Manly Exercises*, 1839.

PLATE 29

Hawking: tall top-hats. Servant in cap and long gaiters. 1839.

*Engraving by R. G. Reeve after F. C. Turner, "Disgorging". Photograph
by courtesy of Parker Gallery.*

PLATE 30

Shooting: left-hand figure in short sporting frock, brown:
"highlows": round hat. Right-hand figure in long grey frock:
"highlows": hat trimmed green bow. 1763.

*Arthur Devis, "The Shoot at Tabley Park". 1763. By courtesy of Messrs
Leggatt Bros.*

The "plain Scotch tweeds" above contrast strongly with this description of a young man's costume about 1850:

> . . . a shooting jacket . . . its waist, being prolonged to a strange and un-
> accountable extent had . . . invaded the region of the skirt . . . this
> wonderful garment . . . embracing all the tints of the rainbow, and a few
> more besides . . . embellished by a plentiful supply of gent's sporting
> buttons . . . not quite so large as cheese-plates, and represented in bas-
> relief a series of moving incidents by flood and field. His nether man exhibited
> a complicated arrangement of corduroys, leather gaiters, and waterproof
> boots . . . his head was adorned with one of those round felt hats, which
> exactly resemble a boiled apple-pudding and are known by the sobriquet of
> "wide-awakes". . . .

> Frank Smedley, *Frank Fairlegh*, 1850.

In the early 1850s large checked trousers also brightened the shooting scene (Fig. 135).

135. Shooting in top hat and loud trousers.
1852.

In 1858 the shooting costume consisted of

> a light single breasted jacket, cut in the same style as worn in the country on
> other occasions . . . breeches reaching to the calf, easy on the thigh, and

long gaiters buttoning at the side, and fastened under the knee with a strap and buckle.

Minster's Gazette of Fashion, 1858.

There seemed to be some danger in wearing gaiters despite their popularity, at the hands of some, perhaps unskilled shots, who mistook them in the under-growth for their legitimate target

under the same hare delusion which made Professor Sedgwick fire fourteen times in one afternoon at a keeper's gaiters.

"The Druid", Post and Paddock, 1856.

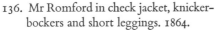

136. Mr Romford in check jacket, knicker-bockers and short leggings. 1864.

137. Shooter in trousers and short leggings: top hat. 1860.

Occasionally "overalls" in the form of light-weight material trousers, buttoning up the sides, were worn over normal trousers. Short gaiters, or spats, could be worn under the trousers and over the boot.

Knickerbockers, introduced about 1860, became popular with shooters. The knickerbockers were loose breeches with the legs gathered into a knee-band which buckled below the knee, and were well adapted to the uses of country pursuits (Fig. 136). A variety of head-wear was to be seen, and the top-hat still had its place (Fig. 137) as well as the bonnets adopted by those whole-hearted English who clad in appropriate local dress, went to Scotland to pursue the stag and grouse.

Trousers were also worn, sometimes with short ankle gaiters, or spats; such an attire (Fig. 138) was described in 1866 as

might be worn by any quiet dressing gentleman.

Minster's Gazette of Fashion, 1866.

138. A "quiet dressing gentleman". See text. 1866.

The Norfolk shirt, or blouse, a forerunner of the Norfolk jacket, was introduced in the mid-sixties and was sometimes worn with knickerbockers for shooting. It was a short jacket with a box-pleat down the back and one down each side of the front: it had a belt of the same material.

In the 1870s the Norfolk shirt, single- or double-breasted jackets with side or back vents, and a morning-coat style shooting coat were all popular. Breeches or knickerbockers with stockings and gaiters at one end were complemented by bowler-hats, cloth helmets and deer-stalkers at the other (Fig. 144).

The evolution of the modern breech-loading shot-gun during the years 1867/73 had obviated the necessity of the powder flask and separate shot container. Cartridges were carried in the pockets or in a leather or canvas cartridge bag.

139. Shooting coat with leather patches reinforcing shoulders, knickerbockers, long laced boots. 1880.

The general style of shooting coats that had developed by the 1880s (Fig. 139) persisted through the 1890s, made in tweeds and stout cloths. Knickerbockers and stockings with calf-length leather or canvas gaiters or canvas spats were the usual leg wear, but breeches might be worn. The range of head-gear was widened by the introduction of the Homburg and trilby hats and by the soft cloth cap with peak (Fig. 140). For protection from the weather large and voluminous Inverness capes were popular.

In 1905 an alternative to the Inverness was offered in the form of the "Balmacaan" Conduit Coat which was claimed

> an ideal sporting coat for shooting, racing, etc. as it gives perfect freedom in any position. It is made from real undyed Harris, Donegal and Kenmore hand woven tweeds.
>
> Advertisement, 1905.

The coat or jacket of the pre-1914 years followed generally the fashionable line of the day, the front fastening less high to the neck as the twentieth century advanced. Knickerbockers or breeches continued in favour, sometimes with puttees replacing or supplementing stockings and spats:

Shaped to wind on spirally from ankle to knee without any turns or twists . . . For ladies and children, light weight with spats 7/6 per pair. Without spats 5/- per pair . . . For men with spats from 10/6 to 12/- per pair . . . Without spats, from 6/- to 7/6 per pair.

Advertisement, Fox Bros & Co. 1905.

140. Shooter: tweed cap, jacket, breeches and stockings. 1897.

141. Sporting gent. 1911.

As in all ages the enthusiastic newcomer tended to overdress the part as the sketch of 1911 indicates (Fig. 141) even wearing shooting kit for a country walk, a habit we have seen recorded a century earlier. On the other hand at the end of our period the rough-shooter was arrayed much as Mr Punch's cartoon of 1916 showed John Bull in action (Fig. 142).

Women did not take to the gun as eagerly as they did to the saddle, and it is the late nineteenth century before they became active members of shooting parties in any numbers. In earlier days their participation was limited to joining the guns for lunch, or accompanying them for part of the day as spectators.

142. Shooter: soft felt hat: knitted waistcoat or cardigan: cartridge belt round waist.

The Duchess of Marlborough, however, was a pioneer in the field and in 1846

brought down eight head of game with her own gun.

Aylesbury News, quoted in *Punch,* November, 1846.

In commemoration of this feat Mr Punch presented his design for a lady's shooting costume (Fig. 143). As is so often the case fact followed fiction and in 1847 the Duchess of Montrose when out with the guns

. . . wears plaid trousers and a short petticoat [skirt] about half way down below her knees.

Edmund Stanley, letter to his wife, quoted in Alison Adburgham,

Shops & Shopping, 1964.

143. "Sporting for ladies". See text. 1846.

Both these outfits bear a striking resemblance to that which some years later acquired fame, or notoriety, in association with Mrs Amelia Jenks Bloomer.

For their excursions with shooting parties the ladies of the mid-nineteenth century shortened their skirts, a fashion much appreciated by their men folk, for

> I ask you, when do the fair sex look more bewitching than they do after a walk or drive to the luncheon tent. . . . It is on these occasions that the well-turned-out walking-costume, its skirt short enough to prevent its draggling in the mud, treats you to a glimpse of a well-turned ankle and arched instep, and, perchance, the well-developed limb that keeps the stockings from wrinkling. . . .
>
> Sir John Astley, *Fifty Years of my Life*, 1894.

The tailor-made costume, advertised first in about 1873, rapidly gained favour and a lady shooter of 1879 dressed in a version with a straight ankle-length skirt and Norfolk blouse (Fig. 144). By 1882 the short skirt to the knees with knickerbockers, and gaiters, was again in fashion, worn with a Norfolk jacket.

In 1890

> those gowns intended for hard wear, have no foundation at all, so that they have little weight—the most comfortable kind of skirt that can be had for shooting on Scotch moors.
>
> *Cassell's Family Magazine*, 1890.

144. She in Norfolk blouse and short skirt with tweed hat: he in
knickerbocker suit and tweed helmet. 1879.

The foundation was a waist-length flounced petticoat attached to the skirt
at the waist.

Leather was used for trimming to collar and cuffs and a strip of it was
often attached to the bottom of the skirt, which was again in the 1890s ankle
length. Deerstalker hats, waist belts, and cartridge bags were to be seen (Fig.
145).

In 1902 the bolero, introduced in the 1890s, was sometimes worn closed,
and found its way on to the moors (Fig. 146), although the Norfolk jacket was
still in vogue:

> If you intend to walk with the guns you must have a properly made tweed
> Norfolk coat and short skirt with regulation pockets, and sensible boots. . . .
>
> Mrs Eric Pritchard, *The Cult of Chiffon*, 1902.

Throughout the 1890s and early years of the twentieth century a waistcoat
was worn with the shooting coat and skirt.

The use of leather trimmings persisted. In 1906 a coat, skirt and waistcoat
was described as:

PLATE 31

Wildfowling: frock-coat, long gaiters, top-hat: mud-pattens. (See text.)
c. 1820–30.

Henry Alken, aquatint "A signal of Distress".

PLATE 32

(a) "Mersea Pattens." 20th century.

The Author's Collection.

(b) Shooting: shooting-coats: short and long leggings: top-boots: top-hats: straw hat with blue ribbon and bow. 1830.

H. Alken, lithograph "I have a strong idea we shall hit something this time". 1830. Photograph by courtesy of University of London Library.

A gown for the Moors. This is the dress for hard wear built in firm tweed, faced up and trimmed with leather.

Advertisement, 1906.

145. Lady shooter: deerstalker; Norfolk jacket: cartridge or game bag. 1890.

146. Shooting dress of bolero-type jacket and skirt: buttoned gaiters: felt hat with feathers: short skirt. 1902.

147. Ladies on the moors; one in Norfolk jacket, the other in knitted cardigan and leather edged skirt. 1914.

The uncompromising flavour of "built in firm tweed" contrasts strongly with the "extravagant frou-frou of frills" of the drawing-rooms of the same period. The sportswoman had in shooting, as in other sports and pastimes, adopted the masculine style that she considered a proper tribute to the male world which she was invading. As illustrated in 1905, a very long, almost knee length coat appears with an ankle-length skirt, shirt, collar and tie, and a flat, peaked cloth cap. A trilby or Homburg hat with a small feather was an alternative head-gear. The cardigan which started as a male garment was to be seen on the woman shooter by 1914 (Fig. 147).

Bibliography

Blome, R. *The Gentleman's Recreation*, 1686.
Cunnington, C. W. and P. *Handbook of English Costume in the Nineteenth Century*. Faber and Faber. 2nd ed., 1966.
"Stonehenge". *Manual of British Rural Sports*. 1857.
Turberville, G. *The Booke of Falconrie*. 1575.

CHAPTER 12

ANGLING

BY PHILLIS CUNNINGTON

> Of recreation there is none
>   So free as fishing is alone;
> All other pastimes do no less
>   Than mind and body both possess;
>   My hand alone my work can do
>   So I can fish and study too.
>
>   The Angler's Song, 3rd verse, in Izaak Walton's
>   *The Compleat Angler*, 1653.

Angling, or catching fish with "a rod, a line and a hook" is a very ancient practice. An Egyptian wall painting of a rod fisherman dates back to 2000 B.C.

Many references to fishing occur in the Bible, but these fishermen were not, of course, angling for sport but "for bread".

> The fishers also shall mourn, and all they that cast angle into the brooks shall lament and they that spread nets upon the waters shall languish.
>
>   *Isaiah,* 19:8.

Fishing as a sport was practised in England during the late fifteenth century (Fig. 148), and it became popular with Tudor Englishmen in the sixteenth, when it was also encouraged by the University authorities (Fig. 149). The development of angling as a sport in the seventeenth century in Britain was probably due to the influence of Isaac Walton. A contemporary of his, Richard Frank, was the first to describe an angling holiday. In 1614 Gervase Markham had this to say concerning suitable clothes for anglers:

Angler's Apparell

Touching the Angler's apparell (for it is a respect as necessary as any other whatsoever) it would by no means be garrish, light coloured, or shining, for whatever with a glittering here reflecteth upon the water, immediately it frighteth the Fish, and maketh them flye from his presence, no hunger being able to tempt them to bite, when their eye is offended . . .

⸿ Here begynnyth the treatyse of fysshynge wyth an Angle.

148. Long-skirted jacket typical of 15th century country wear. Long
hose, shoes, large hat, probably straw.

Let your apparell be plaine and comely, of *dark colour,* as Russet, Tawny
or such like, close to your body without any new fashioned slashes, or
hanging sleeves waving loose like sayles about you, for they are like Blinks[1]
which will ever chase your game farre from you: let it for your owne health
and ease sake, be warme and well lyned, that neither coldnesse of the ayre,
nor the moystnesse of the water may offend you. Keepe your head and feet
drye, for from the offence of them springeth Agues and worse infirmities.

Gervase Markham, *The Pleasures of Princes
or Good Men's Recreations,* 1614.

The warning against "garrish" wear was repeated in the eighteenth century

---

[1] Feathers etc. on a string, for scaring birds.

The Angler's clothes should be of a grave dark colour, and not bright and glaring, for that would fright away the Fish.

> R. Brookes, *The Art of Angling*, 1740.

This warning is repeated yet once more in 1802, as will be seen.

149. Jerkin and sleeved cloak, for warmth. Long-skirted jerkin. Both wear Venetians (i.e. breeches) first introduced *c.* 1570, and probably "littell felts lyned with vellett" on their heads.

How to keep the feet dry when wading was a serious problem, since the invention of rubber boots did not come to the rescue before the nineteenth century.

> In small Brooks you may angle upwards [upstream] or else in great Rivers you must wade as I have known some who thereby got Sciatica, and I would not wish you to purchase pleasure at so dear a rate.
>
> Col. R. Venables, *The Experienced Angler*, 1662.

Thomas Barker in *The Art of Angling* in 1659 has the following advice to give:

> I have a willing mind with God's help to preserve all those that love this recreation to go dry in their boots and shoes, to preserve their healths, which one receit is worth much more than this book will cost.

First, they must take a pint of Linseed oyle, with half a pound of mutton fat, six or eight ounces of bees wax, and half a penniworth of rosin, boyle all this in a pipkin together, so let it coole untill it be milk warm then take a little hairbrush and lay it on your new boots; but it's best that this stuff be laid on before the boot maker makes the boots, then brush them once over after they come from him; as for old boots you must lay it on when your boots be dry.

150. "The honest labouring swaine" in doublet, sleeves with wings, small ruff, and on his head a cap, usually called a night cap, though worn for comfort by day. He wears full breeches with a pocket. 1620–30.

Protective rubber boots for wading came into use after the invention of rubber galoshes in the 1830s, but although these rubber waders were ideal, fishermen were slow to adopt them until the end of the nineteenth century. Rubber boots were advertised in the 1890s.

A woodcut of 1850 after Edward Duncan, reproduced in Sparrow's *Angling in Art* shows an angler wearing waders which reach well above the knee and are fastened to his belt by a front strap. These waders however were probably of leather.

The same author in his book *Angling in British Art*, writes about Francis Barlow's work in 1666–71. Referring to a plate on "Salmon Fishing" he says:

> Three of the fishermen have wading boots but the tops do not protect enough of the thigh. They cover the knees somewhat flappily, leaving abundant space wherein the knees can bend. Though useless for deepish wading they enable us to see that if these boots were water proof, Walton might have been a wader had he wished to throw a fly from a shallow place in a river.

As regards another plate he says:

> It has been said that several of the figures are too well dressed for sport . . . There is no need for us to suppose any such thing.

In Plate 33 the figure on the left is dressed in the height of fashion. He wears a long loose coat with elbow-length sleeves and turned back cuffs. The bunch of ribbon loops known as a shoulder-knot was a favourite ornament at this time.

> I admire the mode of your shoulder-knot, methinks it hangs very emphatically and carries an air of travel in it.
>
> G. Farquhar, *The Constant Couple*, 1699.

His hat, wig and be-ribboned garters and shoes are also *à la mode*. The other men, probably attendants, wear short out-door jackets known as jumps,[1] and knee breeches tied below the knee.

Fishing in the eighteenth century was also enjoyed by women, despite their fashionable clothes. It could be undertaken leisurely and "force" was not necessary. James Saunders in his book *Complete Fisherman* 1724 states:

> Fresh water or River fishing and more particularly that part of it which we rightly call Sport viz. Angling; which as 'tis chiefly the diversion of the ingenious, so it must be acknowledged, that it is a most ingenious diversion. . . . Force is of no use in this War, for the fish are so swift in their motions, so sharp sighted, so shy, and have such secure retreats that . . . nothing but stratagem can bring them to land . . .

---

[1] "A jacket, jump or loose coat reaching to the thighs, buttoned down before, open or slit up behind halfway with sleeves to the wrist." R. Holme, *Armory*, 1688.

151. Ladies in sack-backed gowns. 1760–70.

Saunders goes on to say that an angler "is one that does not angle as a trade . . . or for his Bread, but for sport", and a sport that can only be enjoyed by "a man of leisure", but alas, not as old age approaches.

> The sport of angling . . . never abates; but after sixty much less at seventy the Banks of Rivers and low Meadows and unwholesome marshes, begin to be too damp, too aguish, too cold for the gentlemen to sit close to their sport, or to hold it too long at a time; so they begin to decline the old tracks and haunt the Barble Hole or the Trout Stream no longer, or at least but a little and that in fine Weather.

PLATE 33

Gentleman angler in the height of fashion; other man wearing "jumps". 1671.

From The Severall Wayes of Hunting, Hawking and Fishing According to the English Manner. *Etched by Hollar after F. Barlow.*

PLATE 34

Men and Women anglers all dressed in the fashion of their day. 1788.

After George Morland, engraved in mezzotint by G. Keating. 1788.

The antient sportsmen thus by Necessity of Constitution and Infirmity of Age, dropping off from the Sport, the young anglers are destitute of good Direction.

Anglers of any age, however, appear to have enjoyed the sport (Fig. 152).

152. Fashionable gentlemen, two wearing bicorne hats, more usual for riding, at this date. Boy punting, in trousers. 1792.

Parson Woodforde also enjoyed it. In 1781 he wrote in his Diary:

> Called on my Mercer, Mr. Smith and bespoke a Coat, Waistcoat and pr. of Breeches, and a fishing frock.

The frock at this date was an "undress" coat for morning wear with a turn-down collar.

Fly-fishing was the sport of the aristocracy from the late eighteenth century on. Richard Bowlker writes in *The Art of Angling*, 1758:

> I am now come to the most entertaining and delightful part of the sportsman's diversion, Fly Fishing of which nothing can be said too much in its

recommendation . . . It is the cleanest and neatest that can possibly be imagined, being quite free of the trouble of baiting your hook or fowling your fingers.

The flies were frequently carried by sticking them on to the head-gear. See Plate 35 where the young man is wearing a top-hat, and Fig. 153 where the enraged angler wears a country hat known as a hemispherical or bollinger. The latter was made of firm felt and flies would adhere to this satisfactorily.

153. Man wearing a jacket known as a paletot, trousers and a bollinger hat to which flies adhere. 1858.

The warning against getting the feet wet was also emphasized in the nineteenth century. The Rev. Wm. B. Daniel in his book *Rural Sports*, Vol. II, in 1802, says:

The soles of his shoes should be thick, the leather well seasoned, and now and then rubbed over with Mutton Suet, which will not only keep out the water, but render them soft and pliable.

The Angler's imagination is generally so busied with the hopes of success, that when the distance is considerable, his eagerness influences his pace in

walking and he cannot in warm weather, well avoid being heated before he
arrives at the spot; the air near rivers and pools being cooler than in other
places, occasioned by the motion of the water, *flannel* next the body is
recommended to be worn which will guard against the dangerous con-
sequences of suddenly checked perspiration. Sitting upon the ground, altho'
it appears dry, should be carefully shunned. . . . If the Angler is fishing for
Barbel, Roach and Dace where he is confined to one spot and must sit down,
a piece of coarse woollen cloth doubled two or three times may be carried in
the pannier, and used for this purpose. In common angling never go into the
water without boots that are thoroughly proof against it and in which you
can remain perfectly dry.

154. Angler in short overcoat, breeches and gaiters, carrying the
accessories of his sport. 1830.

An Angler, a century and a half back, must have his *Fishing coat,* which
if not black, was at least a very dark colour, a black velvet cap, like those
which jockeys now wear, only larger, and a Rod with a stock as long as a
Halbert; thus equipped he stalked forth, followed by the eyes of the whole

neighbourhood; but in these later days, *bag* rods have been invented, which the angler may easily convey, so as not to proclaim to everyone he meets where he is going . . . A pocket in the lining of the coat will easily conceal and carry such a (jointed) rod.

155. "I say Jack, are there any fish in the pond?" "There may be, but I should think they were werry small, cause there was no vater in this here pond afore that there rain yesterday." 1834–6.

Tackle

He (angler) will not be without worms . . . in canvas and woollen bags and a larger one for malt or other *ground-bait;* to hold the baits it is far better to have something like a fisherwoman's *apron* with three or four partitions than to dangle the gentle-case or worm bags from a button. A piece of coarse cloth three quarters in length and breadth doubled to within three inches at one side, which three inches must be doubled back again and sewed all along close to the first doubling to receive a belt. The great doubling at each side is then to be sewed up, so that the *foreside* may allow room for the hand to go easily into the pockets, which will be ten inches deep, and when stitched in three places will leave four divisions each four inches broad.

Never angle in glaring clothes, perhaps *green* is that which the fish discern least, as varying less from those objects such as trees and herbage on the sides to which they are familiarized.

The advice given to anglers to wear dark clothes was not always carried out See Plate 36. Here the men are wearing fashionable day clothes of 1831. From left to right (*a*) has a blue coat, white trousers and a black top-hat, (*b*) has a green coat, striped trousers and a white top-hat, (*c*) wears a brown coat, pale blue trousers and black top-hat.

156. Angler wearing an "ugly". 1853.

An angler's requirements are summed up in a song entitled "The Jolly Angler" of 1832;

> We have gentles in our horns
>   We have worms and paste too,
> Great coats we have to stand a storm,
>   Baskets at our waists too.

See Fig. 154.

In spite, however, of the joys of fishing as a sport, there were hazards. The old gentleman in Fig. 155.

157. More hazards of angling. 1852.

158. Angler in check suit and cap. 1856.

Donning his best wig and spectacles he sallied forth, defended from the weather by a short Spencer [a type of overcoat] and a pair of double-soled shoes and short gaiters.

He asked the urchin if there were any fish in the pond.

There may be [was the answer], but I should think they were werry small, cause there vos no water in this here pond afore that there rain yesterday.

159. Introduces rubber waders. 1900.

Anglers by the river-side might be pestered by wasps or flies and this might require a form of protective head-wear often affected by women, but unheard of on a man. This was the "ugly", an extra brim worn over the front of a woman's bonnet as a protection against the sun. It was made up of half hoops of cane covered with silk and when not in use could be folded flat. The lady in the picture does look surprised at what she sees—a man in an ugly! (Fig. 156). The angler in Fig. 157 is so pestered by wasps that he covers his head completely with a large handkerchief. Three boys on the farther bank, however, are wearing uglies. Fig. 158 shows the dangers to spectators. Finally the man in Fig. 159, shows another hazard "when strong language may be excusable". He is dressed perfectly for his sport, a thick overcoat, breeches and strong rubber boots, but:

Well, I'm—! dropped my matchbox into the river, left my flask and chicken sandwiches on the sideboard at home, and I'm a good five miles from anywhere.

The following items for fishermen are advertised in *The Fisherman's Magazine* (Vol. I) of 1864.

Fishing Boots and Stockings, Coats, Capes, Leggings, Fishing Trousers, Petticoats, Ladies Cloaks and every description of waterproof and air-proof covers of best quality.
Edmiston's Waterproofs.
Stout waterproof coats for heavy work, Fishing Stockings, the best that can be made.

Have the people in Fig. 160 availed themselves of any of the above goods?
In 1874 *The Tailor and Cutter* was advising the following for fishing wear:

Coats generally of Scotch Cheviot or tweed. Coat S–B sac with belt. Sometimes has an outside breast pocket but not necessary if bag is carried. Knickerbockers, striped stockings.

160. Fishing in ordinary clothes. 1864.

PLATE 35

Trout Fishing. Young man wearing a top-hat to which the "flies" adhere. *c.* 1840.

Detail of an engraving by A. W. Warren after A. Cooper. The photograph on loan from the Mansell Collection.

PLATE 36

"Bottom Fishing"

Detail from a coloured print, 1831.

Advertisements in 1889 from Edward Kennard's *Fishing in Strange Waters* are given (with illustrations) as follows:

Tarred twill and sateen fishing trousers 31/6—37/6 per pair. Will not get hard. Wading stocking 17/6 per pair.
Waders, socks, Boots fastened by straps and buckles.
Anderson's "Buckland" waders stocking and brogues combined.
The "Buckland" improved waterproof fishing and shooting jacket.
"Test" fishing brogues.

See Fig. 161.

As will be seen in the illustrations women anglers even in the twentieth century dressed in the style of their day, long skirt and all (Fig. 162).

161. Tarred twill and sateen fishing trousers. Waders, stockings and brogues combined. Waders. Waterproof fishing jacket. Fishing brogues. 1889.

How not to dress when fishing is graphically described by W. Henderson in his book *My Life as an Angler*, 1880:

> A fishing trip even appeared to X a favourable opportunity for exercising what he termed a wise economy . . .
>
> "If a fellow may not wear his old clothes on a fishing trip, I should like to know when he may wear them."

162. Tailor-made brown coat. Brown hat, trimmed with bunch of ribbons. 1908.

I must explain that our friend in earlier days hunted the fox. His "wise economy" now dictated to him that the garb which so well became the field was not unsuitable for the flood. So he shone resplendent this summer morning in a bright green coat with velvet collar, gilt buttons, white cord breeches, a purple satin waistcoat figured with gold, well known some years before at many a dinner table, a pair of pale blue worsted stockings and a white hat whose brim was faced with green. But the climax of absurdity was reached in the boots that had seen much service in the chase and were now minus their polished tops.

Perhaps many anglers like those in Fig. 163, would agree in principle with what the *Habits of Good Society* had to say in 1859:

> The less change we make (in dress) the better in the present day, particularly with scrupulous accuracy, we are liable to be subjected to a comparison between our clothes and our skill. A man who wears a red coat to hunt in should be able to hunt, and not sneak through gates . . . A strict accuracy of sporting costume is no longer in good taste, . . . we can dismiss shooting and fishing at once, with the warning that we must not dress *well* for either. An old coat with large pockets, gaiters in one case, and if necessary large boots in the other . . . a wide-awake . . . make up a respectable sportsman.

See Fig. 163.

163. Fishing match on the river Lea. 1875. "The less change we make in dress, the better!"

Bibliography

Barker, Thomas. *Barker's Delight or The Art of Angling,* 2nd edn. Marriott, 1657 (1st edn. 1653).

Briggs, Ernest. *Angling and Art in Scotland.* Longmans Green, 1908.

Brookes, R. *The Art of Angling, Rock and Sea Fishing.* John Watts, 1740.

Howitt, Samuel. *Angler's Manual.* Liverpool, 1808.

Kennard, Edward. *Fishing in Strange Waters.* London, Chapman and Hall, 1889.

Koller, Larry. *The Treasury of Angling.* London, Hamlyn, 1966.

Markham, Gervase. *The Pleasures of Princes,* in *The English Husbandman.* Cresset Press, 1927. (1st publ. 1614).

Sparrow, Walter Shaw. *Angling in British Art through five centuries.* London, John Lane, the Bodley Head, 1923.

Walton, Isaak, and Cotton, Charles. *The Compleat Angler or the Contemplative Man's Recreation.* London, Oxford University Press, 1935 (first publ. 1653).

CHAPTER 13

CYCLING

BY PHILLIS CUNNINGTON

Cycling for pleasure or sport began with the nineteenth century. The early forms from which the bicycle finally developed were crude. The velocipede invented by a Frenchman in 1779 was the first of its kind. It consisted of a wooden bar, rigidly connecting two wooden wheels placed one in front of the other. Handle-bars were fixed to the front wheel and a saddle was fixed to the bar. This machine was propelled by the rider seated astride the bar, pushing against the ground with his feet.

Next came the "draisine" with the front wheel pivoted on the frame so as to be turned from side to side by the handle.

These machines were very popular in England in 1819, when they were also much caricatured and called hobbyhorses, dandy horses, accelerators or bone-shakers. There is a Staffordshire plate in York Castle Museum depicting a "Pedestrian Hobby Horse". The rider wears a tail-coat, trousers with in-step straps, a shirt with a frilled front popularly known as chitterlings, and a top-hat. The date is given as 1825. In a race on velocipedes, called "Modern Olympics" (Plate 37), three dandies are dressed for display. The first has a maroon-coloured tail-coat and blue trousers, the second has a blue coat and buff trousers, while the third wears an orange-coloured coat, white breeches and top-boots with spurs. Spurs at this date were not necessarily part of riding dress, but were worn with walking dress by dandies.

All three of these racing dandies wear fashionable top-hats.

For ladies to attempt riding on a hobby-horse, skirts had to be shortened. See the illustration of "The Ladies' Accelerator", 1819. (Fig. 164).

> Two pretty women run towards each other on velocipedes . . . their short full skirts do not impede their action and they wear long frilled drawers above neat ankle boots. Both are very décolletée; one wears a round cap with feathers and tassell, the other is in an enormous feathered bonnet with flowers under the scoop. The more voluptuous lady says:—"I do not see why ladies shouldn't have a lark as well as the gentlemen."
>
> M. D. George. *English Political Satires.*

In order to save the ladies from riding astride, a hobby-horse with two back wheels was invented, becoming the forerunner of the tricycle. In that known as the Pilentum a seat was provided and a footplate with a propulsion mechanism. The caption to a colour print of 1820 (Plate 38a) reads as follows:

> The elegant little vehicle is peculiarly adapted for use of the ladies. It is impelled by the slightest touch of either the hands or feet at a rate truly astonishing: and it is so completely secured from upsetting that the most timid person might use it with the greatest confidence.

164. The Ladies' Accelerator. "I do not see why Ladies should not have a lark as well as the Gentlemen." 1819.

There was no need now to adapt costume to machine and this lady is dressed in the height of fashion. Her short-waisted, long-skirted white dress is topped by a low-necked spencer (a short out-door jacket) and her large yellow bonnet is trimmed on the tall crown with blue and pink flowers.

Another more complicated machine was the "Pedestrian Carriage" called also a velocimanipede. The front of normal shape would be ridden by the gentleman, behind there was a seat for the lady and at the rear a small seat for a child or a groom. In our illustration (Plate 38(b)):

> A John Bull rides a Velocimanipede in Bushy Park. . . . His wig and hat are on a stick fixed in front of the stearing bar. He is mopping his brow. Behind are his wife and child, at rear the little boy working the handles which turn the back wheel.

165. Tricycling Costume. Ladies wearing jackets and skirts of thin tweed and peaked caps. 1889.

John Bull in a blue coat wears his red-and-yellow striped waistcoat unbuttoned exposing his shirt in an effort to keep cool. His wife's silk dress is short for the fashion, but the large pink feather in her hat is *à la mode*. The child has a white dress with a blue sash and she holds a doll dressed in yellow. The small boy is all in blue.

The next advance, in 1834, was the development of the tricycle, no longer made of wood and having pedals with connecting rods working on the rear axle. The wheels were fitted with narrow, solid rubber tyres. Tricycles made for two, varied in design and were constructed so that the riders sat side by side or one in front of the other. These were popular in the 1880s (Fig. 165).

In about 1865 there appeared the high "ordinary" with a large driving wheel in front and a small trailing one behind. This machine came to be known as the "penny farthing" (Fig. 166).

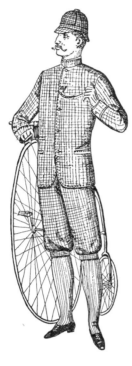

166. Gentleman, with "penny farthing", wearing a lounge jacket, knickerbockers and a deerstalker hat. 1888.

Then followed the safety bicycle, also often called a bone-shaker, in which the wheels were of equal size and finally the tandem, the bicycle made for two, immortalized by Harry Dacre in 1892:

Daisy, Daisy . . .
You'll look sweet, upon the seat
Of a bicycle made for two.

Tricycling or bicycling was not a popular pastime, however, until the second half of the nineteenth century, possibly due to the uncomfortable jolting experienced from solid tyres and rough country roads. When these tyres were replaced by the pneumatic tyres invented by J. B. Dunlop (a veterinary surgeon from Belfast) in 1888, cycling was taken up with enthusiasm by women as well as men, and suitable clothing had to be considered.

Men's outfit was comparatively easy, but women's, in those days gave rise to many problems.

The following are the cycling clothes advised for men by Professor Hoffmann in 1887. In his *Tips for Tricyclists* he wrote:

> The question of dress is a point of first importance in cycling, not merely as a matter of appearance but of health. Cycling indeed has done more than any other sport to spread sound notions as to rational principles of dress. Side by side with the Jaeger movement in Germany, cyclists have been finding out for themselves that the only truly hygienic system of dress is the "all woollen". . .
>
> The costume adopted by the Cyclists' Touring Club (organized in 1878 as the "Bicycle Touring Club") is upon the "all woollen" lines and may be recommended as at once neat, sanitary and durable. A special West-of-England tweed has been adopted for the outer garments, the pattern being a small grey check. Flannel, in two different thicknesses and *all wool* . . . is made of the same pattern, so that if the rider wears a shirt of this material the absence of a waistcoat is not noticeable, a material gain in very warm weather . . .
>
> The coat may be either a "Lounge" jacket or a "Norfolk": vest present or absent; and the nether garments, breeches, trousers, or knickerbockers, at pleasure. The headgear may be either a helmet, hard or soft, a deerstalker or a wide-awake, a cricket-cap or a polo; and in summer, a white straw hat may be used instead, the lining or band being in each case pure woollen felt.
>
> The prices . . . may be gathered from the accompanying list, at which rates any of the official tailors are bound to supply (to members of the club only) the articles referred to.

	£	s	d
Lounge jacket	1	12	0
Norfolk jacket	1	17	6
Breeches and knickerbockers		16	0
Trousers	1	1	0
Waistcoat		10	0
Grey merino combination garments large		15	6
medium		14	6
small		13	6
Grey woollen "Sweaters" same shade as uniform		8	6
Shirt of No: 4 flannel		11	6

	s	d
Ditto of No: 5 (superfine) ditto	14	6
Suspenders to match the club cloth per pr.	3	6
Gaiters per pr.	8	6
Helmets of club cloth, any size, each	6	6
Soft knock-about helmets, ditto	4	6
White straw hats, rough or smooth plait, with club ribbon complete	4	6
Club ribbon	2	0
Straw hats without the ribbon	3	6
Polo hats of club cloth	2	9
Cricket caps of ditto	2	9
Deerstalkers or wide-awakes of club cloth	5	9
Puggarees[1] for helmets	2	0
Linen cap covers	1	9
Stockings, any size per pr.	3	3
Silk pocket handkerchiefs in club colours 24 inches square, each	6	6
Silk muffler or waist kerchief 30″ sq.	9	0
Lounge jacket, vest and breeches make up the most useful costume . . .		

The helmet of the C.T.C. is a capital head-dress, being neat, durable, and effective as a protection from sun and rain.

Trousers may be worn in place of breeches or knickerbockers, but unless the rider has some cogent reason for veiling his calves, Mokanna-like, from public gaze, the latter are to be preferred for many reasons. Trousers are apt to drag at the knees, and soon become baggy and disreputable. Further, an oily pedal-crank will irreparably damage a pair of trousers. Stockings are far less likely to pick up oil, and, if they do, the next time they are washed all is set right again.

The shirt and other underclothing (if any) must also be of pure wool . . .

In respect of stockings, we know none better, for cycling purposes, than Pile's "Perfecta" hose, made specially for cyclists' use. They are shaped to the leg, and extend as should all cycling hose, far enough above the knee to avoid the need of garters, the strap and buckle of the breeches serving to keep them in position . . .

The best kind of collar to wear is a moot point. The ordinary linen collar is out of the question, for it usually becomes a limp and flabby rag before the

---

[1] A thin scarf worn round hat and sometimes falling behind to keep off the sun.

rider has passed his fifth milestone. Dr. Jaeger, true to his principles, is all for woollen, but a flannel collar, though well enough for riding in, has rather a slovenly appearance in the coffee room of a hotel afterwards. The wheelman may meet both conditions by wearing a woollen collar to match his shirt while actually riding and carrying in his bag a celluloid collar for evening use.

The breeches or knickerbockers should be drawn in at the waist with a strap (cloth) and buckle, so as to be independent of other support. We note with astonishment that two such eminent authorities as Viscount Bury and Mr. Lacy Hillier, in their recent work *Cycling* advise riding in braces. We firmly believe that the verdict of nine cyclists out of ten would be the other way. As for ourselves we will none of them. The only brace with which we are acquainted that gives free play to the shoulders is the argosy, and the argosy, unfortunately, is not to be had in a woollen material. . . . we would nearly as soon, when awheel, wear a tall hat and an ulster, as . . . submit to the bondage of the brace.

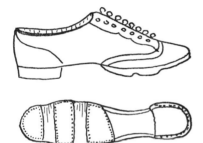

167. Cycling shoes and cycling hat, Pile's "Perfecta". See text.

The last point to be considered is that of head-gear. For winter riding, we should recommend a stiff helmet, as much like that of the C.T.C. as possible; and for summer use, either a soft flannel cap or a straw hat. A very good sample of the latter is *Pile's "Perfecta"*. It is exceptionally light, weighing only $2\frac{1}{2}$ ounces, and has a half-inch opening all round the crown for ventilation—an inexpressible comfort in hot weather [Fig. 167].

Shoes . . . In buying cycling shoes, . . . it should be ascertained that the sole does fit the pedal . . . Shoes are preferable to boots as being cooler, and harmonizing better with breeches and stockings. They should be square-toed and with a broad flat tread, so as to give the foot ample play. The heel should be low, and the waist moderately flexible. On the other hand a fairly stiff sole is an advantage, much fatigue being thereby saved to the wearer.

In spite of Professor Hoffmann's condemnation of waterproof capes for cyclists, a writer in 1890 has this to say on the subject:

Tricycle riders will be glad to hear of a well-ventilated cape (cut sufficiently long to cover the handles in front) which can be stowed away in a water-proof case and weighs from twelve to thirteen ounces.

A waterproof faced cloth is a capital invention both for dresses and cloaks, and some of the brocaded silk waterproofs, being admirably ventilated, are fit for wearing on any occasion.

Cassell's Family Magazine. 1890.

168. Youth in patrol jacket, tight knee breeches and round cap. He holds a bugle in place of a bicycle bell. 1880.

From the 1880s on, the most suitable costume for cyclists was carefully considered and inevitably more so for women than for men. According to the *Tailor and Cutter*, in 1878, men cyclists wore:

A close-fitting patrol jacket, straight waistcoat and breeches or knicker-bockers. The jacket double-breasted buttoned 5 [Fig. 168].

In 1878 it was

> A modified patrol jacket, knickers, stockings and boots or breeches and gaiters.

In 1888

> Lounge jacket and breeches, buttoning three at the knee, ribbed stockings to match; high buttoned boots and peaked polo cap. But "knickers are more usual than breeches", and a Norfolk jacket.

Shoes were often worn instead of boots.

In 1890

> A marked difference from the style adopted in the early days of cycling when the Military braided patrol jacket and tight knee breeches were looked upon as the proper thing. The jacket is an ordinary lounge with the usual pockets and turn down collar made of grey cloth. Knickers cut fairly loose 18″ to 19″ at the knee, made with band and buckle.

169. Bicycling suit at 24/6. Lounge jacket and knickerbockers to match. No waistcoat or braces. Cricket cap. 1897.

In 1894 we have suggestions as to suitable head-gear.

> The "Ventilating Cap . . . exceedingly light and well suited for cycling and holiday purposes. The price we think is marvellous—4/6 per dozen; this is of course wholesale."

> It is a very neat cap, one of the ordinary eightpieced caps in shape . . . made of . . . slate or drab vest linen, taking the form of an ornamental pattern in the crown which forms the ventilation.

Cloth caps, however, seem to have been the most popular.

> These are being worn for almost any kind of sport and pleasure, cycling, cricket, tennis, boating, golfing, shooting and what not. They are even largely adopted as the négligé headgear of everyday life. . . .
> Caps with small peaks and which fit the head close and low down behind are the prevailing shape [Fig. 169].

The *Tailor and Cutter* also recommended in 1894 the Rosebury Belt.

> Made from a mixture of spun silk woven into exquisite designs in a variety of fancy colours.

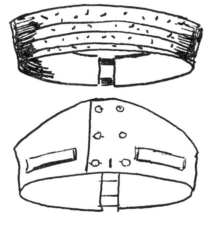

170. Drill vest belt. Cummerbund for cyclists.

Instead of a waistcoat, a cummerbund might be worn, six inches wide and fastened with a buckle at the back, 30s per dozen (Fig. 170). Another choice was a Drill Vest Belt

> made in a variety of colours suitable for summer wear, they fasten at the front with 3 buttons . . . there are two pockets [Fig. 170].

In 1900 we are told:

How to dress a Gentleman for Cycling or Golf

Norfolk jacket, or a single breasted or double-breasted lounge or reefer, knickers or flannel trousers. Shirt of Regatta or Oxford stripe, turndown collar or linen stand or turn-down Golf cap. Hose with fancy tops; tan lace boots; gloves of tan or white chamois.

For riding, breeches of Bedford or whip cord, leggings, brown top boots.

The Norfolk jacket suit was, on the whole, the most popular for cyclists in the 1890s.

He had on his new brown cycling suit—a handsome Norfolk jacket thing for 30s.—and his legs . . . were more than consoled by thick chequered stockings, thin in the foot, thick in the leg.

H. G. Wells, The Wheels of Chance, 1896.

From men's cycling suits, we must now turn to the problem which arose for devising suitable clothes for the woman cyclist, "without shewing her legs to the public".

Professor Hoffmann in 1887 gives his opinion on the best clothes for women cyclists as follows:

Dress—Ladies'

This is a matter of some delicacy to be approached by a masculine writer. The C.T.C. uniform list is as under, and will give a fair notion of the kind of garments which are found most suitable for lady riders.

	£	s	d
Coat bodice, or Norfolk jacket	1	15	6
Skirt plain	1	10	0
Skirt with pannier and apron	2	6	0
Knickerbockers or trousers		18	6
Merino or lamb's wool combination garments		12	6
Dark grey worsted stockings per pr.		4	0
Special ventilated tan gloves per pr.		3	3
"Alpine" or "Deerstalker" hat of club cloth		5	9
Helmet of club cloth		6	8
Puggaree for ditto		2	0
White straw hats, rough or smooth plait with club ribbon complete		4	6
Registered ribbon without hat (colours same as for gentlemen)		2	0
Straw hat without ribbon		3	6
Silk pocket handkerchiefs in club colours 24" square		6	6
Silk muffler 30" square		9	0

It will be observed that the list contemplates, at any rate as a possibility, the use of trousers (!) by ladies. If the lady tricyclist be seventy years of age and rheumatic, by all means let her wear trousers, but we can conceive no other case in which they would be even tolerable. If they were made long enough to be visible, they would be extremely unsightly, besides seriously hampering and thereby fatiguing the rider. If they are not intended to be visible, they can have no possible advantage over knickerbockers, which will be cooler, freer, and in every way more comfortable. Ladies are already at a disadvantage in point of costume when compared with the male rider. Why then should they handicap themselves still further by adopting a garment which the male rider is only too glad to escape from?

171. Jacket bodice, draped skirt, bustle.　172. Norfolk jacket, plain skirt, small hat.
Straw hat. 1887.　1887.

Our observations as to the clothing being throughout "all wool" apply with equal force to ladies . . . The Sanitary Woollen Company also cater in great variety for ladies, and among their specialities will be found woollen corsets, a great boon to ladies who insist on tricycling in such a garment, and who, perhaps from habit, could not safely dispense with it. It is hardly necessary to remark that anything like tight lacing must be strictly avoided.

Next follows advice to Lady Tricyclists:

> Don't ride unattended by a male relative or friend. Don't accompany club runs unless specially small and select. Always ride in correct cycling costume. Stick to the "all wool" principle, and don't have your skirt either too long or too full, these being fertile sources of accident. Don't lace tightly. Use a saddle, not a seat, and preferably a saddle with a short neck, as specially constructed for ladies' use. . . .
>
> When touring carry your own soap, also a box of Brand's or Johnson's meat lozenges, and a few tablets of chocolate or good Muscatel raisins. These by way of roadside "pick-me-ups". Carry a waterproof cape, but don't ride in it.
>
> Carry a menthol cone. Drawn gently over the forehead it is a capital thing for headache or to soothe the nerves when over-fatigue won't let you sleep.

From the reminiscences of Elizabeth Haldane we read:

> In 1879, I wrote from London of an extraordinary sight, a lady attired in a sort of riding habit, tricycling, unconcerned down Oxford Street. That was the beginning of what developed during the next ten or twelve years, till in the nineties, bicycling not tricycling, became the rage. . . .
>
> A woman had to take her courage in her hands to mount even a safety bicycle for it betokened something fast and our full skirts and petticoats were not well adapted for the work. Mercifully coats and skirts came into vogue before long . . . and along with them came sailor hats; and hence the lady cyclist, in the end presented quite a good and tidy appearance though various means had to be adopted of so fastening her skirts on her legs as to prevent them entangling in the back wheel, or worse still showing her legs to the public, an unforgivable offence.
>
> *From One Century to Another*, A. Maclehose & Co., London, 1937.

One method of preventing cycling skirts from blowing up and exposing the legs was to sew a piece of looped elastic to the hem of the skirt on either side. The feet were slipped through this loop before reaching the pedals. This method was used by Royalty. Another method was by having the hems heavily weighted with pieces of lead.

> He saw her go out on her bicycle in the simple grey homespun dress which her own dextrous hands had fashioned—the skirt, heavily weighted round the hem, just covering the little feet, her Norfolk jacket setting trimly to the graceful figure, and the smart little toque resting on her crisp dark hair. 1894.
>
> *The Housewife*, 1894.

173. Jacket and skirt in grey or blue tweed or serge, blouse bodice in thin white flannel, cloth gaiters and peaked cap to correspond, the latter being decorated in front with a club device. 1889.

A writer in 1895 gives an amusing description of ladies cycling with difficulty in the People's Park.

> We must admit we have not been at all struck with the ladies' costumes. In the first place how can any woman ride with ordinary corsets confining the waist to about eighteen inches, or less, when evidently without them the measurement would be at least twenty to twenty three inches? How can she breathe properly or with comfort?
>
> Again why ride with flower gardens on one's head, and yards of dress flowing, anything but gracefully, round the back wheel of the bicycle, to the great danger of the fair rider.
>
> In the Park we have seen some costumes in which, if the owners could only have seen themselves on the wheel, they would never have appeared in public, one riding with a skirt pinned up round the waist under which could be seen white underwear and gaiterless legs; a cloth jacket and huge white

frilled muslin collar and a big straw hat trimmed with orange coloured chiffon and cornflowers completed the attire. Would any sane person go on horseback in such a garb? In our opinion we need to give as much attention to cycling costumes as to riding habits. Both require to be neat and plain—no flowers, frills or furbelows, no tight waists. Where the cycle is concerned a skirt barely reaching to the ankle, not full; gaiters and knickers all to match the skirt: in summer a well fitting plain blouse or better still a golf jersey, relieved by white at neck and wrists, and a plain sailor or other simple hat.

The Housewife, 1895.

In 1885 Miss Ballin in her *Science of Dress* was already giving much thought to the most suitable clothes for women cyclists. She strongly recommended the divided skirt as one possibility. (See p. 341.) This argument was, however, a failure.

Oscar Wilde wrote in 1884:

The "Girl Graduate" with a pathos to which I am not insensible, entreats me not to apotheosize "that awful, befringed, beflounced, and bekilted divided skirt." Well, I will acknowledge that the fringes, the flounces, and kilting do certainly defeat the whole object of the dress, which is that of ease and liberty; but I regard these things as mere wicked superfluities, tragic proofs that the divided skirt is ashamed of its own division. The principle of the dress is good, and though it is not by any means perfection, it is a step towards it.

Pall Mall Gazette, 14th October, 1884.

Another style recommended by Miss Ballin is described as follows:

On the dress of ladies, the tricycle is likely also to have a salutary effect, for to ride it comfortably the dress must be light and easy in every part. Heavy skirts hanging from the waist would be too painful to be borne. Neat, dark cloth costumes, ulsters or jackets, with small felt or cloth hats to match, are suitable for tricycle wear, or dresses of those brownish materials which do not show the dust of the road.

The dress worn by the members of the Ladies' Cyclist Touring Club is made of dark grey tweed and consists of a Norfolk jacket, a long skirt covering knickerbockers and a hat to match.

For the feet she recommended

boots or shoes made to fit the foot . . . the toes should be broad, to allow full play to the toes of the foot; the heels, if any are worn, should be low and broad, and under the natural heel instead of being a sort of peg pushed forward right into the middle of the foot like the fashionable Wurtenburg heels.

174. Tricycling dress which obtained a medal at the Health Exhibition in 1884. See text.

Again another cycling dress recommended, gave the wearer the satisfaction of appearing in the height of fashion. It "obtained a medal at the Health Exhibition and two medals at the National Health Society's Exhibition" in 1884. It

> is a dark blue cloth Princess robe, with the ordinary drapery at the back and a scarf round the hips: at the right side of the skirt are some bows of ribbon, and these, when the wearer is walking, hide the secret of the dress. When she mounts her iron steed, all she has to do is to unfasten some buttons which are cunningly concealed beneath the bows, and at once she has a skirt perfectly adapted for tricycle riding. It is constructed on the same principle as the riding habit now worn, with room for the raised knee, so that the skirt does not draw up with the movements necessary to propel the machine [Fig. 174].

This was probably the dress recommended by Professor Hoffmann in his list of dresses for ladies, under the heading of "Skirt with panier and apron".

PLATE 37

"*Modern Olympics*"—Riders on velocipedes. 1819.

*Engraving (artist unknown). Coloured impression, B.M. (M. D. George's Catalogue of
. . . Satires, No. 13399.)*

PLATE 38

(*a*) "A Pilentum" or "Lady's accelerator". 1820.

Aquatint. B.M. "Sporting Print", No. 1917-13-8-4564.

(*b*) Riders on a Veloc manipede.

Cruikshank, 1819. Colour impression, B.M.

Variations of this style are described and Miss Ballin tells us that:

> these dresses are lined with flannel, and the ideal way of wearing them is with woollen combinations next the skin, a flannel body fitting closely to the figure to take the place of stays, and buttoned on to this a pair of knickerbockers or trousers of cloth to match the dress. Of course, these unmentionables[1] do not show.

RATIONAL COSTUME.

The Vicar of St. Winifred-in-the-Wold (to fair Bicyclists). "IT IS CUSTOMARY FOR MEN, I WILL NOT SAY GENTLEMEN, TO REMOVE THEIR HATS ON ENTERING A CHURCH!" [Confusion of the Ladies Rota and Ixiona Bykewell.

175. Rational costume, worn with Norfolk jackets and straw hats. 1896.

The shock came a few years later when they did show and were not only mentioned but were widely discussed. They took the form of baggy knickerbockers and were called "rationals" (Fig. 175), but the popular name for them was "Bloomers", after Mrs Bloomer who in 1851 tried to introduce rational dress for women. These garments however were very different from her Turkish trousers, which were long and frilled round the ankle:

[1] One of the many euphemisms for a man's trousers or knickerbockers.

. . . the legs are clothed in roomy knickerbockers down to the knees and encased in cloth gaiters for the rest, buttoned down to the ankles . . . As for the attenuated skirts of the Prophet Bloomer, Rational Dress replaces them with a species of frantic frock-coat, spreading as to its ample skirts but tightened round the waist. A "Robin Hood" hat crowns the confection. . . . [This] the very latest development is not pretty: but there! 'tis "pretty Fanny's way" and so an end to all discussion.

Charles Harper, The Revolted Woman, 1894.

. . . if the cycle had not been so democratic a plaything, this latest experiment in dress reform would have been little heard of. Rational Dress as seen on the flying females who pedal down the roads today, is only Bloomerism with a difference.

Ibid., 1894.

176. This lady, in blouse and rationals, wears a Robin Hood hat. Gentleman in Norfolk jacket and knickerbockers. 1896.

The following is a comment in *The Housewife* of 1896:

> The so-called rational dressers go in for comfort and convenience only, without regard to appearance, but it must be said that many succeed in looking not ungraceful or at least, as graceful as any woman can look in an essentially male attire. But the majority by common consent, cannot avoid looking somewhat ludicrous.

FASHION À LA SHAKSPEARE.

" I have a Suit wherein I mean to touch your Love indeed."—*Othello*, Act III., Scene 3

177. Girl in rationals and coat, as described in text, but she wears a
man's bicycling cap. 1897.

For this reason the majority preferred skirts, with knickerbockers as an under garment.

An unknown writer in the late 1890s recommended

> skirt of water-proofed cloth made closely fitting and rather long in front so as not to display a too liberal allowance of ankle, with Norfolk jacket and a small felt hat. Thus equipped the rider can brave any kind of weather and need not be afraid of accident.

But there were other accidents apart from the weather. In an article, in 1897, one of "the old school" laments the modern bicycling craze, not only is it far beyond a girl's strength,

> but it tends to destroy the sweet simplicity of her girlish nature; besides how dreadful it would be if, by some accident, she were to fall off into the arms of a strange man!

178. Lady in jacket, long skirt and sailor hat. Gentleman in Norfolk
jacket, knickerbockers and boater. 1895.

As C. W. Cunnington remarks in *Feminine Attitudes in the 19th Century*: "The phrase expresses, in a nutshell, the feminine psychology of the 1890s, the eternal fear of falling into the arms of a strange man: modern psychologists have taught us that a persistent fear is, in reality, a disguised wish."

Most women, however, could not face appearing in knickerbockers, and bicycling skirts continued into the twentieth century; but the joy of riding in rationals with complete freedom of movement for the legs is summed up in this rhyme:

Some folks think bicycling a thing
   A girl should not go in for;
But their idea of fun for one
   I do not care a pin for!
So if your figure's trim and slim
   Put on your knickerbockers
And shut your ears to cheers and jeers
   From rude street-Arab mockers.

                 Gentleman Joe, musical comedy produced in 1895.

Bibliography

Belloc, Hilaire. *Highway*. London, Studio Ltd. 1926.
Bowden, F. *Points for Cyclists*. Leicester, 1891.
Cook, R. *Handbook of the Bicycle Clubs of Essex*. Chelmsford, 1883 etc.
Davidson, L. C. *Handbook for Lady Cyclists*. London, 1896.
Erskine, Miss F. J. *Tricycling for Ladies*. London, Iliffe, 1885.
Hoffmann, Professor. *Tips for Tricyclists*. London, Warne, 1887.
Hoffmann, Professor. *The Cyclists Indispensable Hand Book and Year Book*. London,
   Iliffe & Sturmey, 1899.
Wells, H. G. *The Wheels of Chance*. 1896, London, Dent, 1914.

CHAPTER 14

MOTORING AND FLYING

BY ALAN MANSFIELD

I. MOTORING

I don't know a silencer from a clutch,
    A sparking plug from a bearing,
But no one, I think, is in closer touch
    With the caps the women are wearing;
I'm au fait with the trim of the tailor made brim,
    The crown and machine stitched strap;
Though I've neither the motor, the sable-lined coat, nor
    The goggles—I wear the cap.

                                                        Anon.

In 1895 the Motor Car Club was formed in London, and suggested a uniform modelled on that of Royal Naval officers for its members. Most of the early motorists seem not to have adopted this attire, however, and a group in a Peugeot photographed at Tunbridge Wells in that same year wore conventional dark suits topped by bowler, silk and Homburg hats. Bowlers were again seen on the Brighton Run in 1896, together with ladies in fashionably decorated hats, and at least one gentleman in a yachting cap. A similar stiff, shiny-peaked cap together with a leather jacket adorned the Belgian winner of a race in 1899. In 1897 the Hon. C. S. Rolls was photographed in a tri-car wearing a close fitting soft-peaked cap.

With increased speed and longer journeys the short-comings of the early motor's protective capacity were shown up, and a variety of specific motoring garments for both men and women were developed in the first years of the present century.

In 1902 Lady Jeune wrote:

> A warm gown should be adopted, made of a material that will not catch the dust, and it is also important to wear warm clothing under the gown . . . jerseys and bodices. The best material for excluding the cold is leather, kid or chamois leather . . . The best coats I have seen come from Vienna and are

both cheap and comfortable . . . the lining is opossum . . . they are to be had of any length . . . button up the front, are double breasted and have two warm pockets . . . in front.

Motors and Motor Driving, Badminton Library, 1902.

A similar type of coat is shown in Fig. 179.

179. Lady's fur lined leather motoring coat: veil: goggles. 1903.

In the same year, 1902, a motoring costume with a long trained skirt had a

double-breasted jacket with pouched front . . . trimmed with ermine . . . giving ample protection to the chest . . . wind cuffs inside sleeves.

The Ladies Tailor, 1902. (Fig. 180).

Mrs Eric Pritchard advised that

In winter fur-lined garments are indispensable, and even on mild days we shall not find a practical cloth wrap any too warm.

The Cult of Chiffon, 1902.

But from today's viewpoint one doubts the practicality of the garment she illustrates (Fig. 181).

By 1905 the dress of men had become stereotyped, almost, into soft, peaked caps, goggles, dust-coats or stormcoats or greatcoats, and either trousers or, more often, knickerbockers or breeches, boots, leggings, and gloves. Innumerable types of motor coat were produced for men, as for women, some fiendishly ingenious, such as the double-breasted motor overcoat with vertical pockets, from the bottom of which

> inverted pleats are pressed down, so that when walking the coat takes its normal shape, while when driving the pleats expand over the knees thus enabling the wearer to protect his legs from the cold.
>
> *Minster's Gazette of Fashion, 1905.*

180. Lady's motoring costume trimmed with ermine. See text. 1902.

181. Lady's motoring wrap. See text. 1902.

In default of such a garment the legs were often protected by a rug, sometimes shared with a passenger (Fig. 182), a device fraught with complexities when dealing with pedals and levers. Passengers, of course, could also indulge in a foot muff.

> Foot Muffs, Fur, Extra Large Size, £1.9.6 to £2.12.0.
>
> *Army and Navy Stores, 1912.*

Dust-coats for both sexes were essential to keep the clothes free of the clouds of dust sent up in dry weather from the macadam surfaces: even in winter a dry day posed problems, one reason for ladies' motoring coats being fur-*lined*—fur coats proper would catch and hold too much dust although by about 1910 fur coats, cloth lined, were worn in closed motor-cars. The summer dust-coat (Fig. 183), was of linen, cotton, alpaca, etc. generally loosely fitting; for women

Smart semi-fitting dust coats, of alpaca, with revers and corded silk ties. 49/6.

Advertisement, 1910.

182. Motorist sharing rug. 1905.

The dust problem, together with that of wind and rain, also necessitated the wearing of goggles in the days of motor cars without wind screens. Stone breakers working by the side of the road had long worn protective goggles of mica or wire gauze and these probably served as the model for the earliest motorists.

Writing of the year 1899 Charles Jarrott said:

To make matters worse, the goggles with which I had provided myself were of a very primitive description. It was the first year that goggles had been considered necessary [in the Paris-Bordeaux Motor Tricycle Race], and I found that those I had gave me very little protection.

Charles Jarrott, *Ten Years of Motor and Motor Racing,* 1906
(2nd Edit. 1912).

Three years later

> . . . Perhaps the hardest concession a woman can make if she is going to motor, and that is that she must wear glasses,—not small dainty glasses, but veritable goggles.

Lady Jeune op. cit.

183. Lady's long linen or cotton dust coat.
Flat cap and veil. *c.* 1908.

Efforts were, of course, made to lessen the concession necessary, and in 1903 there was a

> motor veil and face hood with mica mask in which a woman feels she is looking as nice as she can look under the circumstances.

Fashion Article 1903 quoted in C. W. Cunnington,
Englishwomen's Dress in the Present Century, 1951.

The most common type of goggles were of leather, covering closely the upper parts of the face, with inset glass eye-pieces. The ladies' version was of chamois, lined with silk and edged with fur or fur-fabric (Plate 39).

Another problem facing the female automobilist was that of hair and hat in the rush of air created by her progress. The answer was found in the motoring veil, and numerous hair and hat pins (Plate 39).

> The veil can be varied from gauze in summer to a long grey Shetland cloud in winter . . . two yards long and three quarters of a yard wide. Pinned to hat or bonnet, pulled over ears, crossed behind, bring ends to front and tie in bow under chin. Two or three pins behind. Pull down over face if necessary.
>
> Lady Jeune, op. cit.

Grey was the recommended colour as it showed dust the least. Later motoring veils were made gathered at the centre with a large self-covered button.

Small hats were recommended

> . . . the blue Glengarry cap is the best head dress for the motor-car.
>
> Ibid.

But the fashionable wide-brimmed hat was also worn:

> Molly had changed herself from a radiant girl into a cream-coloured mushroom with a thick, straight, pale brown stem . . . her eyes laughing through a triangular talc window.
>
> C. N. and A. M. Williamson, *The Princess Passes*, 1904.

Perhaps the most practical type of hat for a woman was the Tam-o' Shanter which was popular, as was a man's peaked cloth cap.

Various novel designs of head-gear were introduced, though they did not seem to gain much ground:

> Aunt Mary invested in a kind of patent helmet with curtains that unfurl on the sides, to cover the ears; and I found myself so fetching in a hood that I bought one, as well as a toque, to provide for all weathers.
>
> C. N. and A. M. Williamson, *The Lightning Conductor*, 1903.

Hoods ranged from fur for the winter to silk for summer wear (Fig. 184), including various waterproof materials.

For men various types of caps and helmets were introduced, in addition to the popular cloth peaked cap. Leather was a usual material.

> . . . an automobile flew past us . . . there were two men in it, both in leather caps and coats. . . .
>
> Ibid.

> Tan leather caps with wind shields. Each 8/6.
>
> *Army and Navy Stores*, 1912.

184. Motoring hoods (*a*) of fur and (*b*) of silk.

The soft cap was often worn with the peak to the rear to prevent the cap being blown off—a habit also observable in early flyers. When not in use the goggles were often pushed up over the cap (Fig. 185 Plate 39).

185. Male motirists. One with cap on back to front, and goggles pushed up. One with very long overcoat. See text. 1914.

Leather coats were worn by both men and women but do not seem to have been as popular as cloth ones. One such was advertised as the "Auto" coat:

> . . . made from brown calf or tan sheepskin and is worn by gentlemen who take the more strenuous pleasures of motoring by acting as their own driver, the chauffeur acting as mechanician.

. . . Chiefly used when touring . . . add a leather cap, with covering for the back of the head and ears, a pair of sound goggles, boots, leggings, and gauntlets . . . and the ardent motorist may face any weather. . . .

Tailor and Cutter, 1908.

Motor cycles, with or without sidecars, had their place on the road from early days; in 1896 the magazine *The Housewife* describes a motor cycle whose "general appearance is that of a ladies wheel".

186. Gentleman's motor or motor cycle suit. Double-breasted, high collar jacket in leather or waterproof cloth, breeches, leather gaiters. 1912.

Ladies, however, were generally sidecar passengers; their dress, that worn when in a motor car, though in 1913 a fashion magazine was demanding coats less cumbersome than the motor-coat.

For men also the dress was similar, cap, goggles, jacket or coat, perhaps of leather; breeches and gaiters to protect the legs (Fig. 186). By 1910 a weather-proof motor-cycle suit was on the market, consisting of thigh-length loose double-breasted jacket or coat with straps at the wrist to close the cuffs, and a deep collar. Fairly tight overall trousers were cut to shape over the feet, like spats.

Gloves were often of the gauntlet type, both for motor car and motor cycle and of course worn by both sexes.

> The best gloves to wear are white knitted worsted.
> They are warm and easy to wash.
>
> Lady Jeune, op. cit.

A point of interest about the male motorist is the wrist watch. Although "bracelet" watches for women were advertised in the 1880s, they do not appear on men's wrists until much later—it is probable that the South African War, ending in 1902, originated the use of leather holders to strap a pocket watch on to the wrist. The well-nigh impossible feat of disinterring a watch from the waistcoat pocket when clad in motoring garb, and controlling a motor car or cycle no doubt contributed to the popularity of this practice. Certainly in 1910 the smart motor cyclist had a small watch strapped to his wrist.

187. Lady driver: no distinctive feature except gauntlet gloves. 1916.

From about the year 1908 motor cars had been constructed with greater regard to the comfort and protection of their passengers, and by the end of our period, the Great War, except for racing or long touring journeys in open cars little really distinctive clothing was required (Fig. 187). Despite this, however, the motor car has had a greater effect on the sartorial habits of men in the twentieth century than, perhaps, any other single cause.

2. FLYING

Up in a balloon, up in a balloon,
All among the little stars
Sailing round the moon,
Its something very jolly
To be up in a balloon.

Nineteenth Century Popular Song.

The first successful balloonist in—or over—England was an Italian, Vincent Lunardi, who in 1784 had made an aerial voyage from the ground of the Honourable Artillery Company to Ware, Hertfordshire. Among other rewards of the flight was an honorary commission in the H.A.C.

It has been said that Lunardi had always shown a liking for uniforms, and certainly on more than one subsequent flight he wore that of the Honourable Artillery Company: scarlet and blue coat, white breeches and waistcoat, and three-cornered black cocked hat. Occasionally he also wore a sword when flying.

In 1785 he took as a passenger the first Englishwoman to fly—Mrs Sage. The lady is portrayed as wearing an elegant gown and a large picture hat with white plumes (Plate 40).

In the same year an Anglo-American, Dr John Hunter Jeffries, accompanied the French balloonist Jean Blanchard on a flight across the English Channel. Their clothing seems to have been normal, except that Jeffries was shown in one engraving wearing a fur cap, a sort of fur waistcoat, and fur wristlets, or muffetees (Fig. 188). Blanchard also took an extra coat, as well as a surtout. Cork life-jackets were also taken. Owing to adverse conditions necessitating the jettisoning of all surplus weight, Blanchard threw his coats overboard—Jeffries followed his example, and Blanchard then discarded his trousers, an action which Jeffries apparently thought went too far.

Balloonists on the whole did not clothe themselves in any particular way.

Major Money and Sir Richard MacGuire (or plain Robert McQuin—the accounts differ) both found themselves deposited by their balloons in the sea in the same year, 1785 again, but in different waters: Money was rescued from his basket with dishevelled hair, but otherwise impeccable in coat, waistcoat, pantaloons and cravat. MacGuire (McQuin?) was pulled out of the sea in coat and breeches, his three-cornered hat still fixed firmly on his head.

The unfortunate accident in 1824 which killed the aeronaut James Harris, was survived by the passenger, a young lady, who flew in a high waisted Empire dress and large bonnet.

188. Flying doctor; fur cap and waistcoat. See text. 1785.

Charles Green, one of the most successful and active balloonists ascended in 1828 clad in a cut-away coat, trousers, and a top-hat, but in 1836, on his long-distance European flight which ended at Nassau he and his companions wore forage caps and greatcoats with capes.

Mrs Graham, who with her husband, was a professional aeronaut during the middle years of the nineteenth century was billed in 1850 to make "The first ascent at night ever attempted by a female" and depicted, somewhat romanticized, in a long-sleeved, wide-skirted dress and a bonnet.

Ballooning remained during the nineteenth century as a popular entertainment, with occasional sporting and scientific flights as well: in Edwardian days it acquired renewed popularity as a "smart" addition to week-end parties, and balloon racing across country became a feature of the sporting world. Most people taking part in flights in the early twentieth century wore plain country clothes. Cloth caps or yachting caps were favourites with the men; for the ladies hats and veils worn with costumes or dresses, sometimes with furs worn round the neck.

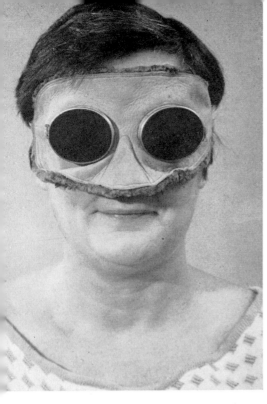

PLATE 39

(*a*) Ladies' motoring goggles: green glass lenses, metal frames secured by elastic band with clip. *c. 1910.*

Author's collection.

(*b*) Motorists' and Golfers' motor caps and veils: dust coat, goggles; male golfer in breeches and stockings, lady in short skirt, blouse and jacket. 1907.

Graphic, *July 1907.*

PLATE 40

Elegant Aeronaut: Vincent Lunardi in H.A.C. uniform with
Mr Biggin and Mrs Sage wearing fashionable gown and large
hat. 1784.

Engraving by Bartolozzi. 1785.

The early aviators in aeroplanes tended to dress rather like their contemporaries of the motor car. Men wore tweed peaked caps, often worn with the peak to the rear so as to prevent wind pressure from lifting it off the head, and suits, or double-breasted jackets buttoning up to the neck with trousers or knee-breeches. Scarves, balaclava helmets, and goggles were usual. Overalls or boiler-suits also were popular, and later, from about 1910, leather flying helmets with ear flaps.

189. Aeronaut; tweed suit and cap. Lady passenger in costume with skirt tied round legs. See text. Early 20th century.

For the ladies, a costume with hat and motoring veil was worn by an American, Mrs Hart O. Berg (Fig. 189); the skirt is tied round the legs below the knees to prevent draughts and preserve decency. A similar device was sometimes practised by men with their trouser legs to achieve the first object above (Fig. 190).

A French woman in 1910 recommended a woollen motor hood, sweater, short divided skirt and brown stockings and shoes. In the following year an "English female pilot" was shown in her winter flying kit consisting of very baggy knickerbockers, gaiters, a double-breasted, waist-length leather jacket, fur gloves and woollen balaclava helmet.

Apart from the leather flying helmet there was apparently no development of protective or other clothing peculiar to the sport of early aeroplaning: the leather jackets etc. were equally worn by motorists, who were just as exposed to the weather as the aviators.

190. Flyer: wearing balaclava helmet and life jacket, trousers tied round ankles. 1910.

As for the balloonists, Lunardi-of-the-uniforms was probably delighted to have named after him a fashionable ladies' hat. The "Lunardi" or "Balloon" hat was an immense balloon-like crown of gauze over a wire frame, surrounded by a wide brim, popular in the late 1780s.

Bibliography

Badminton Library. *Motors and Motor Driving*. Longmans, Green and Co., 1902.
Jarrott, Charles. *Ten Years of Motors and Motor Racing*. Grant, Richards, 2nd ed, 1912.
Rolt, L. T. C. *The Aeronauts*. Longmans, Green and Co., 1966.
Wallace, Graham. *Flying Witness*. Putnam, 1958.

CHAPTER 15

BATHING AND BEACHWEAR

BY PHILLIS CUNNINGTON

BATHING

Sea bathing in the early eighteenth century was advocated as health giving, especially in the winter, and seaside places such as Scarborough and Margate were looked upon as Spas. This followed on the seventeenth-century custom of visiting inland spas such as Bath, for curative purposes, and there bathing in an indoor pool. Celia Fiennes records in 1687 that at Bath:

> The ladyes goes into the bath with garments made of a fine yellow canvas, with great sleeves like a parson's gown, the water fills it up so that its borne off that your shape is not seen, it does not cling close as other linning which looks sadly, in the poorer sort that go in their own linning. . . .
> The Gentlemen have drawers and wastcoates of the same sort of canvas.
>
> *The Journeys of Celia Fiennes*, 1687.

In 1771 the bathing attire at Bath had changed to the following:

> The ladies wear jackets and petticoats of brown linen, with chip hats, in which they fix their handkerchiefs to wipe the sweat from their faces; . . . My aunt . . . contrived to wear a cap with cherry-coloured ribbons to suit her complexion and obliged Win [the maid] to attend her yesterday morning in the water . . . as for poor Win who wore a hat trimmed with blue . . .
>
> T. Smollett, *Humphrey Clinker*, 1771.

In open water, however, such dresses would be extremely hampering, and for a long time both men and women preferred nudity when bathing in the sea or river.

> The four and twentieth day of May
> Of all times in the year,
> A virgin lady bright and gay
> Did privately appear

Close by the river side which she
    Did single out the rather,
'Cause she was sure it was secure
    And had intent to bathe her.

With glittering glance, her jealous eyes
    Did slyly look about
To see if any lurking spies
    Were hid to find her out:
And being well resolved that none
    Could view her nakedness,
She puts her robes off, one by one,
    And doth herself undress.

The Swimming Lady (Anon.) Late seventeenth Century.

The sexes were always separated, but "lurking spies" were the problem, and the subject of much ribaldry until the practice of bathing naked came to an end.

Men, with exceptions, continued to bathe naked until the 1870s but women began to provide themselves with bathing dresses towards the end of the eighteenth century, though nudity was braved by some during the first years of the nineteenth.

Naked women bathers are depicted at Scarborough in an engraving by John Setterington in 1735, and again by another artist in 1805. In *Poetical Sketches of Scarborough*, 1813, illustrated by Rowlandson and others, there is a plate showing naked women bathers. Here are a few extracts from the poem "Sea Bathing" which it illustrates:

Caroline her glass was trimming
To see the gentlemen a swimming.

The man with a bathing machine tells a lady that his wife will "undress and dress you in a trice".
The maiden aunt replies:

The thought of bathing thus I hate
Nought can be so indelicate.

Finally a bathing machine woman persuaded the aunt to bathe, by saying (apparently without truth) that although gentlemen bathers were about the place,

> They do no harm, my Lady they
> Here in the waves, but frisk and play,
> The Ladies, dress'd in flannel cases
> Show nothing but their handsome faces.

Evidently although ladies could bathe naked, as the picture shows, some did wear flannel bathing dresses which at this date were long loose gowns, like chemises, tied round the neck. The attendant woman finally defeated the old aunt's excuse that she could not bathe because she was bald and had to wear a wig, by saying:

> Oh no—here's Lady Bumpkin's tresses
> In which to bathe, she always dresses
> For grey her hair has long been grown.

Which shows that bathing caps were not available here. Nudes wearing white bathing caps, however, are shown in a caricature "Salt Water" *c.* 1802. In a drawing by J. I. Marks *c.* 1820 called "Nymphs Bathing", the ladies are all naked, with their hair streaming down their backs. In the distance a naval officer looks at them through his telescope.

WOMEN

We now continue with the women bathers, whose costumes became more and more complicated, and return to the men later.

Bathing dresses were worn by some women before the nineteenth century, but whatever the material, these continued as long loose sacks until *c.* 1860.

> The guides who attend the ladies in the water are of their own sex and they and the female bathers have a dress of flannel for the sea; nay, they are pro-
> vided with other conveniences for the support of decorum. A certain number of the machines are fitted with tilts that project from the seaward ends of them so as to screen the bathers from the view of all persons whatsoever.
>
> T. Smollett, Humphrey Clinker, 1771.

This addition to the bathing machine was said to be invented by a Quaker, Benjamin Beale, who was disturbed by the thought that ladies might be seen entering or emerging from the sea at Margate in their "flannel cases". This awning was then known as the "Modesty Hood" (Fig. 191).

The guides, whose career began and ended with the bathing machines, were usually middle-aged women, wearing dark voluminous dresses, slouch hats or bonnets and head scarves. Their function was to dip the timid, and for this reason they were known as "dippers" and also to scare off inquisitive males (Plate 41). Fanny Burney tells us that in 1789 after the recovery of George III from a breakdown, ladies in the Royal service wore the words "God Save the King"

> in their bandeaus, on their bonnets to go into the sea; and have it again, in large letters round their waists to meet the waves.

191. "Mermaids at play". Bathing machines fitted with "Modesty Hoods". 1848.

Elizabeth Ham in *c.* 1802 wrote:

> I never enjoyed such bathing before or since. We had made our bathing dresses of green baize, and used to threaten to trim them with sea weed and cockle shells, but this we never did.

> What we used to do was to rise early, put on our bathing dresses, with a loose wrapper and a shawl over, slip our feet in warm slippers, and with a bonnet on our heads our toilet was done. The servant girl with a bundle containing our linen and petticoats, with sheets and towels followed us to the shore . . . We were ready to take to the water in a minute. We used to stoop

and let the rolling waves sweep over us, or throw ourselves head foremost into the deepest, and tumble over to our feet again somehow or other.

Elizabeth Ham, 1783–1820 by herself, ed. E. G. Gillett, 1945.

A more daring garment worn by a lady in 1814, is recorded by John Ashton in his *Social Life in the Regency*.

The wife of a respectable citizen has excited a good deal of curiosity at Margate. She bathes in a green dress without a cap; and attached to the shoulders of the dress is something resembling fins. She swims remarkably well, and the peculiarity of her paraphernalia, together with her long black hair, have occasioned many to believe that she was a mermaid.

One wonders how she managed to swim in the sack-like garment then in vogue. Perhaps she wore the "Bathing Preserver" brought out at this date.

The Bathing Preserver is a most ingenious and useful novelty for ladies who frequent the seaside; as it is intended to provide them with a dress for bathing far more adapted to such purposes than anything of the kind at present in use, and it will be found most necessary and desirable to those ladies who go to the seaside unprovided with bathing dresses and will relieve them from the nauseous idea of wearing the bathing coverings furnished by the guides. Mrs Bell's Bathing Preserver is made in quite a novel manner, to which is attached a cap to be removed at pleasure, made of a delicate silk to keep the head dry. The preserver is made of such light materials that a lady may carry it in a tasteful oiled silk bag of the same size as an ordinary lady's reticule. (1814.)

Possibly this is what it looked like in the water—

"There", said the captain, pointing to one of the young ladies before noticed, who in her bathing costume looked as if she was enveloped in a patent Mackintosh of scanty dimensions.

Charles Dickens, *Sketches by Boz*, 1834–6.

In 1856 *The Observer* had this to say about bathing at Ramsgate:

The water is black with bathers—should the sea be rather rough, the females do not venture beyond the serf, and lay themselves on their backs, waiting for the coming waves, with their bathing dresses in a most dégagée style. The waves come, and in the majority of instances, not only cover the fair bathers, but literally carry their dresses up to their neck, so that, as far as decency is concerned, they might as well be without any dresses at all . . . and all this takes place in the presence of thousands of spectators . . . the gentlemen come to look at the ladies bathing, it is equally the fact, that ladies pay as much attention to the performances of the gentlemen. The portion of the beach allotted to the men is crowded with well dressed females . . . who calmly look on without a blush or a giggle.

The authorities ought to compel gentlemen to wear, as in France, caleçons and the ladies' dresses should at least be so constructed as to prevent a wholesale exposure of their natural perfections or imperfections, as now momentarily takes place.

The sack like garments, still worn at that date, made this exposure possible. Surtees comments:

What lady would traverse the passages of a house with nothing on but a bathing gown and slippers? What peeping and prying and listening there would be at the door before she broke cover, and what hurrying and scuttling there would be after she once got away. If she should happen to meet a man she would never get over it. Yet here in the broad face of day, with myriads of gazers and regiments of telescopes, they come out with the greatest coolness and deliberation, and walk unconcernedly into the sea.

R. S. Surtees, *Plain or Ringlets,* 1860.

A change to slightly more practical bathing dresses for women, took place in the 1860s. The quotations given below, all from contemporary magazines, indicate some of the changes.

The ugly loose blue gown like a bottomless sack is no longer considered the right thing for a bathing costume and a little more attention is paid by fair bathers to avoid looking downright frights.

Some dresses were made with trousers to the ankles worn with a blouse tunic. The material might be "flannel or rep, black with blue or red worsted braid; white is to be avoided for obvious reasons". 1863.

Another style was "The Zouave Marine Swimming costume, a body and trousers cut in one secures perfect liberty of action and does not expose the figure." 1866.

Bathing dresses in the seventies were becoming more elaborate.

A basque bodice and drawers fastened below the knee with scarlet ribbon: some with short skirts; short puffed sleeve, bathing cap with net. 1870.

Should be made with a tunic and worn with a waistbelt and deep sailor collar not open at the throat if you wish to preserve the whiteness of your

192. Bathing dress consisting of a short-sleeved jacket and long loose
trousers. 1875.

neck. Buttons down the front. The drawers should button on each side but a
string should be added for safety, and they should be gathered just above the
ankle.   1874.

Bathing costumes . . . are made more stylishly every season: pink, cream
and even blue flannel are used, but the most durable is bunting; loose full
trousers to the ankle, and a short blouse fastened at the waist or a long jacket.
                                                                                  1877.

Bathing costumes in the form of combinations, gathered just above the ankles,
with short overskirt to conceal the figure.   1878.

In the eighties women frequently bathed in hats (Fig. 193).

Bathing Costumes this season are very neat; a loose blouse of dark blue serge;
elbow sleeves and collar; wide drawers a few inches above the ankle, all
trimmed with wide braid; and a red woollen sash and coarse straw hat.
                                                                1880 [Fig. 194].

Bathing Costumes, some of stockinette, in one piece with detachable short
skirt, or tunic (Plate 41(b)) over knickerbockers (care should be taken lest they
reveal the figure when wet).

In spite of this last remark, some women wore corsets under their bathing dresses in order to show off the small waist of the wearer (Plate 42).

193. Women bathing in hats. 1880.

"Swimming Stays" are actually advertised in the *Daily Advertiser* of 18th May, 1742. What purpose these could have served is difficult to say, in the days of nudity or a "bottomless sack". Possibly they were a form of support such as a swimming girdle. (See page 271.)

> It is becoming the custom to wear shoes with straw soles and embroidered linen uppers kept on by sandals. The trousers are now seldom made as knickerbockers.   1887.

194. "The dress represented is very pretty . . ., it can be made of linen and woollen fabrics. Blue serge is usual." 1885.

In the 1890s bathing dresses were similar, but caps or bare heads were more usual than hats (Fig. 195).

An American lady is surprised that English bathers do not wear black stockings as worn in the U.S.A. for mixed bathing. "You have no idea how decent they make the whole proceedings." 1893.

So, in the early years of the twentieth century English women bathers took to wearing stockings, black or sometimes white.

195. "Southend Mermaid" 1891.

It is interesting to note that in 1880 an old-fashioned bathing gown appears to have been considered almost as indecent as nudity, by the *beau monde*:

"May I swim here?" asked Vere. "Of course it's the thing to do. Can you dive?" "Oh yes! I am used to the water." "Very well then—But wait: you can't have any bathing dress?" "Yes, I brought it, Would you wish to see it?"

Lady Dolly looked. Gradually an expression of horror . . . spread itself over her countenance and seemed to change it to stone.

"That thing," she gasped. What she saw was the long indigo coloured linen gown—high to the throat and down to the feet—of the uneducated British bather whose mind has not been opened by the sweetness and light of continental shores.

"That thing!" gasped Lady Dolly.

"What is the matter with it?" said Vere, timidly perplexed.

"Matter? It is indecent!"

"Indecent?" Vere coloured all over the white rose leaf beauty of her face.

"Indecent," reiterated Lady Dolly. "If it isn't worse! Good gracious! It must have been worn at the deluge. The very children would stone you! Of course I know you couldn't have any decent dress. You shall have one like mine made tomorrow, and then you can kick about as you like. Blue and white or blue and pink. You shall see mine."

She rang and sent one of her maids for one of her bathing costumes, which were many and of all hues. Vere looked at the brilliant object when it arrived, puzzled and troubled by it. She could not understand it. It appeared to be cut off at the shoulders and knees.

"It is like what the circus riders wear," she said, with a deep breath.

"Well it is, now you name it," said Lady Dolly, amused. "You shall have one tomorrow."

Vere's face crimsoned.

"But what covers one's legs and arms?"

"Nothing: what a little silly you are!"

. . . "I would never wear a costume like that," she (Vere) said quietly . . .

"You will wear what I tell you," said her sweet little mother sharply, "and for goodness sake, child, don't be a prude, whatever you are. Prudes belong to Noah's ark like your bathing gown."

Vere was silent.

Ouida, Moths, 1880.

In the last decade of the nineteenth century when women were becoming much more active, bathing costumes were being designed, that were supposedly more convenient for swimming. Bathing caps of various kinds were recommended in *The Housewife*, 1894.

For those who indulge in bathing and swimming, some manufacturers have invented a charmingly becoming seaside cap. It is called the "Normandy" and is intended to be worn by girls on the sands and as a speciality or distinguishing badge for club swimmers and those who compete in swimming contests. It is both pretty and quaint and is made in satin in all the art shades. The front forms a box-pleated frill eminently becoming to the face of the wearer. The outline, both of pleats and curtain, is bound with brocaded ribbon of contrasting tints to the main portion of the cap . . . strings of the brocade . . . tie the cap into position under the chin.

These caps are also made in satin with india-rubber linings, also in delight-ful patterns of sateen . . . with rubber linings and trimmings and bows of fancy or self coloured ribbons. The different colours are intended as badges of swimming clubs and competitors.

196. Bathing cap. "Made in pink, yellow and white jaconet, check twill, fancy sateen, ordinary check silk in various tints." 1894.

Another was

a round bathing cap . . . made in pink, yellow, and white jaconet, in check twill, turkey red twill, fancy sateen, ordinary check, silk in various tints and some few other fabrics [Fig. 196].

The Housewife, 1894.

197. Bathing dress. "Made in scarlet twill flannel trimmed with white braid." 1896.

The dress of ladies is a very important one. Many a bather finds herself extremely tired very soon and that is solely because her attire is unsuited to what she is doing. We strongly disapprove of flannel as a bathing dress. It fills with water and the weight is enormous. A very fine serge is the best and for swimming a jacket and trousers is the best shape.

The Housewife, 1895.

Finally a word of advice:

Always carefully dry the hair after bathing: those who do not wet the hair with salt water ought to place a cloth wet with fresh water round the head while bathing . . . Dress and undress quite leisurely and avoid undue excitement.

Ibid.

MEN

We now come to the far simpler subject of bathing costumes for men, who until mid-nineteenth century preferred nudity. There were of course exceptions. The *Morning Post* in September 1788 states:

The fashionable bathing dress at Brighton is chiefly a pair of buff trousers and a slight jacket.

This may have been due to the presence of Royalty.

The Prince of Wales does not slumber in dull indolence at his retreat at Brighton, but promotes and participates in many manly exercises.

Morning Post, September 1788.

Since men not only bathed, but swam, much attention was paid to accessories such as swimming aids and various methods for keeping afloat.

. . . I have ventured
Like little wanton boys that swim on *bladders*
This many summers in a sea of glory.

Shakespeare, *Henry VIII* Act III, Sc. ii, 359 (1613).

In *The Art of Swimming* by Monsieur Thévenot ("Done out of French" in 1699) advice is given to bathers, especially on keeping oneself above water by several small portable engines, in cases of danger.

The next place among such Enquiries might be alloted to Artificial Swimming. Besides the common helps of Cork and Bladders, etc. that young beginners make use of to learn, there might be invented several Small Machines of different uses to different purposes. . . .

Girdles of several sorts . . . of any materials that are flexible and impervious to the water, such as oyl'd cloths, and several sorts of Leather. A Cylindrical Case made of oyl'd cloth and kept open on the inside by iron-rings fastened in it at a moderate distance from one another, so that clapping them together it might go into ones pocket, might be so contrived as to tye round ones wast and fastened to keep the water out and that alone would save from being drowned.

Several little Machines might be found very diverting in Swimming to promote Expedition and make the motions of one single man in the water swifter than any boat: Contrivances of thin small Planes of Wood with Valves, or otherwise small thinges fastened to the Legs or Feet might be very serviceable to that end, and perform the part of Fishes fins.

Swimming girdles are mentioned throughout the seventeenth, eighteenth and nineteenth centuries. They were worn round the chest and under the arms and from later descriptions were presumably made up of corks or bladders.

Wee have Shipps and Boates for going under Water and Brooking of Seas; also Swimming-Girdles and Supporters.

Sir Francis Bacon, *New Atlantis*, 1626.

I whips on my swimming-girdle . . . and sails me away like an egg in a duck's belly.

G. Farquhar, *The Constant Couple*, 1699.

Under the bulk was a Projector clicking off his Swimming Girdles, to keep up Merchants Credits from sinking.

Thomas Brown, *Amusements Serious and Comical*, 1700.

The Swimming Girdle, about five inches wide is placed round the pupil's breast.

Partington's British Cyclopaedia of Arts and Science, 1835.

Various kinds of apparatus have been recommended for sustaining the body as cork-jackets, swimming-belts, bladders, etc.

"Stonehenge's" *British Sports*, 1856.

Walker in his book on *Manly Exercise* has this to say in 1839:

The aid of the hand is much more preferable to cork or bladders, because it can be withdrawn gradually and insensibly . . . When the aid of the hand cannot be obtained, inflated membranes or corks may be employed. The only argument for their use is that attitudes and action may be perfected while the body is thus supported. . . .

The best mode of employing corks is to choose a piece about a foot long and six or seven inches broad: to fasten a band across the middle of it: to place it on the back so that the upper end may come between the shoulder blades, where the edge may be rounded: and to tie the band over the breast. Over this several other pieces of corks, each smaller than the preceding, may be fixed, so that, as the swimmer improves, he may leave them off one by one.

But a writer in 1872 in a *Handbook of Swimming* gives a word of warning:

Aids to Swimming

Many aids have been used for the benefit of young swimmers. Corks and bladders fastened under the arms are the common ones; but they offer dangerous temptations for bathers to go out of their depth . . . collapsing of bladders and of air jackets is by no means uncommon.

Bathing in the nude was enjoyed by men until the 1830s and less openly until the 1870s. In Everarde Digby's *De Arte Natandi* 1587, there is a delightful illustration showing two naked bathers and one man dressing beside the stream. He is pulling on his stockings. He is already half dressed in trunk hose and shirt, but his doublet and shoes are on the ground beside him (Fig. 198).

From the mid-eighteenth century on, naked bathers in the sea were less exposed to public view by the provision of bathing machines.

At Aldeburgh in Suffolk, . . . for the convenience of those who choose Bathing in the real Ocean there is a curious Machine that by the assistance of a single Person may be run into the sea to any depth proper for bathing.

Advert. in *Ipswich Journal*, 1763.

About eight years later Scarborough was providing a horse-drawn vehicle.

Scarborough, though a paltry town is romantic . . .

Imagine to yourself a small snug wooden chamber fixed upon a wheel carriage, having a door at each end, and on each side a little window above, a bench below. The bather ascending into the apartment by wooden steps, shuts himself in and begins to undress, while the attendant yokes a horse to the end next the sea and draws the carriage forwards till the surface of the water is on a level with the floor of the dressing room, then he moves and fixes the horse to the other end. The person within being stripped, opens the

PLATE 41

(*a*) Women in buff-coloured flannel bathing gowns and caps. Bathing-women "dippers", one in black hat, pink neckerchief and blue dress, the other in red spotted dress. 1830.

Caricature by W. Heath. c. 1830. Coloured impression at B.M.

(*b*) Bathing dresses with short detachable skirts.

An advertisement of Beechams' Pills in the Illustrated London News, *1887*.

PLATE 42

Bathing dresses and boots. Bathing hat, the usual style. Bathing stays. 1880.

Funny Feller, *31 July 1880*.

door to the seaward, where he finds the guide ready and plunges headlong into the water.

T. Smollett, Humphry Clinker, 1771.

198. Bathing naked. 1587.

It is wonderful what a difference the locality makes in these Apollo Belvedere matters. If these great naked men we now see proceeding so leisurely from Underdown Cliff to the sea were to exhibit themselves that way in a secluded wood in the country there would be such a running and shrieking . . . But because they come down upon the open coast with a grand sea before them people think nothing of it.

R. S. Surtees, Plain or Ringlets, 1860.

In 1872 the Rev. Francis Kilvert was enjoying the same delight in bathing nude but not from a bathing machine.

> I was out early this morning bathing from the sands. There was a delicious feeling of freedom in stripping in the open air and running down naked to the sea where the waves were curling white with foam and the red morning sunshine glowing upon the naked limbs of the bathers.

199. Bathing drawers. 1847.

Although bathing drawers had become the mode in the early forties (Fig. 199) many men disliked them intensely and when Parson Kilvert was forced to bathe in them he describes his experiences most vividly.

> Thursday, July 24, 1873.
>
> At Seaton, while Dora was sitting on the beach, I had a bathe. A boy brought me to the machine door two towels as I thought, but when I came out of the water and began to use them I found that one of the rags he had given me was a pair of very short red and white striped drawers to cover my nakedness. Unaccustomed to such things and customs, I had in my ignorance bathed naked and set at nought the conventionalities of the place and scandalized the beach. However some little boys who were looking on at the rude naked man, appeared to be much interested in the spectacle, and the young ladies who were strolling near, seemed to have no objection.

Next year, in 1874, Kilvert gives a graphic account of his first attempt at being "breeched".

> At Shanklin one has to adopt the detestable custom of bathing in drawers. If ladies dont like to see men naked why dont they keep away from the sight? Today I had a pair of drawers given me which I could not keep on. The rough waves stripped them off and tore them down round my ankles. While

200. The misery of bathing
drawers. 1898.

> thus fettered I was seized and flung down by a heavy sea, which retreating suddenly left me lying naked on the sharp shingle from which I rose streaming with blood. After this I took the wretched and dangerous rag off and of course there were some ladies looking on as I came up out of the water.

Kilvert's Diary, 1870–1879.

Even in the 1860s a protest against bathing suits for men had been voiced.

> Rather let the preposterous exhibition of our bather go on, than condemn
> the Briton rushing into his native sea to feel instead of the vigorous hug of
> Neptune, a clammy clutch from shoulder to knee . . . But let us have none
> of your damp, unpleasant, clinging garments.
>
> *Letters and Memoirs of Sir William Hardman*, 1863.

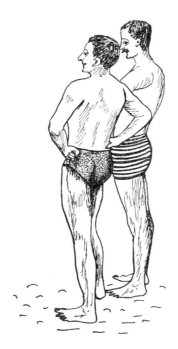

201. Bathing drawers. 1901.

In spite of conventions nude bathing continued.

> The bathing is delightful . . . you see half a dozen fat men at a time scam-
> pering out of the machines. . . . Then they dive, they rise, there is a
> glistening on the right cheek and the left—too distant to offend the most
> gingerly—I opine so, for I have beheld antique virgins, spy-glass in hand to-
> wards the roguish sport.
>
> Letter from George Meredith to Sir William Hardman, 1870,
>   quoted in above.

PLATE 43

Beach wear. *c.* 1862.

"Seaside Attractions" by Erskine Nicol.

PLATE 44

Family group on the beach (Nanny on the left). Little girl in
tam-o'-shanter, baby in sun bonnet. 1902.

Photograph kindly lent by Mrs J. Matthews.

Even as late as 1882 nude bathing must have continued in view of the following notice:

Boro' of Colchester, Municipal Corporations Act 1882. Bye Laws for the Good Rule and Government of the Boro' of Colchester.

Indecent Bathing.

No person shall bathe from any Highway, Street, or public place without wearing drawers or such other dress covering as is necessary to prevent indecent exposure.

202. Bathing suits for men and women. 1877.

Sergent Leahy in his *Art of Swimming in the Eton Style* 1875, makes this surprising comment:

I find that ladies in their bathing dresses are much more buoyant in the water than persons with nothing on them but bathing drawers. This I account for from the flow of water, more or less, through the bathing dresses and because they can stand the coldness of the water better than those who have no clothes on . . . the bathing dress keeps out the repeated cold shocks that the naked body has to incur.

The conventional bathing dress for men started in the late 1830s and consisted of short pants sometimes called *caleçons*. Walker in 1839 states:

> Every swimmer should use short drawers, and might, in particular places, use canvas slippers. It is even of great importance to be able to swim in jacket and trousers,

presumably in case of falling into the sea fully dressed.

203. "Seaside dresses". Black top hat, dark green frock coat, white trousers, white waistcoat. 1830.

By the 1860s *caleçons* were fully established and continued as men's bathing costume to the end of our period (Fig. 201). An alternative style, consisting of bathing suits in one piece with shoulder straps were popular in the 1870s when they were often striped (Fig. 202). This type, dark and plain, the University costume, was used for public swimming contests and became universal from the 1880s on.

So

Bathing is a sport
   Enjoyed by great and small
In suits of any sort
   Though better none at all.

Anon.

BEACHWEAR

Seaside costume both for men and women was usually the ordinary day wear in the fashion of the period, whether appropriate or not. Occasionally special advice as to what was suitable, was given, but whether any gentleman in 1787 acted on the following is perhaps doubtful.

> For the morning provide yourself with a very large round hat. This will preserve your face from the sun and wind, both of which are very prejudicial to the complexion. Let your hair be well filled with pomatum, powder and

204. On Brighton beach. 1861.

> bear's greese, and tuck it under your hat. Have an enormous chitterlin [frill] to your shirt the broader the better; and pull it up to look as like the powter pigeon as you possibly can. A white waistcoat without skirts, and a coat with a collar up to your ears, will do for an early hour; and if they say your head looks like that of John the Baptist in a charger, tell them you are not ashamed to look like an Apostle, whatever they are.
>
> Your first appearance must be in red morocco slippers with yellow heels your second in shoes with the Vandyke tie; your third in cordovan boots

with very long rowelled spurs, which are useful to walk in, for, if you tear a lady's apron it gives you a good opportunity of shewing how gracefully you can ask pardon.

Your fourth dress must be the three-cornered hat, the Paris pump and the Artois buckle.

London Chronicle, Aug. 1787.
(Article concerning dress to be worn at the seaside.)

205. Beachwear in 1864. The lady wears a very large crinoline even when riding a donkey.

The Artois buckle was a very large decorative shoe buckle, extremely fashionable between 1775 and 1788. As to the wearing of spurs with a walking costume, this was not unusual. It was the fashion at this date, whether a man could ride or not. Again the mention of a lady's apron refers to a decorative panel to the front of her dress and not to a protective accessory.

In *Poetical Sketches of Scarborough*, 1813, there is a poem entitled "The Shoe Shop". Here the shoemaker gives advice as to the best footwear for the beach.

Fair Ella and her sister came
To Leatherum's of Crispin fame,
To purchase shoes—experience taught her
They must be made to keep out water.

Leatherum
   "Yes Ma'am, of course you want—some boots."
Ella
   "No sir: I rather choose
   To have a pair of walking shoes."

206. Teenage beachwear in 1887.

Leatherum
   "Why Ma'am, there's nothing Scarboro' suits
   For walking, half so well as boots.
   I make them now—ah here you see,
   Boots that will reach you to the knee:
   With ease to wear and strength of leather
   Suited to every kind of weather,
   To bid defiance to the sea
   Though you should ford it to the knee
   And keep your feet, though rain should fall
   As dry as dancing at a ball . . ."

Ella
  "Well as you choose—
  But let my sister see some shoes."

207. Striped blazers, 1893.

  Strolling in fancy dress by the sea was a custom during the early years of the nineteenth century.

  Among the personages who lately attracted public attention at Brighton was an original, or would-be original, generally known by the appellation of "The Green Man."

  A spruce little man in a doublet of green,
  Perambulates daily, the streets and the Steyne.
  Green striped is his waistcoat, his small clothes are green
  And oft, round his neck, a green 'kerchief is seen.
  Green watch string, green seals, and for certain I've heard,
  (Tho' they're powdered) green whiskers and eke a green beard;
  Green garters, green hose, and deny it who can
  The Brains, too, are green, of this little green man.
                                              Annual Register, 1806.

In a fashion plate dated July 1830 (Fig. 203), standing beside the elegant gentleman depicted, is one in "Fancy Costume, Turkish".

When not dressed to look smart and impress the passers-by, men usually preferred comfortable morning wear for the seaside.

In the 1860s there was a fairly wide range of choice.

208. Bathing machine with "modesty hood". "Well, I'm sure, what a most extraordinary crinoline that creature has on!" says the old lady wearing a talma mantle and a spoon bonnet. Young lady in crinoline dress. 1863.

In Fig. 204, where two men are watching a woman bather with interest, the one with the pipe wears a "lounging jacket" and a "muffin hat", a very popular style mainly worn in this decade. It was a round hat with a flat crown surrounded by a narrow upright brim and made of cloth, for country or seaside wear. The man with the cigar wears a "paletot jacket" and a glengarry.

In Fig. 205, the man on the donkey wears a lounge suit and the country hat peculiar to this date, known as a "bollinger" and featuring a knob on the crown. Without the knob it was called a hemispherical hat. It was a hard felt hat with a bowl-shaped crown.

A great advance in footwear for the beach was made in the mid-nineteenth century and the following account from *The History and Development of Footwear* has been kindly supplied by The Dunlop Company Ltd.

209. "Seaside costume". Skirt and plastron (front panel of bodice) of cream serge trimmed with rows of blue mohair braid. Vest and tunic (i.e. coat bodice and drapery) in blue serge. 1884.

About 1868 the first canvas shoes with rubber soles were introduced, becoming very popular for wear at the seaside. Originally known as sand shoes, they later received the name of Plimsolls, for at about the time of the passing of the Merchant Shipping Act of 1876, through the perseverance of Samuel Plimsoll, the manufacturers had decided to put a band of rubber or golosh around the shoe. Its being likened to the Plimsoll line gave the shoe the name which has passed into common use and has been retained to this day.

An alternative style dress

> to be worn at the sea side in the autumn . . . consists of a short Tweedside jacket . . . waistcoat long . . . no collar and to button up high . . . knickerbockers moderately full, made in the usual style.
>
> *Minister's Gazette of Fashion*, July, 1865.

PLATE 45

Oxford and Cambridge: jerseys, trousers and flat straw hats.
Cox in pilot coat. 1863.

Illustrated London News. *1863.*

PLATE 46

Boating Beauties—with bustles. Draped tunic skirts: fashionable bodices: hats decorated with feathers. 1884.

Cassells Family Magazine. *1884.*

In 1894 the *Tailor and Cutter* tells us that:

> The ruling hat for seaside wear, we were informed, will this season be the
> different kinds of straws . . . while the cloth-covered straw . . . is un-
> doubtedly catching on . . . This hat is made in all shades . . . [and] is
> called the Henley Boater and is expected to be worn more in the autumn
> than during the summer months.

210. Children's seaside clothes in 1865.

Striped blazers started their career for the beach in the 1880s and became
popular seaside wear for men (Fig. 207).

Women appear to have had no let-up. They wore the clothes fashionable
for their day and the head was always covered (Plate 43). The awkwardness of
the crinoline period is laughed at in Fig. 205, where the lady on the donkey
nearly smothers her steed with her enormous crinoline. But as usual, fashion
conquered comfort (Fig. 208). The lady in Fig. 209, wears a seaside costume
described as "skirt and plastron of cream serge trimmed with rows of blue
mohair braid. Vest and tunic in blue serge." The plastron was the front panel
of the bodice. She also wears a bustle.

Children too wore their ordinary clothes, and always some form of head-gear, but in the 1880s comfort began to creep in and:

> For seaside wear, girls as well as boys, have discovered the comfort of the pea-jackets [a short double-breasted jacket] with collar and gold buttons of the most nautical aspect.
>
> *The Lady's World*, 1887.

211. One boy wearing jersey and trousers rolled up; the other in a sailor suit. Both have "brewer's caps". Girl in fashion of the day. 1886.

And the striped flannel jackets, under the familiar name of "blazers" are worn on nearly all occasions [this included the seaside] now by girls and boys.

> Ibid.

Boys might also wear jerseys and knitted "brewer's caps" (Fig. 211). A child's complete outfit for the seaside in 1896 was described as follows:

Next to the skin the child is to wear a thin woollen gauze combination very short in the leg: over that a stay body to which is buttoned a pair of blue serge knickerbockers unlined. Over that only one skirt is worn and that had seven flat buttons sewn on the wrong side near the hem. On the upper part of the skirt are seven corresponding loops so that for paddling the desired shortness is easily attained by buttoning the bottom of the dress to the loops. A little blouse of white serge or washing silk is worn with the skirt and a short blue serge jacket added according to the weather or time of day . . . Long merino stockings should be worn, which should pass under the knickers. To take off the effect of the sun's rays on the head it is well to give the hat a complete green head lining, using a dull green so as to avoid arsenical dyes.

The Housewife.

Even after the turn of the century children playing on the sea shore had to wear hats, caps or sunbonnets. A typical middle-class Edwardian group is shown in Plate 44.

But whatever they wore no doubt they all enjoyed

A mile of warm sea-scented beach.

Robert Browning, *Meeting at Night.*

Bibliography

Bacon, Sir Francis. *New Atlantis*, pub. posthumously in "Sylva Sylvarum" ed. John Haviland, London, Wm. Lea, 1627.
Digby, Everarde. *De Arte Natandi*, London, Thomas Dawson, 1587.
Frost, J. *Scientific Swimming*, London, 1816.
Leahy, "Sergeant". *The Art of Swimming in the Eton Style.* London, Macmillan, 1875.
Percy, William. *The Complete Swimmer.* London, Henry Fletcher, 1658.

CHAPTER 16

ROWING AND SAILING

BY ALAN MANSFIELD

> The halcyons brood around the foamless isles:
> The treacherous ocean has forsworn its wiles:
> The merry mariners are bold and free:
> Say, my heart's sister, wilt thou sail with me   Shelley.

As a maritime nation we have traditionally a working association with the sea and ships: an association which over the last three hundred or so years has extended to embrace our leisure hours also; producing a devoted band of spare time sailors on sea, river and lake, whose existence is occasionally brought into prominence by an event such as Dunkirk or an individual such as Chichester or Rose.

As in other sporting activities the early yachtsman or wet-bob paid little heed to his costume: what he normally wore sufficed, perhaps adapted in some details or supplemented by some acceptable items. These adaptations or additions should not in any way impair his amateur appearance; although, as "Craven" sarcastically condemned there were always

> noblemen and gentlemen who have enough of patriotic ambition to look like smugglers, enough of delicacy to disregard their being thought dirty lubbers by their own men. . . .
>   Walker's *Manly Exercises*, 1839.

In 1661 Evelyn records that he

> sail'd this morning with his Majesty in one of his yachts (or pleasure-boats), vessells not known among us till the Dutch E. India Company presented that curious piece to the King . . .
>   *Diary*, 1st October, 1661.

Pepys also records these early Royal yachts, and five years later speaks of a party arriving from Flanders in "the Catherine yacht", including

> Sir Thomas Liddall, with a very pretty daughter, and in a pretty travelling-dress.
>   Pepys *Diary*, 2nd June, 1666.

A YACHTING COSTUME OF BLUE SERGE.

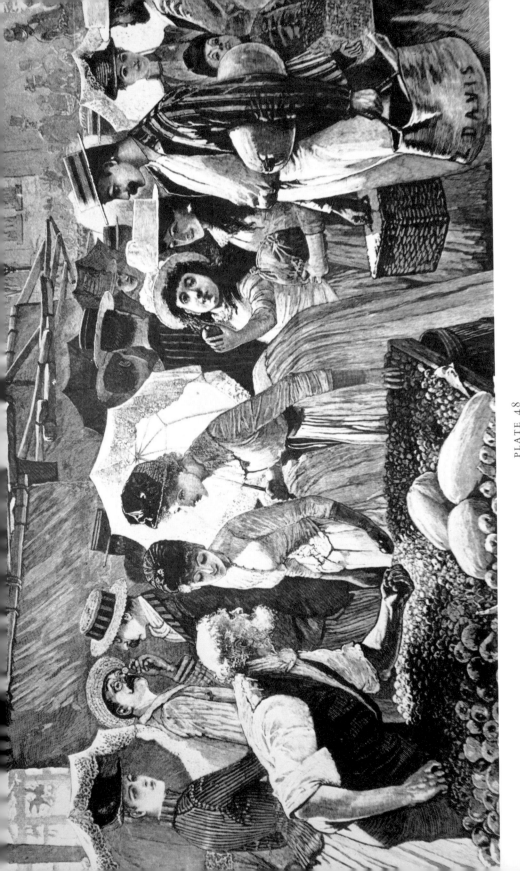

PLATE 48

Blazers. 1887.

Illustrated London News, September 1887.

The pretty daughter's travelling dress might as appropriately have been worn when travelling by road.

These yachts of the seventeenth century were, of course, the toys of the rich and noble, and so they remained for another hundred and fifty or two hundred years. However, during the eighteenth century the use of small boats on the river or at the seaside for pleasure purposes became more common, and water parties with fishing or picnicking as an object were popular in its later years. Three young men painted with a sailing boat on the Waveney in 1780 wore frocks,[1] breeches, stockings and shoes. Their frocks are worn open with waistcoats beneath: two are bareheaded, one wears an uncocked low crowned round hat.

The angling party in Morland's painting are wearing the fashionable and elaborate clothes of the men and women of 1790. (Plate 34.)

The end of the century saw King George III at Weymouth, and in her memoirs Elizabeth Ham recalls that

> Once a week the Royal Party generally went for a sail. The Royal yachts were in attendance for this purpose . . . The Queen and Princesses always wore dark blue Habits on these occasions, and I have often seen them look very miserable and bedraggled on their return.
>
> *Elizabeth Ham by Herself*, Eric Gillett, 1945.

In the early nineteenth century "aquatic sports" of rowing or sailing races attracted spectators in boats wearing top-hats, if men, and elaborate bonnets and parasols if women. For rowing men might wear striped jerseys, and in 1829 the first Oxford and Cambridge boat race, held at Henley, saw the Oxford crew dressed in dark blue striped jerseys, canvas trousers, and black straw hats. The Cambridge rowers wore white shirts and pink sashes. The Cantabs light blue is said to have been introduced in 1836.

Women were not so common a sight on the river, at least as active rowers, but the wives and daughters of fishermen apparently engaged in races. A report of such a match in 1833 rowed on the Thames, commented on the large numbers of spectators and announced that

> the lady who wore a blue bow in her cap as large as a sunflower, and who had her garments tied round her legs with a rope, had the distinguished honour of being declared the victory.
>
> *The Times*, 4th September, 1833.

[1] See page 111

A photograph of 1858 shows the Cambridge crew in white trousers and short-sleeved shirts or jerseys, with round necks, fastening slightly off-centre, and straw hats, or caps. A print of 1863 (Plate 45) shows the same dress, with the cox in a reefer jacket. This style of dress persisted during the 1870s, thick jerseys being worn in addition when not actually racing, if necessary.

212. Reefer or Pilot jackets: (*a*) single-breasted 1889; (*b*) double-breasted 1892. Yachting caps.

From the 1830s "aquatic" shirts had been worn on the river and at the seaside. They were self-coloured, or with stripes or checks in colours on white. They might be collarless or with a large attached collar.

> Bob Jones is a rowing man of the second class. . . . He wears a blue checked shirt without a collar, a coloured neck cloth, a cut-away green coat and in-expressibles that fit as tight as a second skin.
>
> Kenny Meadows, *Heads of the People*, 1841.

> The ties are also as free and as open as the sea; fastened in a loose knot and the ends are allowed to coquet with the idle breeze. Shirts, if not ruled in red lines, they are in blue. Collars are large and hang down on the side à la poodle.
>
> *Punch*, 1848.

Flannel shirts were also to be seen, and braces were as acceptable on the rivers as on the cricket field in the mind-nineteenth century.

> . . . they all went on the river; the popular preacher [Rev. J. M. Bellew] being clothed in a scarlet flannel shirt, with gorgeous braces worked by the fair hands of some female admirer among his congregation.
>
> *Sir William Hardman's Memoirs*, 1862.

213. Yachting: tight bodices; draped overskirts; bustles; yachting caps. 1887.

For the yachtsman a jacket was *de rigeur*

> . . . a bunch of portly gentlemen in round jackets and white trousers in the lugger-yacht, who stand consequentially on deck, with, as they think, the eyes of England upon them.
>
> R. S. Surtees, *Plain or Ringlets*, 1860.

Jackets could be single- (Fig. 212a) or double-breasted (Fig. 212b) and went under the name of Reefer or Pilot coat. A shorter unwaisted version was the pea- or monkey-jacket. Blue serge was general.

Hats were generally varieties of the straw sailor, with ribbon bows with long ends, or boaters. In the 1880s the yachting cap, a peaked forage-cap based on the naval officer's, was introduced (Fig. 212). Trousers were often white and were sometimes of the bell-bottom variety, tight above and 22 inches at the ankles. Black or black and white leather, or white canvas shoes were acceptable. In the 1870s and 1880s knickerbockers and Norfolk jackets or Norfolk shirts were sometimes worn.

By the 1890s the accepted yachting dress for men was a blue reefer suit, or reefer jacket and white trousers, yachting cap and black shoes.

214. Sailing in serge: serge dress, straw "boater" hat. See text. 1892.

The ladies of the nineteenth century stepped aboard the yachts clad in all the glories of fashionable dresses with little consideration for their fitness for the occasion: concessions were made in colours, but in little else. The lady of the sixties wore a dress of dark blue serge trimmed with white braid, a small hat, coloured handkerchief at the neck, and, sign and seal of the Perfect Lady, gauntlet gloves.

The Jersey costume of 1879 was worn for tennis, and may also have been seen aboard, for we read that it was extremely popular at Ryde, worn with a serge or flannel skirt.

Ladies in 1884 took to the river in draped and kilted overskirts and skin-tight bodices, feathered and flowered hats and, underneath, woollen combinations, drawers, corset, chemise, and bustle of whalebone, wire or horsehair (Plate 46).

Similar dresses, though less elaborate, were worn when yachting, sometimes with a yachting cap (Fig. 213). Despite their complexity, such outfits
were not unduly expensive:

Yachting Costumes from £1. 15. 0.

Peter Robinson advertisement, 1887.

215. Punting: plain dress with basqued bodice, full sleeves: hat
trimmed with ribbon and artificial flowers. 1892.

Blue serge trimmed with white remained popular in the 1890s, and fashion
plates of the decade show the society yachtswoman in this material (Plate 47),
which was equally popular among her humbler sisters, if less expertly tailored,
and worn on other occasions also. The "badly made serge frock" worn by
the heroine of a tale in *Cassels Family Magazine* for 1892 (Fig. 214) was not
specifically designed for sailing: neither was the morning dress of another
young lady in the same magazine solely worn when punting, an occupation
in which she often indulged (Fig. 215).

At least one contemporary writer was critical of the boating dresses of his day:

> Nothing is more fetching, to my thinking, than a tasteful boating costume. But a "boating costume" it would be well if all ladies would understand, ought to be a costume that can be worn in a boat, and not merely under a glass case . . . all lace and silk stuff, and flowers, and ribbons, and dainty shoes and light gloves . . . They were the "boating costumes" of a French fashion plate. It was ridiculous fooling about in them anywhere near real earth, air, and water.
>
> Jerome K. Jerome, *Three Men in a Boat*, 1889.

216. Yachting: man in knickerbockers and lounge jacket; cloth cap and stockings and gaiters: Woman in double-breasted reefer jacket, with fashionable sleeves, stiff collar, tie, yachting cap. 1897.

Late nineteenth-century fashion plates of boating and yachting costume generally show the models clutching an oar or rope or some other nautical object, without which symbol it would at times be difficult to decide for what occasions the elaborate confections they are wearing were intended.

The advance of women in the 1890s and their increasing invasion of the male domain was reflected on the yacht as elsewhere by the adoption of garments modelled on men's fashions side by side with the purely feminine modes, and the severely cut reefer jacket and peaked cap (Fig. 216) of 1897 continued into the twentieth century. A popular hostess of 1904 appeared at Cowes in an untrimmed dark blue coat and skirt, naval peaked cap, shirt, stiff collar, and tie; a contrast to the "yachting dress of white flannel, a large picture hat and flowing veil" advertised in 1906.

217. "At Henley"—linen or muslin frock; large straw hat decorated with artificial flowers. 1902.

On the river, the flowing draperies of the 1890s were carried over into the Edwardian era, the flared skirt of that period balancing the large, wide-brimmed hat (Fig. 217). A period of gracious curves began to give way in 1908–9 to a straighter line leading to plain, tubular skirts, ankle length, as seen in the 1912 dress "for tennis or river wear" (Fig. 218). Energetic rowers anchored their skirts below the knees with strong rubber bands, an up-to-date version of the rope of 1833.

218. For the river or tennis: Princess dress, hand embroidered, in "washing fabric equal in appearance to linen". See text. *c.* 1912.

219. Boating single-breasted jacket with small turn-down collar; knickerbockers; white leather or canvas shoes; straw "boater" hat. 1874.

Meanwhile, the rowing man had, in the 1870s adopted knickerbockers (Fig. 219) of white flannel, which gave place in the 1880s among serious oarsmen to shorts. Those who took to the river less energetically remained content with trousers—generally of white flannel (Fig. 220).

> Every man with a grain of respectability, on the river puts on white trousers, with white flannel shirt, straw hat, striped flannel coat.
>
> *The Gentleman's Magazine of Fashion*, 1884.

220. Boating: striped shirt or jersey: white flannel trousers, with ends of legs turned up; brewer's cap. 1891.

The striped flannel coat is the blazer. In the 1880s blazers gained great popularity and were seen in all varieties of multi-coloured stripes (Plate 48).

> The latest novelty for the river is flannels, a blazer, and spats.
>
> Durham University, 1885, quoted in *Oxford English Dictionary*.

Cricket caps, Panama or linen hats, sometimes with a veil covering the neck, and occasionally knitted fisherman's caps were seen in addition to the ubiquitous straw boater.

A feature noticeable in the 1890s is the habit of turning up the bottom of the trousers when boating (Fig. 221) to keep the trouser bottoms from getting wetted—a habit probably originating in the 1880s to keep the trousers dry in

wet weather, and also, perhaps, among the smart young men, to show off
their fancy-buttoned boots. By 1896 the fashion had become acceptable with
lounge suits.

Below the trousers would be worn Russian leather or canvas boating shoes.

The yachtswoman of the early twentieth century found the motor-veil
convenient afloat to secure the fashionable large hats, if these were worn
instead of the yachting cap.

221. Punting: striped blazer; white flannel trousers, turned up at legs;
brown or black and white shoes: straw hat with veil shielding neck.
1891.

In 1910 a typical rig for yachting was white skirt and white jersey, yachting cap and white canvas shoes for women; and white trousers, blue reefer,
white shirt, stiff collar, dark tie, yachting cap and white shoes for men. In
wet weather sou'westers and oilskins have been "musts" for small boat
enthusiasts from their introduction in the early nineteenth century until today.

In the early years of the present century the rowing man, as distinct from
the man in a boat, took his exercise in vest and shorts, calf-length socks and
shoes. The neck and sleeves, and sometimes the socks, might bear stripes of

the rowing club colours. The rowing woman is not very evident in our period, but a photograph of about 1920 shows a Ladies Eight wearing white sailor-type blouses worn over dark blue or black knee-length shorts, black stockings and black leather boating shoes. The cox wore also a blazer with club badge and a striped scarf. Several of the girls had hair ribbons or bandeaux around their heads.

Bibliography

Cunnington, C. W. and P. *Handbook of English Costume in the Nineteenth Century.* Faber and Faber, 2nd ed, 1966.

Jerome, Jerome K. *Three Men in a Boat.* Reader's Library Edition, 1927.

CHAPTER 17

SKATING

BY PHILLIS CUNNINGTON

In solitude, such intercourse was mine,
. . . I wheeled about,
Proud and exulting like an untired horse
That cares not for his home. All shod with steel,
We hissed along the polished ice, in games confederate.

William Wordsworth, The Prelude, 1802.

Going "all shod with steel" was practised, of course, long before Wordsworth's time, in fact skating as an outdoor recreation developed in England in the 1660s when the Stuarts made it a fashionable winter sport.

Before this period, in Tudor times and as far back as the Middle Ages, skating of a primitive kind was performed on skates made of bone (Plate 49). The cannon bones of horses and other animals were used. They were pierced with a hole through which a thong was threaded to tie the skate to the wearer's boot or shoe. The skaters usually propelled themselves along the ice with a long stick held in each hand.

Here is a short extract from William Fitz Stephen's account in *Descriptio Londiniae*, translated by H. E. Butler; although written in *c.* 1170, it would apply also to the Tudor period.

> When the great marsh that washes the northern walls of the City is frozen, dense throngs of youths desport themselves upon the ice. Some gathering speed with a run glide side-long with feet set apart . . . Others there are more skilled to sport upon the ice, who fit to their feet the shin-bones of beasts,[1] lashing them beneath their ankles, and with iron-shod poles in their hands, they strike ever and anon against the ice, and are borne along swift as a bird or a bolt shot from a mangonel.

The iron skates of the seventeenth century were introduced from Holland and with these the true sport of skating began. Both Pepys and Evelyn give

---

[1] Specimens of bone skates can be seen in the London Museum, Guildhall Museum and Castle Museum Colchester.

accounts of watching skaters on the new canal in St James's Park during the hard frost of 1662.

> . . . where I first in my life, it being a great frost, did see people sliding with their skeates, which is a very pretty art.
>
> Pepys, Diary, (Entry for December 1662).

> Having seen the strange and wonderfull dexterity of the sliders on the new Canall in St James's Park, perform'd by divers gentlemen and others with skates, after the manner of the Hollanders. . . .
>
> John Evelyn, Diary (Entry for 1662).

These early metal skates were iron-bladed runners, probably fixed to a wooden sole.

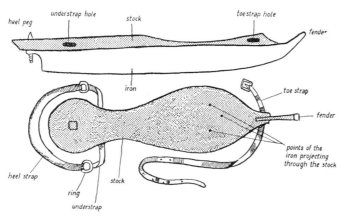

222. Diagrams of 18th century skates.

In 1772 Robert Jones brought out *A Treatise on Skating*, the first manual on skating to be published. In Section I he described various methods used for fastening on the skates (Fig. 222):

> Some have done this by means of a strong tape put through the holes in front of the skate, which is then tied across the toes, and from thence being carried through the rings in the heel strap, is brought back again, and tightly fastened by a knot over the instep; some have their shoes screwed to the stocks of skates, others have them fastened to plates of brass, which are fixed to the skate irons instead of wooden stocks. . . . the common people . . . only make use of buckles, straps, rings, and heel pegs. . . .

A number of other examples are given but he condemns them all and ends by saying:

> All the preceding methods being defective in some particular or other; I shall now give one both safe and simple, which I have practised for many years without the least inconveniency. My method is this: Let the skates be prepared with toe and heel straps, as usual; but instead of heel pegs, let the heel screws be made with flat heads and long enough to go through the heels of the shoes, in which holes must be bored, and the heads of the screws sunk even with the leather so to prevent hurting the feet; to guard against which more effectually, let a piece of leather be sewed to the quarter of the shoe, which will defend it sufficiently from the screw.

It is interesting to note that at this date shoes and not boots were worn for skating (Fig. 223).

223. Gentleman in frock (day coat with turn-down collar), waistcoat and breeches. "Tricorne" hat and shoes. 1772.

An exception to the wearing of shoes is seen in an aquatint showing skating in Hyde Park in 1787, where an old gentleman in a red greatcoat wears top-boots.

The front curve up (fender) of the blade in the eighteenth-century skates continued into the nineteenth, a change taking place towards the 1860s;

though some skates continued with the old pattern still later. Compare Figs. 225 and 227.

The costume worn by skaters was purely the fashionable winter wear of the period. The delightful portrait by Gilbert Stuart of William Grant[1] skating on the Serpentine in 1782, shows him in a coat with a turn-down collar, then known as a frock (not frock-coat); a short waistcoat, knee breeches and a "round hat" of beaver. Even children wore their ordinary clothes (Fig. 224).

224. (*a*) In "skeleton" suit, i.e. trousers buttoned to a short tight jacket, a favourite boy's wear at this date. 1816. (*b*) Tail coat, breeches, round beaver hat and turn down frilled collar.

In 1815, the skaters from "*Les Patineurs Anglais*" (Fig. 225), all wear round hats, most are in tail coats and one man has a spencer—a waist-length overcoat—but now they all wear boots of the style called Hessians.

Poor Mr Winkle (of *Pickwick Papers* fame) found skates too complicated an accessory of footwear to adjust:

> All this time, Mr Winkle, with his face and hands blue with the cold, had been forcing a gimlet into the soles of his feet and putting his skates on with the points behind, and getting the straps into a very complicated and entan-

[1] Mellon Collection.

gled state with the assistance of Mr Snodgrass who knew rather less about skates than a Hindoo. At length however . . . the unfortunate skates were firmly screwed and buckled on.   (1837.)

225. The skaters wear round hats and Hessian boots. The central figure wears a Spencer, i.e. a very short overcoat. The others have cut-away tailcoats. 1815.

In 1839 a man's skating dress is described as follows by Walker in his *Manly Exercises*:

> A skater's dress should be as close and unincumbered as possible. Large skirts get entangled with his own limbs or those of the persons who pass near him; and all fulness is exposed to the wind. Loose trousers, frocks, and more especially great coats, must be avoided; and indeed, by wearing additional underclothing, they can always be dispensed with.
>
> As the exercise of skating produces perspiration, flannel next the chest, shoulders and loins is necessary to avoid the evils produced by sudden chills in cold weather. The best dress is what is called a dress coat, buttoned, tight pantaloons, and laced boots (having the heel no higher than is necessary for the peg) which hold the foot tightly and steadily in its place, as well as give the support to the ankle: for it is of no use to draw the straps of the skate hard, if the boot or shoe be loose.

Fig. 226 shows how not to dress.

PLATE 49

(*a*) Bone skates as used in medieval and Tudor times.

Colchester Castle Museum.

(*b*) "As for her to whose neat bottines the gimlet is applied at
this moment for the purpose of fixing a pair of skates . . . we
hope she will enjoy this intended pastime." 1875.

Illustrated London News, *2 January 1875. "Winter Amusements"*
(*Detail*).

PLATE 50

Edwardian skating fashions.

James Laver Collection. "Sketched at Prince's Club" in 1906. An illustration from The New Album.

A decided advance was made in the 1860s when further thought was given regarding costume suitable for skaters. In *A System of Figure-Skating* by H. E. Vandervell and T. Maxwell in 1869 "The Dress of the Skater" is contemplated.

> In considering how the skater should be attired, we have to observe that fashion and custom have not sanctioned, as in other athletic pastimes, a special dress for him, the probable reason being that men rush to the ice before and after business hours, and any peculiar (though comfortable) costume would thus be inconvenient. We need hardly remark that the white cravat, swallow-tailed coat, and pantaloons (the old dress of the Skating Club) are things of the past.

226. Amateurs, 1826. The right-hand figure wears an outgrown coat, tight "gaiter-pantaloons" and a bright red waistcoat.

We may also remark that, when a man is about to take violent exercise, no matter what the temperature may be, he, if possible, divests himself with great eagerness of all clothing likely to impede him . . . let the skater take care that his clothes are well fitted, so that the action of the arms and legs is not interfered with. The coat, such as the Beaufort [Fig. 227], with rounded skirts and buttoned across the chest to prevent flapping of the said skirts, will do very well, and better indeed than the frock coat, though, perhaps, not so well as the dress coat. We also recommend a warm vest, flannel shirt, and under jersey, with the trousers tight round the waist, whatever fashion is given to the legs, ordinary warm drawers, and socks of cotton, merino or silk.

227. Beaufort coat, trousers and top hat.
1868.

The overcoat should be used for coming and going, and standing still, but not when skating, as it is not only unnecessary but apt to make the skater so warm that standing still for a few minutes even may give a chill that will cause a cold.

We must absolutely forbid the use on the ice of the walking-stick, as it is utterly useless as an artificial support for the learner, and excessively dangerous to everyone in the immediate vicinity . . . We now come to

The Boots

We prefer, after numerous trials of all kinds of boots, those of the lace–up kind, with good stiff, or even double, upper leathers, and moderately thick sole and heel. . . . The next best boot in our opinion is the one with elastic sides . . . if the skates are fastened with the modern cramps, instead of straps, it is absolutely necessary that the boot should fit tight to the foot otherwise the foot "wrings over" in the boot when the edges are being skated.

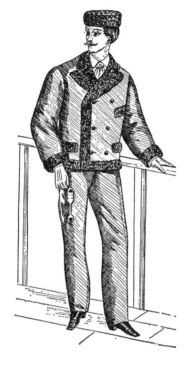

228. Short fur-trimmed jacket without skirts. Fur cap, style known as a "muffin cap". 1870.

Finally various types of skates are described:

The skate most generally in use is made after this fashion: a wooden bed, hollowed out to fit the boot as closely as possible; three small spikes in the front part of it to enter the sole and a good screw or pike to go into the heel; the iron of the skate extending but a trifle beyond the length of the foot, and rounded fore and aft [Plate 49]. The fastening may be one strap passing under the wood, and crossed over the foot. There are a variety of fastenings, however, but the reader must remember . . . that the object is to firmly attach the skate without cumbering the foot and . . . if contrary to our advice, he intends to skate in a Wellington or other boot of like character, he must have more straps in order to fasten both it and the skate securely on.

It is here that the great advantage of the lace-up boot is apparent, for it permits the straps to be reduced to a minimum or eliminated altogether.

The writer mentions and disapproves of

> skates entirely of metal—the metallic ring of which can be easily distin-
> guished.

He then describes several varieties.

> We now arrive at a very old-fashioned skate without straps. This has the
> iron fastened permanently into the sole of the boot, and thus causes the
> trouble of taking off the regular boots with the thermometer, perhaps, at
> ten degrees.
>   The next skate on our list is a patent one which has recently appeared in the
> shop windows; it is entirely metallic, with an open toe-cap and bed, and
> adjusting screw at the heel, which projects slightly behind, by means of which
> the skate is tightened longitudinally and two pikes enter the front part of the
> heel . . . on the same plan as the Halifax skate.
>   The last skate on our list is called the "Ladies' Clog Skate" [Compare
> Fig. 229] . . .

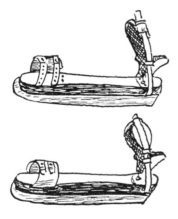

229. "Wooden skates shod with iron or steel, used universally by both sexes." 1878.

Skates that are used exclusively for running are made longer in the irons
. . . the irons are very thin; the ends beyond the toes also turn up, and often
project very much in front.
    Altogether, then there is a vast variety of skates, varying as much in
appearance as in price, from 3s. 6d. to 56s. (including the boot fittings but not
the boots); and considering that the outfit of the skater costs so little, it is
good policy to avoid purchasing those of so low a price as would exclude
good materials and workmanship.

The "boot skate"—also called the "skate boot"—was recommended for ladies by George Anderson in his *Art of Skating*, 1868.

> For ladies, I should consider them by far the best . . . The skate iron is just inserted in the thick sole of a lacing ankle boot and there is no fastening beyond putting on the boot and lacing it firmly [Fig. 230].

230. Lady in small hat, a full-skirted green paletot with a shawl-like collar. A short buff-coloured skirt, "boot skates". Gentleman in a short dark coat and a thick white woollen muffler round his neck. Trousers pale bluish grey. 1874.

An anonymous writer in 1870 states:

> The "skate boot" invented in the great frost some years ago, is highly recommended. Another in use by the London Skating Club called the "elastic skate" is also good, from a spring being introduced at the bottom of the foot, which keeps it firmly in its place. . . . Skates of gutta percha are also worthy of notice for young skaters.

This writer also considers clothes suitable for skating worn by ladies.

> It is indispensable that extra warm clothing should be worn, and a close-fitting dress, but not too tight; the skirt short and narrow, and of warm heavy material [Fig. 231].
>
> Article in *The Young Lady's Book*.

Although the following account describes the costume worn by fashionable women on a covered ice rink, similar garments might equally be seen in the open air, in the 1890s when skating was becoming very popular. (Compare Plate 50.)

> A skating costume furnishes an opportunity for the display of handsome furs, and an electric-blue dress trimmed with golden beaver, and a biscuit coloured gown with an ermine waistcoat have both been much admired at the Real Ice Rink of artificial ice which will keep the skating furore up yet for some months to come in town. A good many ladies come in heavy carriage wraps, which they throw aside in order to appear in the smartest of blouses, in company with plain black skirts. A beautiful blouse was in cornflower blue chiffon, tucked to fit the figure with a broad box pleat down the front, fastened with diamond studs. Another was in heliotrope silk with cut-steel buttons, and a beaver collar, finished off with a bunch of Neapolitan violets on one side, and a heliotrope chiffon rosette at the other.
>
> *The Housewife*, Vol. X (1895).

231. Polonaise (overskirt) and skirt of waterproof tweed. Military trimming. 1872.

The whims of fashion have certainly dictated some startling variations in the upper garments of skaters; yet the essential item, the skate itself, has not radically changed since the far-off days when the sport was so young that Swift could write to Stella:

The Canal and Rosamond's Pond full of the rabble sliding and with *skates* if you know what they are.

> Swift's *Journal to Stella* (Letter headed "London, Jan: 31, 1711").

Bibliography

Anderson, George (="Cyclos"). *The Art of Skating.* 2nd Ed., London, Horace Cox, 1868.

Brown, Nigel. *Ice Skating.* London, Nicholas Karf, 1959.

Jones, Robert ("A Gentleman"). *Treatise on Skating*, London, 1775 (1st pubd. 1772).

Vandervell, H. F. and Witham, T. Maxwell. *A System of Figure-Skating.* London, Macmillan, 1869.

CHAPTER 18

RUNNING AND ATHLETICS

BY ALAN MANSFIELD

. . . neither delighteth He in any man's legs.	Psalm 147.

Th'athletic fool, to whom what Heaven denied
Of soul, is well compensated in limbs.   John Armstrong.

From remote ages trials of physical strength and skill have been a natural feature where men gathered together, either as incidentals to the purpose of the gathering, or as its purpose *per se*. Village wakes and fairs, and licensed assemblies for games all provided opportunities for running, jumping, wrestling, as well as archery and such forgotten sports as tilting at the quintain.

A document of Queen Elizabeth I dated 1569 refers to John Powlter as organizing in Middlesex Sunday games, including

> . . . the Lepping [leaping=jumping] for Men, the Running for Men, the Wrastlinge, the Throwing of the Sledge and the Pytchinge of the Barre, with all such other games as have at anytime heretofore or now be licenced, used, or played.
>
> *Gentleman's Magazine,* 1813 (said to have been in possession of
> Sir John Evelyn).

The *Spectator* in 1711 notes a country wake with

> Cudgel-players . . . a foot-ball match . . . a ring of wrestlers. . . .

and goes on to say

> A country fellow that throws his rival upon his back, has generally as good success with their common mistress; as nothing is more usual than for a nimble-footed wench to get a husband at the same time she wins a smock.
>
> *Spectator,* 4th September, 1711.

Running races with a smock as a prize was common among young women at fairs and on other occasions. Brand says that

These races were frequent among the young country wenches in the North. The prize, a fine Holland chemise was usually decorated with ribands. The Sport is still continued at Newburn, near Newcastle.

Brand, *Popular Antiquities*, 3rd edit. Preface dated 1848.

Quoting a poem referring to a smock race in Ireland:

Stript for the race how bright she did appear
No covering hid her feet, her bosom bare
And to the wind she gave her flowing hair.

Steele Poetical Miscellanies 1714, quoted in Brand, op. cit.

An eighteenth-century print, "Smock Race at Tottenham", shows the contestants, some fully dressed and wearing caps, but one bare-headed and exposing her breasts, all wearing shoes.

A seventeenth-century ballad describes a smock race where

In half-shirts and drawers these Maids did run.

The Virgins' Race, or Yorkshire's Glory,
quoted in Ashton, *Ballads etc. of the 17th century*.

This is unusual as drawers were not usually worn by women in the seventeenth century.

Men at the same period, according to the illustration in Annalia Dubrensia jumped and wrestled and hurled the hammer wearing doublet, breeches, stockings and shoes, but not hats (Fig. 88).

A foreign traveller visiting England in 1782 speaks of the "fine, ruddy, slim, active boys, with their bosoms open" and says that

free, loose, and natural dress is worn till they are eighteen, or even 'till they are twenty. It is then indeed discontinued by the higher ranks but with the common people it always remains the same.

Travels of C. P. Moritz in England 1782—English translation, 1795.

A painting attributed to A. W. Devas of a Lord Harris, aged 12, pole-jumping in 1794 does not convey such a free and easy picture of dress. The boy wears a tight, striped, waistcoat, frilled shirt, breeches buttoned at the knee, stockings and shoes, although he wears neither coat nor hat. He is vaulting with a pole over a 6-foot gate.

Hats were often awarded to the winners of wrestling matches and also to the victors at back-sword play, which was much the same as cudgel play, fought with wooden sticks, like single sticks, the object being to graze the opponent's forehead (Fig. 232):

> the old farmer . . . who is master of the revels . . . announces . . . that a half-sovereign in money will be forthcoming . . . to which the Squire and he have added a new hat.
>
> T. Hughes, *Tom Brown's Schooldays*, 1857.

232. Backsword play: open-necked shirts, breeches and braces: left-hand tied to thigh by handkerchief. Early 19th century.

Hughes is writing of the 1830s, and two of the back-sword competitors are thus described:

> Joe's white shirt and spotless drab breeches and boots contrasting with the gipsy's coarse blue shirt and dirty green velveteen breeches and leather gaiters.
>
> Ibid.

Cornish wrestlers in the seventeenth century

> set forthe stripped into their dublets and hosen, and untrussed, that they may so the better command the use of their lymmes . . .
>
> R. Carew, *Survey of Cornwall*, 1602.

At the same time men were reported to run races in Derbyshire, naked: a contrast to the boys racing the stage-coach in *Tom Brown's Schooldays*—

they had "their jackets buttoned tight". But when running with the Big-side Hare-and-Hounds Tom

> girded himself with a leather strap, and left all superfluous clothing behind.
>
> T. Hughes, op. cit.

As in many other cases, athletics did not acquire a distinctive form of dress until the middle of the nineteenth century—up to then, as we have seen, the discarding of more or less of the normal clothing was deemed sufficient; as the celebrated match in Paris between Mr Jorrocks and the Baron demonstrates:

> Mr Jorrocks ungirded his sword and depositing it with his frock coat in the cab . . . Mr Jorrocks action was not very capital, his jack-boots and leathers rather impeding his limbs, while the Baron had as little on him as decency would allow.
>
> R. S. Surtees, *Jorrocks' Jaunts and Jollities*, 1831–34.

233. Vaulting: open-necked shirts, tight trousers: belt and round hat.
1839.

In the 1830s it was recommended that

> the coat and all unnecessary clothes should be laid aside; and all hard or sharp things should be taken from the pockets of the remaining dress. A very light covering on the head, as a straw hat, is best; the shirt collar should be open,

the breast being either exposed or thinly covered; the waistband of the trousers should not be tight, and the boots or shoes should have no iron about them [Fig. 233].

> "Craven", *Walker's Manly Exercises*, 1839.

In addition, says "Craven", "a belt or cincture is of utility" and he advocates a belt five or six inches wide (or eight or ten for wrestlers) with buckle and strap to fasten it, a pocket and an iron ring, which last two are

> to inclose the articles that may be wanted according to the class of exercises performing.

and to

> suspend, by means of hooks, anything we wish to carry, so as to leave the hands at liberty.

> Ibid.

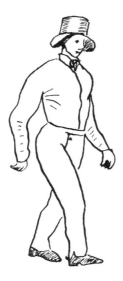

234. Walking: tight jacket, trousers, tall-crowned hat with wide brim. *c.* 1820s.

This advice, as we have seen, was followed by Tom Brown. Similarly, his school fellows with their buttoned jackets had examples in the walking champions who were a feature of the first half of the nineteenth century (Fig. 234), though not all of them went as far as Captain John Campbell who marched ten miles in under two hours wearing a complete soldier's kit, small arms, and ammunition; with heavy bets placed on the result.

Similar kit was worn by Sir John Astly in 1856, in his case running two hundred yards at the Army athletic meeting at Aldershot. Astly was a noted amateur runner, and normally his attire was of a scantier nature:

> I alluded to the light and airy costume I used to run my races in, which consisted (if no ladies were present) of a tiny pair of drawers—made of silk— with a pattern like the plaid band round the Scots Guards forage caps. If the fair ones were to the fore, the same little gems were pulled over silk tights.
>
> Sir J. D. Astly, *Fifty Years of my Life*, 1894.

235. Perkins walking against time: vest, drawers, and gloves. 1875.

Astly used to carry his silk shorts in a cigar case, and on one occasion, being asked to open a Working Men's Club, he produced cigar case and shorts and pointed out the great advantage running had as a sport in that so little luggage was needed to be carried about. Alas, his ideas were too advanced for some of his audience, and the following day a letter appeared in the local paper from a clergyman who had been present complaining that

Anything more ungentlemanly than the way in which he (Astly) spoke of and displayed his luggage, I never heard, and considering that half his audience were ladies, he might have spared us that part of his speech. For my own part—having a lady with me—the only thing to do was to leave the hall at once.

Ibid.

236. Inter-University Athletics: hurdlers in vests and knickerbockers.
1875.

Other drawers, not in the Scots Guards plaid, were worn in 1875 (Fig. 235), but in the meantime runners and athletes in the 1860s were wearing very modern looking shorts. Vests, stockings and light boots or shoes made up the athlete's outfit, often with a cap in addition. Vests and shorts were sometimes edged with stripes in club colours.

Shorts were worn at the Inter-University Athletic meetings of the 1860s and 1870s, but they were apparently not considered essential at least for domestic contests: W. Allison writes of Balliol in 1871:

So little did I really think of the Athletics, being then the merest novice, that I never troubled to get shorts or running shoes, and went to run in baggy flannels, tucked into my socks, and boating shoes.

William Allison, *My Kingdom for a Horse*, 1919.

Of the previous year, when still at Rugby, Allison notes that at the school athletics

we ran on grass and had no proper running shoes or shorts.

Ibid.

237. Walkers: shorts over tights: vests, one long sleeved: scarf round neck; bowler hat and cap. See text. 1878.

Knickerbockers were also sometimes worn for cross-country running, hurdling or hare-and-hounds (Fig. 236) and a type of shorts which appear to have elastic in the legs appeared at the Agricultural Hall in 1878 (Fig. 237). These shorts are shown as worn over tights, and one feels that ladies present or not, the addition of a bowler-hat as worn by one of the contestants shows a gentlemanliness sufficient to satisfy the most critical of parsons.

At the end of the nineteenth century and during the years up to the Great War the athelete and runner were clad in very similar garments to those worn today. Shorts varied in length, some being three or four inches below the knee, others as many inches above. Vests had short sleeves. Club colours were often shown in coloured stripes at the neck and sleeves of vests, and round the edges of the legs of the shorts (Fig. 238, Plate 51).

238. Hare and Hounds: vest buttoned at neck, long shorts with contrasting braiding. 1891.

Rubber shoes, and spikes for running were in use in the mid-nineteenth century; writing of the 1850s Astly speaks of

a lovely little pair of spiked shoes,

and of

india rubber shoes which fitted him like gloves, but they had no spikes.

Sir J. Astly, op. cit.

Bibliography

"Craven". *Walker's Manly Exercises*. W. S. Orr & Co. 1839.
Hole, Christina. *English Sports and Pastimes*. B. T. Batsford Ltd. 1949.

PLATE 51

School Sports. Round-necked vests with short sleeves: knee-
length shorts. 1902.

Illustration by R. Noel Pocock to P. G. Wodehouse, The Pothunters. 1902.

PLATE 52

Portrait of John Barrow (see p. 323).

Reproduced in his Expeditions on the Glaciers. *1861.*

CHAPTER 19

CLIMBING

BY PHILLIS CUNNINGTON

And hey! then up we go.

Francis Quarles, *The Shepherd's Oracles,* 1644.

This section will include English costume for climbing whether in the British Isles or abroad.

Interest in mountaineering began to be shown in the early years of the nineteenth century, but it was then considered a somewhat eccentric pastime. It was in the 1850s and 1860s that it was recognized as a magnificent sport and it was during these years that the great peaks were conquered by a relatively small number of Englishmen. The Alpine Club was founded in 1857. The years 1854 to 1865 were known as the "Golden Age". This ended with the first successful ascent of the Matterhorn, "the unconquered peak of the central Alps", when on the descent a slip caused the death of four men. The only survivors were two guides and the famous Edward Whymper. This caused a lull, but soon after 1865 interest in mountain climbing was revived, especially in climbing old mountains by new routes both in Britain and abroad.

The clothes selected were usually simply those worn during winter walks in Britain. Boots were frequently ordinary hob-nailed boots and very little specialized equipment was used. It is extremely unlikely, however, that mountaineers ever dressed in the style described by this dandy in 1819!

> I endeavoured to ascend some mountains, but my stay-lace gave way, my Morocco boots burst and my dowlas trousers got wet through . . . might I trouble you to tell my man to get me a new Cumberland corset?
>
> Capt McDonough, *The Hermit in London,* 1819.

Dowlas was a coarse linen and the Cumberland corset was one worn by dandies and had a whalebone back.

The growing popularity of mountaineering tempted the more venture-some women to join in the sport, but even with this arduous form of exercise, they continued to wear skirts. Sometimes the skirts were so arranged that they could be shortened or let down at will. Lieut-Col H. Westmorland wrote, *c.* 1873:

> The amusing part of the "advanced" costumes of my aunts was that they wore buttons round the waist and button holes round the bottom hem, so that should the figure of a strange man appear in the distance, the buttons could be undone and the skirt let fall to a discreet length (*c.* 1873).
>
> Ronald Clark, Mountaineering in Britain, 1957.

239. Men in ordinary clothes, but one wears hob-nailed boots. 1855.

Lucy's mountaineering dress, described in Claire Eliane's delightful reminiscences, *They Came to the Hills*, published by George Allen & Unwin is decidedly surprising.

> In 1858, the whole [Walker] family . . . decided one day to go up again to the Theodule Pass . . . and while they were planning the climb, someone asked why Lucy should not go with them. Could she do it? She might try. What about her dress and provisions. Everything was quickly settled. Lucy decided that she would do it, that she could do it, and that she would wear

her old white print dress—a strange idea. However she stuck to her decision and apparently the dress survived many years. Of course she would not have dreamt of borrowing a pair of her brother's breeches. All through her life she climbed in skirts.

In *Expeditions on the Glaciers* in 1861, John Barrow (Plate 52) describes the clothing which he considered suitable for mountaineering:

> When fine balancing is necessary, the presence of a very light load to which one is unaccustomed, may introduce an element of danger, and for this reason I here left the residue of my tea and sandwiches behind me.
>
> As far as the Grands Mulets the weight is of little or no moment, nor do I consider that any extra clothing thus far is required, except an overcoat in case of bad weather on the glacier, a pair of woollen or felt gaiters to keep the feet from the snow, and an extra pair of socks, all of which can easily be put on at a moment's notice, if carried loose for the purpose. The hob-nailed shoes, should be well greased, of course: outfit for the ascent I shall reserve till we reach the Grands Mulets.

Here follows his account of the outfit for the ascent.

> A very queer "get up" it was too that many of them appeared in: the greater part wearing skull-caps and calico masks over their faces, with holes cut for the eyes, nostrils and mouth. For my own part, I dispensed with the mask, contenting myself for the present with a handkerchief tied over my "wide-awake" and fastened under my chin, which kept the face and ears warm Couttet having previously given me a black silk skull cap to wear, which, together with the coil of rope in his hand, I thought looked rather ominous! (Would that it had been of another colour), and which I would most gladly have dispensed with, but he assured me that it was "bien nécessaire". Indeed I subsequently found that it was so, although if the colour had been different it would have been more cheery. As it was, I felt very much as one must feel on coming out of a condemned cell! I trusted to my beard and moustache for protection of the remainder of my face, my only anxiety being about my nose, across which I was subsequently compelled to tie a handkerchief, to prevent its being frostbitten. A pair of blue spectacles were provided to protect the eyes, but not being used to these disagreeable appendages, I found them liable in ticklish places to make me miss my footing, so that I soon discarded them and was satisfied with my blue veil, which answered every purpose, as my eyes did not get in the least degree inflamed. Knowing that it would be a great object to avoid all weight of clothing, I brought with me sundry vests,

which I thought likely to answer the purpose best. As I doubt if the arrangement could well be improved upon, I will mention, for the benefit of future aspirants, how I ensconced myself—viz. first and foremost was a merino waistcoat, then two light flannel shirts, a chamois leather waistcoat (an appropriate vest i.e. waistcoat for the High Alps), and over these a double-breasted cloth waistcoat, a light kind of "lounging coat", and light over-coat. For the nether garments, a pair of stout trousers, two pairs of drawers, two pairs of socks, a strong pair of felt gaiters to keep the snow out, and hobnail boots, well greased. For the hands, a pair of easy fitting kid gloves, and a pair of stout felt fingerless gauntlets, lined inside with wool. In addition to this, my guides carried for me a light kind of cape in case of need, and glad I was to avail myself of it as will be seen hereafter. The only failure in my outfit

240. Climbing the Malvern Hills in crinolines. 1863.

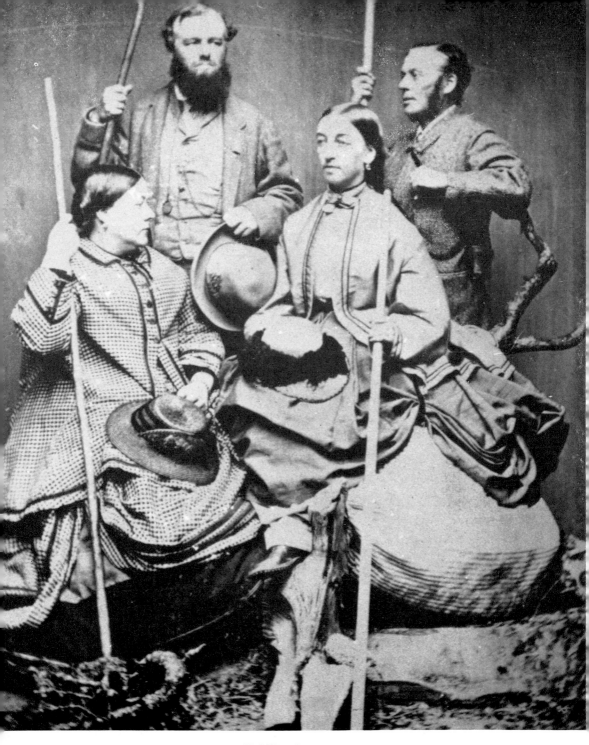

PLATE 54

Non-mountaineering tourists in guided excursions on snow and ice was as regards my feet, and for these I should advise a flannel sock in addition to what I have stated, which, I think, provided the shoes are perfectly easy, might answer the purpose.

An amusing suggestion was made in 1906 when

> someone remembered the story of some famous mountaineers in the 60's who, *in puris naturalibus* ascended a waterfall chasm . . . He suggested the same methods for our present route. However, it was pointed out that there was no excuse for such a proceeding on this occasion; I am glad to say that the instincts of respectability prevailed, so we scrambled up the crags clad in normal garb.
>
> G. and A. Abraham, *Rock-Climbing in North Wales*, 1906.

In the 1860s, as will be seen by the illustrations, women still clung to their crinolines, whether climbing abroad or on the Malvern Hills, and crossed glaciers during the 1870s in skirts down to the ankles (Plates 53 and 54).

In our picture of the climbing of Ben Nevis in 1881 (Fig. 241), the women are fashionably clothed, but the full pleats that emerge round the ankles from the draped overskirt suggest that they are wearing the much disguised divided skirt (see p. 342).

Suitable clothes for rock climbing and mountaineering in Britain, for women, are thus recommended by Miss Ada Ballin in 1885.

> Ever since the Bloomer costume, however, the idea has been gaining popularity, although but slowly, and at the Health Exhibition in South Kensington several divided dresses of the most pronounced type were shewn, and with favourable comment, some of these were very attractive, some not. For example, the Rocky Mountain travelling costume, devised by Mrs Bishop, however useful it may be is far removed from the beautiful. It is made of dark cloth, with a skirt to the knees, below which appear a sort of Turkish trousers gathered in to the ankles and finished with senseless little frills pinked out of the cloth. But this kind of dress need not be either ugly or dismal. Mrs Fleming Baxter exhibited one also intended for highland and mountaineering use, which is really charming. It is made of dark blue cloth with gaiters, knickerbockers, a skirt reaching to the knees, and a very pretty short coat like a gentleman's shooting jacket, with a hat to match . . .
>
> Dresses of this sort save the wearer from the friction and weight of long skirts which form an impediment to the movement of the limbs and are a means of wasting a considerable amount of energy. They moreover, clothe the body evenly and warmly, and are comfortable as well as light. Thus from

a health point of view, these dresses are excellent. They are moreover, extremely chic; but unfortunately they are attended with that great disadvantage inherent in all dresses of the kind—that those ladies who first were brave enough to attire themselves in this way would be called, not *brave* but *bold*.

Miss Ada Ballin, The Science of Dress, 1885.

241. Men in jackets and knickerbockers, one wearing gaiters to match his suit. One wears a tam-o-shanter. The rest have what were known as helmet hats. 1881.

Climbing in clothes that hampered added greatly to the difficulties for women mountaineers (Plate 55). Fanny Bullock Workman, the Himalayan mountaineer, appears to have adopted, by 1899, the most suitable climbing costume for women that has appeared so far in the nineteenth century. But she insisted on wearing her topee even in the Alps (Fig. 242).

Details for the best mountaineering outfit, both for men and women, were carefully considered in the 1890s as shown by the following list:

Clothing [for men]

Tweeds . . . or any woollen fabric in which the fibres are cross-woven . . . Materials such as serge and flannel are too apt to tear. The colour of the suit should be medium, of a "subfusk" hue as the old Oxford University statutes phrase it. . . .

242. Fanny Workman in 1899. Blouse and knee-length skirt. Thick puttees and strong boots. Topee (held on by elastic).

In the Alps, the costume adopted by our countrymen appears to be generally agreed upon. It consists of a Norfolk jacket, waistcoat and knicker-bockers . . . In tropical climates a man would be safer with a waistcoat and no coat . . . A very good form of coat, although no longer fashionable, is that made in the shape of a double-breasted pilot jacket. It should be provided with pockets, one or more being lined with mackintosh . . . A "game" pocket large enough to carry maps is convenient . . . Flaps are also required to all pockets. . . .

The coat, waistcoat, and knickerbockers can be lined with flannel. . . .

Hat   The majority of mountaineers adopt a light-coloured felt hat with a tolerably wide brim. . . . Some have a very high crown to the hat and claim that it is cooler. . . . On a very hot day, it is not a bad plan to make a little depression on the crown of the hat, and to carry in it a small lump of snow. An ordinary tall white hat is considered an eccentricity on the mountains. . . . Hats that fit close to the head are unsuitable—so are solar "topees" or cloth caps.

Boots   Perhaps the most important part of the clothing equipment is the boots.
. . . The uppers should extend well above the ankle and must be absolutely waterproof . . . Laced boots are now invariably adopted . . . the heel should be two thicknesses of leather deeper than the soles.

The boot-nails are a most important part of the equipment. Boot makers in England almost invariably use cast-iron nails. Wrought-iron nails, such as are generally used in Switzerland, are better. Various patterns are adopted. Warm slippers, as a change . . . are a necessity. (In a Swiss hotel.)

Stockings should be hand knitted as thick as possible. Those made of undyed wool are much the best. . . . A thin sock worn underneath the thick stocking will often save sore feet.

Garter   A simple piece of Berlin wool wound three or four times round the leg is the best form of garter.

Shirts should always be of flannel and made to fit loosely round the neck, even though this method be temporarily opposed to the dictates of fashion. A flannel shirt without a collar will look untidy, even though worn by a bishop, but if provided with a collar of fine-wove linen, the wearer can always look respectable without having any discomfort. In the Alps, at any rate, some concessions must be made to the possible prejudices of others, and no man has a right to go about looking like an ostler unless he happens to be one. A shirt of white silk is extremely comfortable and silk underclothing generally, as a change, is the most convenient, as it packs up into an extremely small space.

Pyjama Sleeping suits are . . . the best to take, made either of thin flannel or silk. . . . A woollen knitted jersey, large enough to go over the waistcoat and under the coat is a useful thing in a bivouac or for sleeping out . . . "Cardigan" jackets are warm but bulky . . . A most valuable addition to the clothing store is the ordinary flannel cholera belt, such as is commonly used in tropical climates. . . .

A waterproof coat is unhappily a necessity in the changeful climate of the mountain regions. . . . A knitted woollen Balaclava (Templar) cap is useful for sleeping out. . . .

Thick gloves are required on the mountain side. A perfect glove for mountain purposes is still a desideratum. Woollen gloves . . . hold the wet terribly. . . . Leather gloves get hard when cold. Fur-lined gloves are bulky . . . On rocks, the hand-hold is never so safe when gloves are worn.

Gaiters arc needed for walking in deep snow . . . and to keep stones out of boots. They should come well up to the knee but not above it . . . The strap or string usually provided to pass under the waist of the boot and keep the gaiters in place is useless, as it gets cut to pieces at once on rock. Only a well-made chain will stand the wear. Coarse woollen stuff or box cloth is generally used. . . . The gaiter may either be made to button (horn buttons are best) or strap, or lace at the side.

For walking on loose rubble high spats answer perfectly well and are considered at present to give an elegant appearance to the leg.

Climbing outfit for Ladies

Every garment should be of wool . . . The only exception to this latter point should be the skirt, and this will be found most serviceable if made of cloth, rough in texture and as thick as the wearer can get, provided it is not clumsy. . . . A small check pattern mends neatly if torn. The skirt should be made perfectly plain, except for a deep border of stitching. The pockets should be large, plentiful . . . one . . . nearly in front, two others quite at the back. All the pockets should be made outside and have flaps to button down . . . Three yards round the hem, will be found a good width for a skirt which can be of an ordinary walking length. When climbing, the skirt must whatever its length, be looped up and therefore it is easy to have a skirt which, in the valleys or towns does not look conspicuous. For looping up the skirt . . . an extra belt of strong ribbon is put on over the skirt which is then pinned to it in fish-wife style. . . . One safety pin attaching the two sides and another fastening the back, the hem being pinned on to the outer belt, do the work . . . Dark blue or dark grey are both suitable colours. . . . Under the skirt a short *under-skirt* reaching just to the knees, of the same colour, but of a lighter material, can be worn. A rough cloth coat lined throughout with silk . . . in case of cold.

Knickerbockers of waterproofed cloth, lined with flannel . . . are a great safeguard against a chill when sleeping out. A soft grey flannel blouse, high in the neck, long in the sleeves. . . . A *short jacket* of thick cloth, and lined with . . . fur (squirrel is the best) with the collar rising high all round the neck . . . unusual, extremely comfortable.

A light grey felt hat . . . each wearer must decide on the shape she prefers. A knitted helmet . . . the eyes only being uncovered . . . in very cold weather. A large silk handkerchief . . . to tie the hat on in a high wind. . . . Nailed mountain boots . . . cloth gaiters . . . gloves of wool, and of the shape worn by babies, the fingers being enclosed in a bag and the thumb only having a separate casing. Let the gloves come well up the arms. . . . A very fine woollen mask to protect the face . . . pleasanter than one of linen.

> *Mountaineering*, The Badminton Library of Sports and Pastimes
> edited by His Grace the Duke of Beaufort K.G. assisted by
> Alfred E. T. Watson. Longmans, Green & Co. 1892.

Even in the early years of the twentieth century women climbed in fairly long skirts, but as with other sports, suitable clothes gradually evolved and women at last could mountaineer on more equal terms with men.

Bibliography

Abraham, George and Ashley. *Rock-Climbing in North Wales*. Keswick, G. P. Abraham, 1906.

Barrow, John. *Expeditions on the Glaciers*. London, E. and F. N. Spon *et al*, 1864.

Clark, Ronald, W. *A Picture History of Mountaineering*. London, Hulton Press, 1956.

Clark, Ronald W. and Pyatt, Edward C. *Mountaineering in Britain*. London, Phoenix House, 1957.

Clark, Ronald W. and Pyatt, Edward C. *Victorian Mountaineering*. London, Batsford, 1953.

Longstaff, Tom. *This My Voyage*. London, John Murray, 1950.

Lunn, Sir Arnold. *Matterhorn Centenary*. London, G. Allen & Unwin, 1965.

Smith, Albert Richard. *The Story of Mont Blanc*, Bogue 1854, London.

CHAPTER 20

WALKING AND EXCURSIONS

BY PHILLIS CUNNINGTON

WALKING

Walking for pleasure belongs to the nineteenth century. While suitable clothes for this form of exercise were no problem to men, women were many years making up their minds what to wear. This chapter will therefore be largely devoted to walking costume for women.

Let us start, however, by quoting a description of the clothes worn by "so great a man" as Dr Johnson on his Hebridean Tour, in 1773.

> Dr Johnson wore a full suit of plain brown clothes, with twisted buttons of the same colour, a large bushy greyish wig, a plain shirt, black worsted stockings and silver buckles.
>
> Upon this tour when journeying, he wore boots and a very wide brown cloth greatcoat with pockets which might have almost held the 2 volumes of his folio dictionary; and he carried in his hand a large English oak stick [Fig. 243].
>
> Let me not be censured for mentioning such minute particulars. Everything relative to so great a man is worth observing.
>
> > James Boswell,
> > *The Journal of a Tour to the Hebrides with Samuel Johnson.*

In *Country Life*, April, 1965, a very interesting account is quoted by Miss Mary Corbett Harris of the walking attire worn by John Horseman, a country curate, in August, 1804. He wrote:

> I set out on foot last Thursday morning, from Toddington to Luton, with one shirt, three cravats, and a night cap in my pocket. This summer time I wear, except with canonicals, a white beaver hat green underneath, and a silk umbrella in the sun, as well as in the rain. I had blue pantaloons, hessian boots, with immense tassels, a black lapelled coat, and a black silk waistcoat, single breasted. My hair (unpowdered) is cropt close behind, and porcupined before. A pair of patent periscopics[1] complete this elegant figure.

[1] Spectacles giving a wide view.

He was in fact dressed in the fashion of his day. The pantaloons were close-fitting tights shaped to the leg and the hessians were walking or riding boots, with a tassel in front below the kneecap. The statement that his hair was

243. Dr Samuel Johnson. 1773.

"porcupined before" meant that it was "frizzled" in front above his fore-head. This was a late eighteenth-century style for women and unusual in a man. It was then known as hair dressed à la hérisson—Hedgehog fashion.

> The next who presented her delicate form
> Was the charming Miss Hedgehog
>   whose head looked like a storm,
> The points of her hair like a porcupine's quills
> And her curls stuffed with reams of
>   dup'd shop-keepers' bills.

> *Bath Chronicle*, 1778.

Later in his letter John Horseman says that though he takes snuff he never lets

PLATE 55

Mountaineering in the Tyrol: "Turning a corner" in fashionable dress.

Drawing by R. Caton Woodville in the Illustrated London News
18 September 1886.

PLATE 56

Walking dresses, hampered by trains, having tapes within, producing a hobble-skirt effect.

Sylvia's Home Journal. *1880.*

244. Lady in high waisted dress, cottage mantle and small bonnet.
Gentleman in morning dress, i.e. tail coat, pantaloons and hat with
turned up brim. 1812.

it fall over his clothes as some people do, "so I coast round my handkerchief
for a clean place to blow my nose".

Men had the advantage over women in not being hampered by skirts
when walking, so that descriptions of their walking clothes consist largely of
accessories and details. Miss Ballin[1] tells us of

> a gentleman of a scientific frame of mind, who determined to make the
> experiment of walking in petticoats in order to estimate the disadvantage
> under which women labour in regard to dress. He walked for a mile up hill;
> but was so exhausted by the endeavour that he gave up, with the remark that
> women must be stronger than men or they would never be able to stand it.

[1] *The Science of Dress*, 1885.

The following instructions were given in 1859:

> The best walking dress for non-professional men is a suit of tweed of the same cloth, ordinary boots, gloves not too dark for the coat, a scarf with a pin in winter, or a small tie of one colour in summer, a respectable black hat and a cane . . . the best substitute for a cane is an umbrella, *not* a parasol unless it be given you by a lady to carry. The main point of the walking dress is the harmony of colours . . . it should vary according to the place and hour. In the country or at the seaside a straw hat or wide-awake may take the place of the beaver, and the nuisance of gloves be even dispensed with in the former . . . Very thin boots should be avoided at all times . . . The shirt whether seen or not, should be quite plain. The shirt collar should never have a colour on it, but it may be stiff or turn-down. The scarf, if simple and of modest colours, is perhaps the best thing we can wear round the neck, but the neck-tie, if preferred, should not be too long nor tied in too stiff and studied a manner. The frock coat should be ample and loose . . . and should never be buttoned up.
>
> *Habits of Good Society*, Anon, 1859.

In 1860 the *Gentleman's Herald of Fashion* advised for a Walking Tour:

> Frock coat S.B. [single breasted] Hip Bs. [buttons] 4″ apart. Sleeve wide but narrowing to hand and slit to elbow behind. 8 Bs- pockets in seams, knicker-bocker trousers with leather gaiters.

These, however, are details for the fashionable man's walking costume. As will be seen by the illustrations, many men wore their ordinary clothes, though for country wear knickerbockers or breeches were preferred in the 1890s (Fig. 245).

How did the women dress? Elizabeth Ham describing her predicament when out walking in the early years of the nineteenth century says:

> After I had rested, we set out on our return . . . We had to cross many deep trenches . . . there were places to be crossed where I was compelled to take a good jump. These were the days of scanty skirts, and a sad hindrance they were to gymnastics. In one of my exertions to clear a bog-hole, away went gown and petticoats in rents to the waist nearly. I was in a sad strait to conceal my flannel petticoat. Fortunately we had to pass but few houses before we came to Mrs Jones's. Here I went for a needle and black silk, and then walked decently through the town. (*c.* 1805.)
>
> *Elizabeth Ham* (*1783–1820*) by herself, ed. E. Gillett, 1945.

To free women's legs for exercise was a struggle that continued off and on throughout the second half of the nineteenth century. It began in 1851 when, as we have seen, Mrs Amelia Jenks Bloomer, tried to persuade Englishwomen

245. Tourist in knickerbocker and cap with handkerchief to protect from flies. Farmer in breeches, gaiters and straw hat. 1892.

to adopt a more "rational" costume, which consisted of a form of Turkish trousers, originally frilled at the ankles. See Fig. 246 and compare Fig. 53, p. 91. Only a few of the more daring women ventured to wear them and the garment was much satirized.

> For the Bloomer costume was nothing else but a travesty of male attire . . .
> The year 1851 "witnessed beldame in breeches . . . walking the London Streets".
>
> Charles Harper, *Revolted Woman*, 1894.

The ladies who wore them were sometimes called "Bloomers".

The following are two verses from a broadsheet of 1851:

It will be fun to see
    Ladies possessed of riches
Strutting up and down
    In Wellingtons and breeches
Bloomers are funny folks,
    No ladies can be faster,
They say 'tis almost time
    That petticoats were master.

Female apparel now
    Is gone to pot I vow, sirs,
And ladies will be fined
    Who don't wear coats and trousers;
Blucher boots and hats
    And shirts with handsome stitches,—
Oh dear! What shall we do
    When women wear the breeches?

A frivolous account of this costume is also given by Surtees in *Handley Cross:*

her lovely daughter Constantia in the full-blown costume of a Bloomer . . .
in her silver-buttoned vest, with flowing jacket above a lavender-coloured
tunic and white trousers, fingering her cambric collarette and crimson silk
necktie above her richly figured shirt with mock diamond buttons scattered
freely down the front.   (1854.)

The day for women in trousers, however, was a long way off. An anonymous
writer in 1859 had this advice to give for

walking and country dress.
    The . . . walking dress . . . should be quiet in colour, simple, sub-
stantial . . . For the country the attire should be tasteful and solid and strong.
The bonnet may still, though plain, and perhaps of straw or whalebone, be
becoming. The hat, now so prevalently used, admits some decoration, that
gives both character and elegance . . . it is the most sensible as well as the
most picturesque covering for the head; long feathers in the most tranquil
scenes, are not inappropriate. Cloaks of a light material for summer and stout
in winter, are more elegant and suitable than shawls, which belong rather to
the carriage or visiting dress. One point of dress has been much amended
lately, owing to the good sense of our Queen. It was formerly thought

PLATE 57
Walking costumes. 1909.
Original photograph kindly lent by Mrs T. C. Hart.

PLATE 58

Children of Queen Victoria in goat-cart (with their staff) in 1844.

Victoria and Albert Museum, coloured print published by Dean.

ungenteel to wear anything but thin Morocco shoes, or very slight boots in walking. Clogs and goloshes were necessarily resorted to. "The Genteel disease". . . has however, yeilded to the remedies of example. Victoria has assumed the Balmoral petticoat, than which for health, comfort, warmth, and effect, no invention was ever better. She has courageously accompanied it with the Balmoral boot and even with the mohair and coloured stocking. With these, and the warm cloak, the looped dresses, the shady hat and to complete a country walking dress, soft gloves of the kind termed *gants de siècle* the high-born lady may enjoy the privileges which her inferiors possess—she may take a good walk with pleasure and safety, and not shiver at the aspect of a muddy lane.

246. "The Bloomer Costume". 1851.

As regards gloves, the same writer declares that

> Nothing is so unlady-like as a hand that is either rough, or has become sunburnt, in which case gloves should be used.
>
> Anon., *The Habits of Good Society,* 1859.

The Balmoral petticoat was shorter than usual. The Balmoral boot was a short black boot, laced up the front, often with coloured laces and was generally worn with country or walking dresses.

Walking in the late 1850s and the 1860s was less hampered by clinging skirts owing to the then fashionable cage crinoline which spread the skirt outwards away from the legs. It did, however, add to the weight to be carried. The walking dress in our illustration (Fig. 247) is an example.

> Skirts hitched up on spreading frame
> Petticoats are bright as flame
> Dainty high-heeled boots proclaim
> Fast Young Ladies!   (Song) 1860.

247. Walking skirt, hitched up over red **petticoat** and crinoline. 1860.

On country walks stiles were tiresome obstacles to wearers of crinoline, but also, apparently, another difficulty might arise as shown in a letter to a young woman called Peachblossom:

Peachblossom is advised not to attempt the climbing of stiles in a crinoline for the task is impossible; and if she suffers much from the comments of vulgar little boys it would be better in a high wind to remain indoors.

The Englishwoman's Domestic Magazine, 1856.

Walking in the 1870s and early 1880s in the attire then in vogue must have been reduced to a mere saunter, for at no period in the century was the fashionable woman's dress so complicated. Dresses were overloaded with drapery and trimmings, skirts were tight and often trained (Plate 56) and until 1875 were puffed out behind with a form of bustle known as a crinolette.

In 1876 a surgeon gave the following advice to women:

Ladies who are going to try training for athletic purposes will find some attention to costume expedient. No portion of the garment should restrain the movement of the shoulders . . . [What about the legs?] Stays should fit close on the hips and should of course have no shoulder-straps, till you are a grandmamma. The drawers should not come below the knee, and should hang loose. The best defences to the lower extremities in rough ground are stout Alpine shoes, and light leathern gaiters half way up to the knee supporting the long socks without garters.

A woollen jersey should be worn next the skin. The skirt of the dress should be short and narrow, and the best materials are serge and homespun. Besides these, the less drapery is worn the better.

Thomas King Chambers M.D. (Oxon) F.R.C.P. (Lond.),
A Manual of Diet in Health and Disease, 1876.

Even in 1879 there were young ladies who "were no longer afraid of long walks" in spite of the equipment which they were advised to take for a walking tour; each should have:

two cotton dresses, one cashmere dress, one ulster, one alpaca dustcoat, one parasol, one umbrella, one walking-stick, one pair of shoes, one pair of button boots, six pairs of stockings, two straw hats, one green veil, and a small flask of brandy in case of faintness.

The dress to be worn was:

A costume of navy-blue serge, braided, with polonaise buttoned down the front: Alpaca under-petticoat.

By the time we reach the 1880s, great efforts were being made—without much success—to devise suitable walking dresses for women. Since bloomers or Turkish trousers had failed, the divided skirt was now urged, particularly as the division did not show.

Miss Ada Ballin in her *Science of Dress,* 1885, has described this somewhat complicated attire:

> The bodice should be cut well down over the hips, and the buttons placed round the bones of the hips so that the weight of the clothes may be supported by these bones . . .
>
> A high-necked and long-sleeved woollen combination vest and drawers should be worn next the skin. Over this should be a closely fitting flannel bodice, on to which the suspenders of the stockings should be buttoned, and to which the drawers can be fastened if made separate from the vest. On to the bodice also is fastened what is called the divided skirt—loose trousers made of the material of the dress, the bottom of each leg being finished with a kilting.
>
> These form the whole of the under-clothing, though in very cold weather an extra pair of woollen drawers may be worn under the divided skirt. The advantages of this system of dress are manifold. It clothes every part of the body evenly and warmly, permits perfect freedom of movement, gives the maximum of warmth with the minimum of weight, and, as none of the garments fasten round the waist, injurious pressure on the abdominal and pelvic organs is avoided.

The reason for the kilting at the bottom of each leg of the divided skirt was to ensure that the trouser effect was obscured.

> the skirt [of the dress], falls in loose double box plaits more than half way down the calf and below it the trouser legs show for three or four inches . . . the kilted flounces which fall into each other look like one flounce.

See Figs. 248 and 249.

Miss Ballin remarks that:

> Divided dress skirts . . . may be made so artfully that an outsider would not know the difference between them and an ordinary dress.

She adds that

> A lady friend of mine, wearing one for the first time, told her son what it was and met from that youth the consolatory, if not elegant rejoinder, "Oh bosh! You don't come that sort of hoax on me."

Women's clothing in the 1880s was excessively heavy and Miss Ballin was trying to reduce the amount worn as well as to free the legs.

PLATE 59

"To Brighton and back for 3s. 6d." Men, women and children wrapped
in shawls in an excursion train with open windows.

City of Birmingham Art Gallery, painting by C. Rossiter. 1859.

PLATE 60

Picnic scene at Longleat. 1816.

It must be obvious that each petticoat that is worn not only adds to the weight of the dress, but also impedes the movements of the legs by constantly pressing against them in the act of walking. This is one great reason why girls, when walking with their brothers, become fatigued so much sooner than the boys do.

248. "The petticoat shown is the much-maligned divided skirt." 1885.

Viscountess Harberton when lecturing to the National Dress Society in 1887, herself wore Turkish trousers. But in spite of demonstrating the fatiguing and bad method of walking caused by petticoats and skirts, and the right method permitted by her own dress, she failed to convert the majority of women to her way of thinking. Fashion as usual won the day. A trade journal made this comment.

> There is no need for a woman to be able to do more than use her limbs in a feminine fashion.

The amount of underclothing advocated for women hikers at this period is astonishing and perhaps also is the undercurrent of prudery.

> A companion is highly desirable not so much as a defence against that bug-bear to most women "a man" but in case of mishap. For clothing, flannel next the skin should be the rule; beneath a dust-coloured woollen dress, the woollen undergarment must come up to the neck and down to the middle of the thighs, with long sleeves to the wrists: this with flannel drawers and a light-coloured petticoat is all that is needed for underclothing.
>
> *The Field,* 1885.

Women's day clothing in the last decade of the nineteenth century was less weighty and less complicated than previously, but skirts were long and sometimes trained. An advertisement in 1893 describes a "Walking Dress—bell shirt with slight train, cord edging . . ." . The cord edging was an essential protection for the hem.

249. Divided skirts, as worn with a full dress. 1885.

When out walking along muddy roads or field footpaths, the skirt was usually bunched up at the back and held in one hand. To avoid this tiresome necessity, the "Alston Dress Suspender" was invented (Fig. 251).

> The Alston Dress Suspender is an article that will command much appreciation among all classes of the feminine community. It combines the advantages of both simplicity and security and its lightness and portability render its use applicable on any and every occasion when the wearer wishes to raise her dress from the ground without the necessity of carrying it. For golfing, walking and touring it will be found of invaluable service. It is readily adjusted to any height, and claims to be the only dress suspender which places ladies' skirts in perfect safety . . . it will not injure the finest of dress materials. This unique . . . suspender is but a length of fine chain with larger rings set at regular intervals. The extremity of the two chains that descend the dress are furnished with strong safety pins that are pinned through the skirt. The

chain traverses the waist belt or band at the back of the skirt for the space of
about five inches where it is furnished with two flat hooks that slip securely
over the band. These hooks are also furnished with small exterior hooks over
which the intersecting of the chains are passed to regulate the length of the
dress. Both the band and ring hooks or clips are smooth and flat thus occupy-
ing no material space in waist measurement.

The Housewife, 1895.

250. (*a*) Short coat with leg-of-mutton sleeves, gored skirt. (*b*) Tailor-
made coat and skirt. 1899.

Skirts for walking continued well into the twentieth century (Plate 57).
It was only the women cyclists and cricketers who began to wear what were
popularly known as Rationals. (See Cycling, p. 242–243.)

A party of girls camping out somewhere in America did try the experiment of wearing knickerbockers, to their great satisfaction.

In short Tweed skirts, Norfolk jackets and stout boots they were well equipped for long tramps, white jaunty Tyrolese hats gave a touch of elegance to their appearance to which even our Amazons were not indifferent.

The skirts concealed *loose garments of masculine origin* in which the girls specially rejoiced, having never known before the luxury of perfect freedom of motion.

The Housewife, 1896.

Even here the knickerbocker had to be hidden under a skirt.

251. The Alston dress suspender. 1895.

The Housewife also tells us in 1894 that:

Holiday clothes are indeed a joy in the country, but all trace of them must be rigorously abandoned when once we set foot in the great metropolis.

PLEASURE TRIPS AND EXCURSIONS

Excursions to the seaside or to the races, and pleasure trips by steamboat, became increasingly popular in the nineteenth century owing to the new means of transport. They were further promoted by the passing in 1871 of the Bank Holiday Act. This ordered fixed holidays at Christmas, Easter, Whitsun and the beginning of August and thus enabled thousands more people to go for day excursions.

A steamer excursion is described by Dickens in 1836. The costumes appear to have been somewhat unusual.

> Ten minutes to nine and the committee embarked in a body. These were Mr Hardy in a blue jacket and waistcoat, white trousers, silk stockings and pumps—in full aquatic costume, with a straw hat on his head . . . and there was the young gentleman with the green spectacles, in nankeen inexplicables [trousers] with a ditto waistcoat and bright buttons . . . The remainder of the committee, dressed in white hats, light jackets, waistcoats and trousers, looked something between waiters and West Indian Planters.
>
> *Sketches by Boz.*

"Travelling for a spree" by steamer in 1835 is thus described:

> The City of London Ramsgate Steamer was running gaily down the river . . . "Charming, aint it?" said Joseph Tuggs in a bottle-green great coat, with a velvet collar of the same, and a blue travelling cap with a gold band.
>
> Ibid.

Again from the same source we have the description of:

> A regular Sunday water party . . . It's a Richmond tide, and some dozen boats are preparing for the reception of the parties who have engaged them. . . . the party arrives . . . in full aquatic costume, with round blue jackets, striped shirts, and caps of all sizes and patterns, from the velvet skull cap of French manufacture to the easy head dress familiar to the students of the old spelling books, as having, on the authority of the portrait, formed part of the costume of the Reverend Mr. Dilworth.

A trip to see the Races is described by Albert Smith in 1844.

> Having plunged into various remote regions . . . in search of vans and horses, the price was at last fixed, the party collected and the trip determined upon. . . .
>
> Mr Ledbury who was ever anxious to be in the mode, had mounted one of the celebrated sporting wrappers at twelve and nine pence, of which he had read so much in the fashionable newspapers, and which common every-day people would have called a brown Holland blouse, if they had not been privately informed of the proper name by considerate friends; and under this he had a brown cut-away coat with Conservative buttons, two of which

detached from the rest, but Siamesed together with a bit of shoe string, fastened it across his chest at one point only, after the manner of men about Regent Street in general.

Besides this he had a blue-spotted handkerchief round his neck, white trousers, and new Albert boots[1] of resplendent varnish, and undeniable toes, so that altogether he might be considered rather the thing than otherwise, and decidedly up to a move or two, at least judging from his costume.

The toilets of the other gentlemen were not particularly soignées, but still sufficiently appropriate to throw no discredit upon the expedition.

All the preparations being concluded, they entered the van and commenced the journey.

Albert Smith, *The Adventures of Mr. Ledbury*, 1844.

The children of Queen Victoria were happy to take their trip in a goat chaise (Plate 58).

Excursions by train, however, were perhaps the most popular and certainly the most widespread, especially in summer. A ballad ("Margate Hoy") of the first half of the nineteenth century shows this trend in the *beau monde*:

Bucks who hunt fashion like quick-scented mousers,
Leave town, it exhibits no sport for ye now Sirs,
So pull off your boots, and put on your trousers
To join the gay throng where the sea breezes blow.

Eliza Cook in 1851 shows how the habit had spread to all classes:

This is a new character that has sprung up within the last few years in the manufacturing districts. The Tripper is the growth of railways and monster trains. Before they were, he was not. Tens of thousands of operatives formerly grew old and grey, who had never seen the sea . . . Now, they collect into monster trains of from one to two thousand passengers, and away they go at thirty miles an hour—sometimes to cathedral towns . . . but oftenest of all to the sea-shore . . . During this summer, the Tripper has been in all his glory . . . He is attired in his best, as she (his wife) is in hers. He has a bright blue kerchief round his neck (such being "fashionable", he says) and he sporteth a thorn stick surmounted by a dog's head . . . which he admiringly contemplates at intervals, throwing also an occasional look down his spotted vest, and his new Californian trousers, seeing that they "sit" well. She is no less artistically ornamented—her bonnet with red ribands, her

---

[1] Side-lacing boots with cloth tops and patent leather toe-caps; often with "a close row of little mother-of-pearl buttons down the front" merely ornamental.

person with a new black silk dress, over which a shawl of brilliant device becomingly sits. She carries a boa over her arm, and a heavy reticule basket in her hand. He too, has a basket well packed . . . Under his arm, (for he is a cautious youth) he carries a rather fat umbrella. This is to provide against contingencies. True, it is rather heavy work to bear all this luggage about and he had long contended with himself whether he should relinquish the umbrella or the stick. But he cannot give up the stick; and as for the umbrella—is there not his new hat! And so he determines finally to carry both.

Eliza Cook's Journal, No. 116, 19th July 1851.

Travel was frought with difficulties for ladies wearing the crinolines of the 1860s—but the railway train (Plate 59) was easier than the coach.

Dress has made a marvellous spring since the introduction of railways. Ladies whose mothers used to get all their things into a moderate sized box and a carpet bag, travel with great piano-forte case-like packages so numerous that they are obliged to be numbered for fear they forget how many they have. And the more they take the more they want to take, till each lady looks as if she ought to have a luggage van to herself.

Then to see them attempt the entry of a moderate sized carriage; the utter disproportion of the door to the "object", as it may well be called, that seeks admission! The absurdity of fashion might be tolerated if it inconvenienced only the wearer; but when one lady extends herself to the size of two, she necessarily takes up the room of two, and must exclude some one else from a seat.

A family coach, has now no chance of accommodating a family; one full-blown sister must go instead of two natural sized girls. The only advantage we see in the absurdity is that it forms a sort of graduated scale of gentility; the more extravagant a woman is in her hoops, the less inclined we are to think her a lady. It is only the vulgar who go into extremes, and make themselves look like curtains to bathing machines.

R. S. Surtees, *Plain or Ringlets,* 1860.

Crinolines, whether fashionable or vulgar, were certainly not practical garments for excursions. But an excursion is an "occasion"; just as men trippers were often uncomfortably jaunty, so women trippers were usually uncomfortably smart.

CHAPTER 21

PICNICS

BY PHILLIS CUNNINGTON

A picnic or having a meal out of doors is one of the delights of a pleasure party.

> In life's varied sports
>   There's nothing half so good
> Nothing half so charming
>   As a picnic in the wood.

Herbert Rodwell, The Picnic, a One Act Farce, 1842.

As early as *c.* 1575 we have an illustration of a picnic in a wood, in George Turbervile's book *The Noble Arte of Venerie or Hunting* (Fig. 252). The central figure is Queen Elizabeth I, changed to James I in a later edition. She herself and all her attendants are dressed in the fashion of their day. Royalty is seated on a convenient mound which presumably does not impair the royal attire. A cloth covered with dishes of food is spread at the feet. This, however, is a hunting picnic where food during a pause would be required, and not perhaps a picnic in the modern sense.

Similar picnics are portrayed occasionally in the seventeenth and eighteenth centuries, but picnics as part of a pleasurable pastime developed in the early nineteenth century.

In a beautiful aquatint of a "General View of Longleat from Prospect Hill" in 1816, a picnic is shown in the foreground (see Plate 60). The ladies appear to be sitting on a tablecloth spread on the grass, probably to protect their flimsy dresses. One has a white skirt and white hat, and a yellow bodice; the other wears a dress striped pink and white, and a blue hat. The gentlemen wear black coats; the one pointing at the view is in a cut-away tail-coat, drab breeches, short brown Hessian boots and a grey top-hat. The servant taking bottles from the basket wears a red spencer (i.e. a short out-door coat) white breeches and top-boots, also a wig. The footman on the right wears a brown livery coat with red collar and cuffs, light brown breeches, grey stockings

PLATE 61

Earl of Moray and picnic party. Earl of Moray (central figure) wears dark glasses and the type of shawl known as a plaid and worn as shown. Umbrellas and wraps are required by the rest of the family. 1846.

Water-colour by W. Bucker, in the collection of the Earl of Moray; with kind permission to reproduce.

PLATE 62

Picnic. Fashionable clothes and typical pagoda-shaped parasols of 1834.

Etching by R. Seymour, c. 1834, in "A. Crowquill's" Seymour's
Humorous Sketches. *1866.*

and black highlows (i.e. short country boots). All these clothes are correct for their date without being adapted for sitting on the grass in the open.

252. Picnic for Queen Elizabeth I. 1575.

In 1860, Surtees maintained that:

> A picnic, being an indefinite sort of entertainment, comprises every variety of male costume—morning coats, evening coats, nondescript coats, riding boots, dress boots, jockey whips, and heel spurs.
>
> The ladies only vary their costume by laying aside their bonnets for dinner or the dances, though if they were to take our advice they would keep them on—especially if the bonnets are pretty ones.
>
> Surtees, *Plain or Ringlets*.

If "Sunday pleasures . . . in some well-known Tea gardens" can be counted as picnics for Londoners in 1836, we find a strange assortment of attire:

> What a dust and a noise! Men and women—boys and girls—sweethearts and married people—babies in arms and children in chaises—pipes and shrimps—cigars and periwinkles—tea and tobacco—Gentlemen in alarming waistcoats and steel watch guards . . . ladies with great long white pocket handker-chiefs, like small table clothes, in their hands, chasing one another on the grass in the most playful and interesting manner, with the view of attracting the attention of the aforesaid gentlemen . . . —boys with great silk hats just balanced on the top of their heads, smoking cigars and trying to look as if they liked them—gentlemen in pink shirts and blue waistcoats, occasionally upsetting either themselves or somebody else with their own canes.

Charles Dickens, Sketches by Boz.

For picnics throughout the nineteenth century, there were usually important accessories—apart from the food and drink—such as umbrellas, parasols, shawls and rugs, even sun-glasses. In the picnic on the Culbin Sands in 1846 (see Plate 61) all are needed.

There were other hazards to contend with besides the weather. A picnic scene on the banks of the Lea shows a disaster to the carefully laid tablecloth on the grass (see Plate 62).

> There's that nasty cow walking all over our dinner—Oh dear, oh dear there go his feet into the currant and raspberry pie.

Parasols had other uses than to protect from the sun. Gwen Raverat, in her fascinating book *Period Piece* (1952) has this to say about river picnics in Cambridge in the 1890s.

> For instance, there were the river picnics. All summer Sheep's Green and Coe Fen were pink with boys, as naked as God made them; for bathing drawers did not exist then; or at least not in Sheep's Green. You could see the pinkness, dancing about, quite plain from the end of our Big Island. Now to go Up the River, the goal of all the best picnics, the boats had to go right by the bathing places, which lay on both sides of the narrow stream. These dangerous straits were taken in silence and at full speed. The gentlemen were set to oars . . . and each lady unfurled a parasol and, like an ostrich buried her head in it and gazed earnestly into its silky depths, until the crisis was past and the river was decent again.[1]

[1] With acknowledgements to the publishers, Messrs. Faber & Faber, London.

Without being suitably dressed many picnickers must have had awkward moments, as in the boating picnic of 1852, depicted in *Punch* as "Perils of Picnics" (Fig. 253). Rain, too, was a hazard, (Fig. 254).

253. "Mr Pipkin makes a vigorous but unsuccessful effort to secure
that Darling Water Lily." 1852.

Picnics, no doubt, have always been pleasurable pastimes whatever the clothing worn. A word of warning, however, was given to young ladies in 1870:

Of all delightful outdoor amusements, perhaps there are none so delightful as a well arranged successful picnic . . . It should be composed of persons who are willing to eat and enjoy their dinner under difficulties; who do not think a relay of clean plates, of dinner napkins, plate and glass, necessary; but who can eat with zest pasties and sandwiches in their fingers, and drink out of mugs or glasses without stems; who come in sensible dresses that they do not fear to spoil, and sensible boots that will go through a little mud and damp if needful: ladies who do not have hysterics at a cow or stoutly refuse to get over a stile in case they should show their ankles.

Mrs Henry Mackarness, *The Young Lady's Book*, 1870–4.

254. "It would have been so provoking for us all to have brought our
umbrellas, and then to have had a fine day." 1851.

In Plate 63 they did not mind apparently showing more than their ankles, but
the gentlemen were placed in discreet positions.

Plate 64 shows an interesting picnic party at Stonehenge, the older men
wearing frock-coats and top-hats or straw hats; the women in the ordinary
dresses of the 1870s.

PLATE 63

Picnic. Women wearing cage-crinolines. Men in lounge suits. One (seated) wears a "nautical" hat, the other a "muffin" hat.

A contemporary print. 1858.

PLATE 64

A party at Stonehenge. In charge is Henry Cunnington (second from right), grandson of William Cunnington, the Wiltshire archaeologist. 1873.

Author's collection

CHAPTER 22

GENERAL TOPICS

BY ALAN MANSFIELD

I. SOME SOCIAL AND ECONOMIC FACTORS

Our ladies in those days
In civil habit went;
Broad cloth was then worth praise,
And gave the best content:
French fashions then were scorned,
Fond fangles then none knew;
Then modesty women adorned,
When this old cap was new.   Anon. Seventeenth century.

In the preceding chapters of this book we have traced the clothes adopted for a variety of sports and games during some three and a half centuries. During this time, with very few exceptions, little attempt was made to achieve a practical style of dress suitable to the conditions of those sports and games until the last fifty years or so of the period. Exceptions to this general rule of lack of appropriate clothing are such essential and obvious protective items as the archer's and falconer's gloves, but these are more in the nature of equipment for the sport rather than articles of dress *de facto*.

Perhaps the oldest of all our sports are those varieties of hunting and riding which have evolved from man's efforts to fill the cooking pot and to secure a form of transport other than that of his own legs. If we stretch the term "hunting" in the American manner we can include the sports of shooting and fishing and hawking in this category. These are where we first see a specialization of dress arising—for riding by the sixteenth century; and in the case of hunting and shooting, the introduction in the eighteenth century of the "frock". Based on the loose coat worn by town and country workmen, the frock was a less restrictive and less formal garment than the fashionable coat. (It is interesting to note that the frock was accepted wear on dress occasions by the end of the century—an example of how sports or leisure clothes of one generation become the formal attire of the next generation but one.)

The successive game-laws that had been enacted over the centuries dictated that hunting and shooting, and in certain cases fishing, became pastimes of a privileged class, and a certain sartorial exclusiveness grew up around these sports, so that, eventually

> Men who have not hunted before should begin so quietly dressed that they will attract no notice.
>
> Charles Richardson, op. cit.

The popularity of clubs in the eighteenth century found expression in the hunt and in the cricket clubs that grew up in the latter half of that century, and in both cases uniforms were adopted which became the ancestors of a host of club-coloured blazers, caps, scarves and ties adorning the followers of all types of sports and games, denoting loyalty to clubs and schools and institutions and firms and regiments. These colours, in the case of team games, were not only a sign of loyalty to an organization but also a necessary distinction between friend and foe on the playing field.

The rise of cricket in the eighteenth century was unrivalled by that of any other game, and preceded by a century or more the popularity of football, hockey, lawn tennis or golf. This early supremacy of the game resulted in the cricketer settling down to the standard pattern of white clothing long before the players of other games had got round to considering what they should wear.

Real tennis, pell-mell, and other courtly games never drew large numbers of followers from the masses, and like the royal and ancient game of golf south of the Border, were confined to small numbers of enthusiasts with little influence on the development of sports clothing.

The village varieties of football, handball, and hockey were primitive semi-ritual contests which did not develop into organized sports until the nineteenth century, when they rapidly gained favour among all classes and in every corner of the land. At the same time, the old rural athletics of running and wrestling also acquired immense popularity. Later newly invented or introduced games, such as lawn tennis and croquet, and revivals of old ones such as golf, added to the variety of pastimes available.

The causes of this great and comparatively sudden rise in games' playing and athletic exercise, to which must be added an increase of hunting, shooting and aquatic sports, are many, some easy to see and some less obvious.

The movement of the rural population as a result of the industrial revolution no doubt took the village sports into the city alleys; the spread of the railways enabled the townsman to visit the country more easily for the purpose of holiday recreation, bringing him in contact with the sports of hunting, angling, shooting and the like. The prosperous urban middle and tradesman classes, as exemplified by Mr Jorrocks, joined in these sports, riding out to the nearest countryside, or going further afield by rail.

The development of the reformed public schools pioneered by Arnold at Rugby with their emphasis on muscular Christianity and *esprit de corps* fostered by the playing of team games influenced the ideals of educationalists and spread the cult of sportsmanship among the private and grammar schools, and later the new elementary schools. These games together with simple athletics were carried from schools to the universities. Those who were not so fortunate as to have access to school and university sports banded themselves into clubs. Other clubs were formed by those old boys who wished to continue playing after leaving school or university. Such organized sports and games led to a codification of rules and the wearing of a uniform style of clothes.

Blackheath Rugby Club was founded in 1858 by old boys of Rugby and Blackheath schools; the Football Association followed in 1863. In 1850 an athletic meeting was held at Oxford. The inter-University Boat Race was first held in 1829 and Leander Rowing Club was formed in 1820.

Rowing, sailing and swimming had, of course, been stimulated by the rise of the seaside watering places. Bathing in the sea evolved from a therapy to a pleasure: a process aided by the devotion of King George III to the water at Weymouth. The arts of sailing and rowing were encouraged among the holiday makers by the boatmen and fishermen of the various resorts who found an additional source of revenue in teaching these arts to the visitors. As in the case of the inland countryside, so the railways opened up these seacoast delights to the town dwellers.

The Volunteer movement of the late 1850s, gathering local men into organized groups, playing games in their free time, joined the schools and universities and clubs. Mention has been made of the introduction of golf to Wimbledon by the London Scottish.

The successive Factory and Shop Acts had given to working men and women of Victorian England an increasing amount of leisure time, and as education spread and economic conditions became better, surplus energies were turned to the more easily available games, the playing of which was encouraged by enlightened municipalities providing facilities in local parks and open spaces.

As the nineteenth century progressed there emerged a demand for appropriate clothing for sports and games. To meet this there was an ever increasing stream of new cloths, processes, and inventions at the disposal of a growing ready-made clothing industry, which began to get into its stride in the 1860s and 1870s:

> The tailor's bill shrinks every year through the invention of rough colourless cloths impossible to wear out.
>
> > E. C. Grenville, Murray *Sidelights on an English Society,* 1883 Ed.

> Adjustable spikes on a frame attached to the sole of the shoe for cricket.
>
> > Patent Specification, 1860.

> About 1868 the first canvas shoes with rubber soles were introduced, becoming very popular for wear at the seaside.
>
> > Dunlop Rubber Co., *Making Footwear with Rubber,* 1965.

The clothing trade was not backward in adopting these new lines and catering for the sporting customers:

> Knickerbockers, elastic web figure fitting, 6/6.
>
> > Advertisement in *Football,* season 1882–83.

> In consequence of the increased popularity of golf, the wearing apparel used for this sport is now to be seen in the windows of most of the leading out-fitters both in London and the provinces.
>
> > *Tailor and Cutter,* 1894.

One garment introduced for sports and games which became exceedingly popular in the 1880s and 1890s, and which remains so today, was the blazer.

The word has acquired a dubious etymology, but seems to be derived from "blaze", perhaps with undertones of the heraldic "blazon".

The garment originated in the new "lounge" style jackets of the 1850s such as seen on the cricketer Tom Lockyer in 1863, and later acquired the stripes and designs which in the 1860s and 1870s were such a feature of games clothing. At the beginning of the present century a dark blue version was becoming popular, and this navy coloured blazer, now generally double-breasted, has acquired a place in every-day wear and is not confined to the sports field. The blazer has also become, in its pristine variety of colours, a uniform for both schoolboys and schoolgirls.

The flood of patented garments designed to equip the sportsman against all eventualities is overwhelming, ranging from a pair of braces which easily converts into two cricket belts for the proud owner and a favoured friend, to a garment produced in 1861 under the title of the Knickerbocker Pants, which reached the ankles, combining "Knickerbockers and Leggings". As *Minster's Gazette of Fashion* said at the time, there was "some particular arrangement, which the diagram sent to us does not clearly illustrate" enabling a "flap" to be worn either turned up over the thigh or hanging down to protect the leg, which could "be worn as most convenient for the saddle or the field". A century later this awe-inspiring garment is no more clear to us than it was to Minster's baffled editor.

As the Preface has pointed out, the story of women's sports clothes is shorter than that of men's, and indeed the greatest advances were made after the end of the period covered by this book, and so do not come under our present review.

The first step forward was the adoption of the man-like riding coat in the seventeenth century, and this filching of a male garment set the pattern for most subsequent feminine excursions into sports and games wear: excursions that were few and timorous before the 1880s.

The male influence was apparent in the shooting and tricycling dress of the 1880s and in the jackets and caps of female golfers of the same decade.

This tacit admission of male dominance was, however, tempered by what was described in 1897 as a "spirit of conciliation". This conciliatory spirit, as Anne Buck has pointed out (*La Belle Epoque*, The Costume Society, 1968), cropped up wherever women invaded hitherto exclusive masculine domains in sport. There must be no offence given by their rivalry of the sterner sex; for instance, for many years the tricycle was considered the ladies' machine, even after the inventor of the "safety" bicycle had put two wheels within a woman's grasp. When the bicycle finally ousted the tricycle opinion predominately favoured the same conciliation in costume worn, despite the advocates of Rational dress.

All through the 1890s the fashion writers were worried about the clothes worn on bicycles and the proponents of knickerbockers fought a steadily losing battle. In 1896 the *Housewife* speaking of "Rational dressers" said:

The majority by common consent, cannot avoid looking somewhat ludicrous, and although admitting that

for riding long distances at speed, rational dress is by far the best and safest,

concluded by stating flatly that

Most ladies will not adopt it.

In the United States, that same year, the American Women's Rescue League denounced

bicycle riding by young women because of producing immoral associations, both in language and dress, which have a tendency to make women not only unwomenly, but immodest as well.

On this side of the Atlantic Mrs Lynn Lynton, who once had "thought that the lives of women should be as free as those of men, and that community of pursuits would bring about a fine fraternal condition of things", was so affected at this time by the thought of women playing football that she wrote, in the *Daily Graphic*:

Has, indeed, all sense of fitness, of feminine delicacy—not to say decency— left these misguided girls and women . . . whose sole endeavour seems to be to make themselves bad copies of men while throwing off every attribute that constitutes the claim of woman.

For the majority of women the "spirit of conciliation" was most necessary if strictures such as these were to be avoided or if not avoided lived down.

The principle of exercising this conciliation was, therefore, by maintaining an unswerving devotion to the sign and symbol of the sex—the skirt. And, furthermore, to maintain that symbol in as invulnerable a form as possible. All references to "short" skirts are, up to 1914, to be taken as meaning to within about six inches of the ground, and even the most advanced of riding habits had to include an apron skirt which was of no value to the horsewoman except to conceal, mounted and a-foot, the essential and practical breeches.

Tennis, hockey, cricket, rowing—all were practised in the full and flowing skirts of the period: fishing, shooting, golfing, all meant carrying around yards of surplus, hampering, and often wet, material. As Mrs Pritchard said in her *Cult of Chiffon,* the tennis skirt need not be aggressively short, and it is necessary to cover as much as possible of that flat-footed shoe,

and speaking of yachting,

you cannot comfortably wear very long dresses aboard . . . do not attempt the French shoe with its ridiculously high heel . . . although it is a terrible thing for a woman to sacrifice her long skirt and her high heel.

Whilst the skirt was triumphing over the knickerbockers around the legs, above the waist the male principle was being reinforced by the wearing of shirts, stiff collars and ties, which only gradually gave way to more easy blouses and knitted jerseys as men's shirts and collars themselves became softer.

This uneasy marriage of a masculine top half with a feminine lower half was the inhibiting circumstance which dominated all female sports wear until the Great War freed women physically and mentally from many of the clothes and conventions of the past ages; although it took yet a second and in many ways a greater upheaval a quarter of a century later to enable women to enjoy the freedom in sports and games, as well as in life generally, that they now enjoy—or at least pretend to enjoy.

UNDERCLOTHING FOR SPORTS

But how shall I unblamed, express
The *awful MYSTERIES of DRESS*.

Pierce Egan.

Our book has dealt on the whole with the externals of sports wear. Underneath it is mostly mystery.

Special underclothing for sportsmen and sportswomen developed more slowly and to a far lesser degree than their outer garments; indeed in the majority of cases no special underwear was worn.

In the early days the doffing of the coat or other outer clothing revealed what was worn beneath—shirts or smocks. In the case of men the shirt assumed the functions of an outer garment for many games; in the case of women the disclosures made by the country girl in a smock race, for example, came to be regarded as unseemly and by the time a large number of women engaged in sports and games most strenuous efforts were made to prevent untoward revelations: efforts that are observable as early as the eighteenth century among young ladies enjoying the then popular pastime of swinging —"The lover who swings his lady is to tie her clothes very close together with his hat-band before she admits him to throw up her heels", as Steele reports in the *Spectator* of 24th September, 1712.

Waistcoats were considered an undergarment in the sixteenth and seventeenth centuries and were worn by men and women; as we have seen (Chapter 8) Blome refers to jockeys dressed in "waistcoats and drawers". The drawers, long or short (the jockey's would be long) were a male garment only at this time. The smock race run in "half shirts and drawers" quoted in Chapter 18 may point to women wearing the latter garments, borrowed from their men folk, or made specially for the occasion, as sports wear. That the half-shirt, a short under-shirt, was also a man's garment perhaps adds colour to this theory.

The shirt of the eighteenth-century cricketer was very full with voluminous sleeves, pleated into a wristband, but ruffles do not appear to have been generally worn at the wrist as was then fashionable for normal daily wear.

The ladies of that century appeared in a new under-garment—a habit-shirt—when riding. This was somewhat like the man's shirt, with frilled sleeves and a jabot at the front, and could be made to open like a modern coat-shirt, or be closed. The front was longer than the back—about fifteen inches and twelve inches respectively. At the back hem was attached a long tape for tying round the waist. It was worn underneath the coat and waistcoat.

> Four yards of long Lawn at 3/6 per yd. for Nancy to make her riding habit shirts and 1/2 yd of corded Muslin for ruffles.
>
> Rev. James Woodforde, *Diary of a Country Parson*, 1782.

"Riding hoop-peticoats" and "habit-stays" are other items mentioned in the eighteenth century for the convenience of lady riders. (*Blundel's Diary*, 1723; *Ipswich Journal*, 1786).

Towards the end of the century "false rumps" or "bustles" often made from cork, rivalled hoops as a skirt support and were worn by at least one lady who enjoyed a day on the water. She fell in the sea but "it was impossible she should sink . . . she owed her life to the cork-rump, the use of which I recommend to all ladies who may love boating"—so wrote her husband to the *Gentleman's and London Magazine* for July, 1777.

Ladies took to "Trowsers" or Pantaloons, for riding in the early nineteenth century and drawers (reaching to just below the knee) were advertised in 1811 as "Ladies hunting and opera drawers in elastic Indian cotton". As well as for riding and going to the theatre they were worn when bathing:

> Many ladies when riding wear silk drawers, similar to what is worn when bathing. 1828.
>
> Quoted in Cunnington, *The History of Underclothes.*

Towards the middle of the nineteenth century men began to wear woollen vests underneath the shirt, and the running kit of the 1860s and 1870s seems to owe something to this garment and to the short drawers, which by this time were beginning to be known as "pants".

Woollen underwear gained steadily in favour and was given the seal of science by Dr Jaeger in the early 1880s. Wool next the skin was advocated in the form of flannel and knitted fabrics: "the perspiration passes freely away through pure, porous wool, leaving the skin warm and comparatively dry" as Dr Jaeger said.

"For riding as for other exercises, the body should be clothed entirely in wool. The habit should invariably be lined with flannel . . . The trousers as well . . . all the underclothing that is required is woollen combinations," declared Ada Ballin in 1885. She also recommended a body belt of flannel and stays. Riding stays were shorter than those normally worn: an adaptable design of the 1850s, the Corset Amazone, could be shortened by three inches when required by pulling a cord. In 1893 Alice Hayes stated that the corsets "should be short, and cut away over the hips so as not to interfere with the free working of the hip joints".

Alice Hayes was a dissenter from the woollen school, and recommended tricot or elastic silk long drawers: "I need hardly say that no kind of petticoat should be worn." Nevertheless, petticoats had frequently been worn, even after the introduction of trousers and drawers.

During the nineteenth century the habit-shirt had become a very skimpy garment, little more than a "fill in" to the front of the bodice and an anchorage for the collar. The sleeves, if present, could have cuffs, but these latter were sometimes fastened direct to the inside of the bodice sleeves.

The stock, a high made-up neckcloth of linen began to rival the cravat as men's neckwear in the early eighteenth century. It persisted, influenced by the black style adopted by the army, through the nineteenth century, and crystallized into the hunting-stock by the 1890s.

Men would wear pants under their breeches, but not always—Mr Facey Romford for instance on one occasion had "very indifferent cords [breeches] and no drawers". This was in 1865, and we have seen that thirty years earlier John Mytton "knew not the use of these garments". In 1906 *Practical hints for Hunting Novices* was assuming the use of under-clothing for hunting, and of course, it was recommended to be of wool for both sexes and all ages.

Mrs Pritchard, writing in 1902, suggests gauze combinations for riding "trimmed with lace and made as attractive as possible" to be worn beneath the riding habit and breeches, while for country wear generally "There is a decided fancy, and a very sensible one it is, for wearing silk or satin knickers . . . with detachable linings of flannel, linen or washing silk". Such were also recommended for the bicycle: "gaiters and knickers all to match the skirt", according to *The Housewife* in 1895, whose fashion writer noted with disapproval "a skirt pinned up around the waist, under which could be seen white underwear and gaiterless legs". Bicycling skirts should be so correctly constructed that, to quote another fashion columnist of this same year, "no possible peep" could be obtained of the wonders underneath.

This concern with concealment, with preserving inviolate the hidden depths, was all part of the contemporary skirt technique of conciliatory woman, who, anxious "for equality with man, and for the privilages and independance he enjoys", had, according to Mrs Pritchard, "infinite opportunity of obtaining all she wants through the service of dress, beauty and the subtleties which have never yet failed"—disguising—"the details of dress and toilet in a mask of mystery".

And it is this mystery which, despite such phenomena as mini-skirts, we find, at bottom, in all female fashions: even when its mask took the form of

> Ladies tailor-made leather motoring knickers, fitted with detachable flannel linings.
>
> Advertisement, *c.* 1900/1912.

Bibliography

Cunnington, C. W. *Feminine Attitudes in the Nineteenth Century*. Wm Heinemann Ltd, 1935.

Cunnington, C. W. and P. *The History of Underclothes*. Michael Joseph, 1951.

Costume Society, The. *La Belle Epoque*. Victoria and Albert Museum, 1968.

Douglas, Mrs. *The Gentlewoman's Book of Dress*. Henry & Co., N.D.

Grenville-Murrey, E. C. *Sidelights on English Society*. Vizetelly, 1883.

Pritchard, Mrs Eric. *The Cult of Chiffon*. Grant Richards, 1902.

GENERAL BIBLIOGRAPHY

Publication in London unless otherwise stated.
Abbreviations: ed. = edited by
Ed. = edition.

Adburgham, Alison. *Shops and Shopping*. 1964.

Alken, Henry. *National Sports of Great Britain*. 1821.

Allison, W. *My Kingdom for a Horse*. 1919.

Altham, H. S. and Arlott, John. *Lords and M.C.C.* 1967.

Anon. *Habits of Society*. 1859.

Anon. *Several Wayes of Hunting, Hawking and Fishing According to the English Manner*. 1671.

Ashley-Cooper, F. S. *The Cricket Field*. 1922.

Ashton, John. *Ballads etc. of the 17th Century*. N.D.

Ashton, John. *England a Hundred Years Ago*. 1900.

Ashton, John. *Social England under the Regency*. 1899.

Ashton, John. *Men, Maidens and Manners a Hundred Years Ago*. 1888.

Ashton, John. *Florizel's Folly*. 1899.

Ballin, Ada. *Science of Dress*. 1885.

Blaine, Delabere P. *Encyclopedia of Rural Sports*. (Hunting, Shooting, Fishing, Racing.) 1840.

Blome, R. *The Gentleman's Recreation*. 1686.

Bowlker, Richard. *The Art of Angling*. 1758.

Bowlker, Richard. *Universal Angler*. 1766.

Brand, John. *Popular Antiquities*. Ed. 1848.

Brown, Thomas. *Amusements Serious and Comical*. 1700.

Buck, Anne. *Costume for Sport:* Gallery of English Costume Picture Book. 1962.

Burney, Frances. *The Early Diary, 1768–1778*. Ed. Anne Ellis. 1913.

Cassell's Book of Sports and Pastimes. 1888.

Cassell's Household Guide. N.D. *c.* 1870.

Carew, R. *Survey of Cornwall*. 1602.

Chamberlayne, Edward. *Angliae Notitia or The Present State of England*. 2nd ed. 1669.

Comenius, John Amos. *Visible World*, trans. C. Hoole. Ed. 1664. (1st ed. 1658.)

Cope, A. (ed.). *Cope's Royal Cavalcade of the Turf*. 1953.

Costume Society, The. *La Belle Epoque*. 1968.

Costume of Yorkshire. Leeds. 1814.

Cotgrave, Randle. *Dictionary*. 1611.

"Craven". *Walker's Manly Exercises*, 6th ed. 1840.

Cunnington, C. W. *English Women's Clothing in the 19th Century*. 1937.

Cunnington, C. W. *English Women's Clothing in the Present Century*. 1951.

Cunnington, C. W. & P. *Handbooks of English Costume in the 16th, 17th, 18th and 19th centuries.* 1954–59.

Cunnington, C. W. & P. *The History of Underclothes.* 1951.

Cunnington, C. W. & P. and Beard, C. *A Dictionary of English Costume.* 1968.

Daniel, Rev. W. B. *Rural Sports.* 1801–2.

Ditchfield, P. H. *Old English Sports and Pastimes.* 1890–1.

Douglas, Mrs. *Gentlewoman's Book of Dress.* N.D.

"Druid, The". *The Post and the Paddock.* 1895 (1st ed. 1856).

Egan, Pierce. *The Finish to the Adventures of Tom, Jerry and Logic.* 1828.

Egan, Pierce. *Book of Sports and Mirror of Life.* 1832.

Ellis, S. M. *A Mid-Victorian Pepys (Sir William Hardman).* 1923.

Ellis, S. M. *Letters and Memoirs.* 1925.

Evelyn, John. *Diary* (1620–1706), ed. Wm. Bray. 1907.

Fairfax, T. *The Compleat Sportsman or Country Gentleman's Recreation.* 1758.

"Felix". *Felix on the Bat.* 1845.

Fiennes, Celia. *Journeys,* ed. Christopher Morris. 1949.

Gibson, A. and Pickford, W. *Association Football.* 1905–6.

Grego, Joseph. *Rowlandson the Caricaturist.* 1880.

Ham, Elizabeth. *Elizabeth Ham by Herself (1783–1820).* Ed. 1945.

Harper, Charles G. *Revolted Woman.* 1894.

Harrison, Molly & Royston, O. M. *How They Lived, 1485–1700.* Oxford 1963.

Higgin, L. *Art as Applied to Dress.* 1885.

Hilton, H. H. & Smith G. G. *The Royal and Ancient Game of Golf.* 1912.

Hole, Christina. *English Sports and Pastimes.* 1949.

Holinshed, Raphael. *Chronicles.* 1587.

Holme, Randle. *Academy of Armory.* 1688.

Howitt, S. *The British Sportsman.* 1812.

Hughes, T. *Tom Brown's Schooldays.* 1857.

Hunt, Cecil. *British Customs and Ceremonies.* 1954.

Hutchinson, G. A. *Outdoor Games and Recreations.* 1892.

Jaeger, Gustav. *Health Culture* (trans. by R. S. Tomalin). Ed. 1911.

Kilvert, The Rev. R. F. *Diary (1870–1879),* ed. Wm. Plomer. 1944.

Kohler, Carl. *A History of Costume.* New York. Ed. 1963.

Mackarness, Mrs C. (ed.). *The Young Ladies' Book.* 1870.

Marsh, W. Lockwood. *Aeronautical Prints and Drawings.* 1924.

Martineau, R. *The Jockey Club.* 1958.

Meadows, Kenny. *Heads of the People.* 1841.

M. Misson's Memoirs and Observations in his Travels over England. . . . Trans. John Ozell. 1719.

Newton, G. W. *Rural Sports and How to enjoy them.* 1867.

"Nimrod". *Memoirs of the Life of the late John Mytton.* 1837.

Osbaldeston, W. A. *The British Sportsman.* Ed. 1792.

Pepys, Samuel. *Diary. (1660–1669)*, ed. by H. B. Wheatley. Ed. 1923.

Pritchard, Mrs Eric. *The Cult of Chiffon.* 1902.

Roberts, John A. C. *The Four Seasons of Sport.* 1960.

Routledge. *Handbook of Football.* 1867.

Rowlandson, Thomas. *Poetical Sketches of Scarborough.* 1813.

Salek, John S. *Dictionary of Sports.* 1961.

Scott, J. W. R. *The Day before Yesterday.* 1951.

Smedley, F. E. *Frank Fairleigh.* 1850.

Smith, Albert & Reach, Angus (ed.). *The Man in the Moon.* 1847.

Sparrow, W. S. *British Sporting Artists.* Ed. 1965.

Siltzer, Capt. Frank. *The Story of British Sporting Prints.* New ed. 1929.

Stone, Lilly, G. *English Sports and Recreations.* U.S.A. 1960.

"Stonehenge". *Manual of British Rural Sports.* 1857.

Stow, John. *Annales,* continued by Edmund Howes. 1631.

Stow, John. *A Survey of London,* ed. C. L. Kingsford. 2 Vols. Oxford, 1908.

Turbervile, George. *Noble Arte of Venerie or Hunting.* 1575.

Walbancke, Matthew. *Annalia Dubrensia.* 1636.

Walsh, J. H. *British Rural Sports.* 1888.

Walker, Donald. *Games and Sports.* 1837.

Walker, Donald. *Walker's Manly Exercises,* 6th Ed., ed. by Craven, 1840.

Williamson, C. N. & A. M. *The Princess Passes.* 1904.

Williamson, C. N. & A. M. *The Lightning Conductor.* 1903.

Woodforde, The Rev. James. *Diary. (1758–1803)*, ed. by John Beresford. 1924.

Wright, Thomas. *England Under the House of Hanover.* 1848.

Works of Chaucer, Dickens, Goldsmith, Shakespeare, Smollet and Surtees.

Periodicals

The Autocar.
Bailey's Magazine.
Bath Chronicle, 1770.
Bell's Life in London.
Boys' Own Paper.
Cassell's Family Magazine.
Century Magazine.
Chambers' Book of Days.
Chambers' Journal.
Country Life.
Daily Advertiser.

Derby Mercury.
Englishwomen's Domestic Magazine.
English Illustrated Magazine.
The Family Herald.
The Field.
The Fisherman's Magazine.
Football.
The Gentleman's Herald of Fashion.
The Gentleman's Magazine.
The Gentleman's Magazine of Fashion.
Girls' Own Annual.
Golf Illustrated.
The Graphic.
The Hockey Field.
The Hockey World.
The Housewife.
The Illustrated London News.
The Illustrated Sporting and Dramatic News.
The Ladies' Tailor.
The London Magazine.
London Society.
Minster's Gazette of Fashion.
The Observer.
Outing.
The Pall Mall Gazette.
The Pictorial World.
Punch.
The Queen.
Scores and Biographies.
The Spectator.
Sporting Magazine.
The Tailor and Cutter.
The Tricycling Magazine.
The West End Gazette of Fashion.
The World.
The Young Ladies' Journal.

The above periodicals, together embracing the years from the early eighteenth-century until today, can provide much written and pictorial information on all aspects of dress. Light is also shed by newspapers, national and local.

SOURCES OF FIGURES

CHAPTER I

CHAPTER II

CHAPTER III

CHAPTER IV

CHAPTER V

CHAPTER VI

CHAPTER VII

CHAPTER VIII

CHAPTER IX

CHAPTER X

CHAPTER XI

CHAPTER XII

CHAPTER XIII

CHAPTER XIV

CHAPTER XX

CHAPTER XXI

INDEX

Page numbers in *italics* indicate an illustration in the text, but in the case of articles of clothing, where written reference is made on the same page as an illustration ordinary type is generally used.